THE PRAEGER SINGER-SONGWRITER COLLECTION

The Words and Music of Paul McCartney

The Solo Years

Vincent P. Benitez

James E. Perone, Series Editor

 PRAEGER

AN IMPRINT OF ABC-CLIO, LLC
Santa Barbara, California • Denver, Colorado • Oxford, England

Library of Congress Cataloging-in-Publication Data

Benitez, Vincent Perez, 1955–
    The words and music of Paul McCartney : the solo years / Vincent P. Benitez.
       p. cm. — (Praeger singer-songwriter collection)
    Includes bibliographical references and index.
    ISBN 978-0-313-34969-0 (hard copy : alk. paper) — ISBN 978-0-313-34970-6 (ebook)
    1. McCartney, Paul—Criticism and interpretation. 2. Rock music—History and criticism I. Title.
    ML410.M115B44   2010
    782.42166092—dc22   2009052379

ISBN: 978-0-313-34969-0
EISBN: 978-0-313-34970-6

14 13 12 11 10   1 2 3 4 5

This book is also available on the World Wide Web as an eBook.
Visit www.abc-clio.com for details.

Praeger
An Imprint of ABC-CLIO, LLC

ABC-CLIO, LLC
130 Cremona Drive, P.O. Box 1911
Santa Barbara, California 93116-1911

This book is printed on acid-free paper ∞

Manufactured in the United States of America

For my father, Vincent P. Benitez, Sr. (1917–2009)
"As long as you and I are here, put it there."

Contents

Series Foreword

Although the term *singer-songwriter* might most frequently be associated with a cadre of musicians of the early 1970s such as Paul Simon, James Taylor, Carly Simon, Joni Mitchell, Cat Stevens, and Carole King, the Praeger Singer-Songwriter Collection defines singer-songwriters more broadly, both in terms of style and time period. The series includes volumes on musicians who have been active from approximately the 1960s through the present. Musicians who write and record in folk, rock, soul, hip-hop, country, and various hybrids of these styles are represented. Therefore, some of the early 1970s introspective singer-songwriters named here will be included, but not exclusively.

What do the individuals included in this series have in common? Some have never collaborated as writers, whereas others have, but all have written and recorded commercially successful and/or historically important music *and* lyrics at some point in their careers.

The authors who contribute to the series also exhibit diversity. Some are scholars who are trained primarily as musicians, whereas others have such areas of specialization as American studies, history, sociology, popular culture studies, literature, and rhetoric. The authors share a high level of scholarship, accessibility in their writing, and a true insight into the work of the artists they study. The authors are also focused on the output of their subjects and how it relates to their subject's biography and the society around them; however, biography in and of itself is not a major focus of the books in this series.

Given the diversity of the musicians who are the subject of books in this series, and given the diversity of viewpoint of the authors, volumes in the series differ from book to book. All, however, are organized chronologically around the compositions and recorded performances of their subjects. All of the books in the series should also serve as listeners' guides to the music of their subjects, making them companions to the artists' recorded output.

James E. Perone
Series Editor

Acknowledgments

I want to thank several people who provided me with advice, assistance, and support during the writing of this book. I am especially grateful to Professor Thomas Cody of the Pennsylvania State University for his advice regarding matters related to Paul McCartney's guitar playing. Sincere thanks are also due to Professor Christopher Kiver of the Pennsylvania State University for his encouragement and support of this book.

I would like to thank series editor James Perone and acquisitions editor Daniel Harmon for both their support of my project and their patience and understanding in seeing it come to fruition.

I want to thank my father, Vincent P. Benitez, Sr., for supporting my musical endeavors since childhood. Dad, you did not know how much you changed the life of your young son when you bought him those Beatle records one Christmas a long time ago.

Finally, I should like to extend my deepest appreciation and profound gratitude to my wife, Esther Ann Wingfield Benitez. I introduced you to the music of the Beatles when we first met. When I took you to see Paul McCartney at Gund Arena, Cleveland on 4 October 2002, you got to hear the music I was crazy about for so many years, seeing it played and sung by the person who composed it. You encouraged me during every phase of the writing of this book and helped me with numerous practical matters associated with its completion. I owe you so much.

Vincent P. Benitez
State College, Pennsylvania

Introduction: A Biographical Sketch of Paul McCartney

CHILDHOOD AND YOUTH, 1942–57

James Paul McCartney was born on 18 June 1942 in Liverpool, England, in a private ward in Walton Hospital.[1] He was the firstborn son of James "Jim" McCartney (1902–76), who worked intermittently in the cotton market, and Mary Patricia Mohin McCartney (1909–56), a maternity nurse. McCartney was given the middle name "Paul" by his mother in order to distinguish him from his father and great-grandfather, who were not only both named "James" but also, according to family tradition, did not have middle names.[2] Although baptized a Roman Catholic, perhaps as a concession to his mother and her traditional Irish family, Catholicism had no role in McCartney's upbringing. His father, an Anglican turned agnostic, did not want McCartney sent to Catholic schools because he felt they spent too much time on religion at the expense of education.[3] On 7 January 1944, a brother, Peter Michael, was born. McCartney grew up in a large, extended family. His father had five married sisters, who doted on McCartney and his brother Michael.

In 1947, McCartney entered the Stockton Wood Road Primary School. Due to overcrowding at Stockton because of the English postwar baby boom, he moved to the Joseph Williams Primary School. Few students at Joseph Williams possessed the intellectual abilities to get into grammar school; instead, most went to secondary modern schools, attending classes until they were old enough to work.[4] Only 93 out of several hundred students in McCartney's class opted to take the eleven-plus exam to see if they were not only grammar school material but also eligible to work toward a General Certificate of Education. Of the 93 students, 4 passed, one of whom was McCartney. His passing grade secured him a place at the Liverpool Institute in 1953, an outstanding free grammar school that took special pride in sending more of its students to Oxford and Cambridge than any other state school in Britain.[5]

While attending the Liverpool Institute, McCartney met George Harrison (1943–2001), who enrolled at the school in 1954. They shared the same hour-long bus ride from the Speke district of Liverpool, where they both lived at the time, to the Institute and back.[6] The two future Beatles realized that they were schoolmates by the uniforms they were wearing. According to McCartney, "George was a bus stop away. I would get on the bus for school and he would get on the stop after. So, being close to each other in age [eight months apart], we talked—although I tended to talk down to him, because he was a year younger." According to Harrison, "[McCartney] had a trumpet and he found out that I had a guitar, and we got together. I was about thirteen."[7] Thus, McCartney and Harrison became fast friends after meeting on the bus. In 1957, they got together to learn the guitar at Harrison's home, sharing a passion for American rock 'n' roll. McCartney was especially impressed with Harrison's playing of Bill Justis's "Raunchy."

Mary McCartney was the major breadwinner in the family. In 1955, her job as a domiciliary midwife allowed the McCartneys to move to a small, two-floor brick terrace house at 20 Forthlin Road in the suburb of Allerton. This address was not only closer to the city's center but also located in a better neighborhood than their previous residence at 12 Ardwick Road. As a part of her job, Mary McCartney rode her bicycle to the houses where she was needed. But the move and her work took a toll on her health. Having been diagnosed with breast cancer several years earlier, she underwent a mastectomy on 30 October 1956. She died the next day.

Devastated by the loss of his mother, McCartney found solace in music, practicing his Framus Zenith acoustic guitar for hours on end. In a word, guitar playing and rock 'n' roll became an obsession. Before taking up the guitar, McCartney learned how to play a trumpet bought for him by his father for his 14th birthday (18 June 1956).[8] Although he could eventually play a C–major scale, "The Saints Go Marching In," and a few other things on the trumpet, McCartney quickly realized that it was going to be difficult for him to both sing and play a trumpet at the same time. Accordingly, with his father's permission, he traded in the first instrument he ever owned for that Zenith acoustic guitar.

Because he was left-handed, and after noticing a picture of Slim Whitman playing a guitar left-handed, McCartney restrung the Zenith upside down, learning mirror-image versions of A, D, and E chords.[9] He began to write songs, the first being "I Lost My Little Girl," which is based on G, G7, and C chords, as well as songs made famous when he was a Beatle, such as "Michelle."[10] It was on the Zenith, moreover, that he learned "Twenty Flight Rock," made famous by Eddie Cochran (1938–60). He played the song for John Lennon on 6 July 1957 when they first met, which got him into the Quarry Men.[11]

Inspired by his father's piano playing, McCartney took up the keyboard instrument. He tried to take piano lessons in Liverpool, but eventually ended up teaching himself. As he was learning to play by ear, McCartney began writing songs on the piano, influenced by the British music-hall tradition of his father. Jim McCartney played trumpet and piano in a swing band—the "Masked Melody Makers," which evolved into "Jim Mac's Band"—in the 1920s until bad teeth precluded him from playing trumpet, forcing him to perform only on the piano. McCartney heard his father playing many old jazz and pop standards on the piano while he was growing up. Not surprisingly, at the age of 16, McCartney wrote "When I'm Sixty-Four," a song strongly shaped by the music-hall tradition imparted to him by his father.

THE BEATLE YEARS, 1957–70

On 6 July 1957, Paul McCartney met John Lennon at the village fête at Saint Peter's Church in Woolton, a historic day in music history. Ivan Vaughan, a mutual friend who was aware of the two future Beatles' passion for rock 'n' roll, invited McCartney to the fête not only to hear the Quarry Men but, more importantly, to meet Lennon. The Quarry Men were a struggling skiffle group in Liverpool with Lennon serving as their leader and singer.[12] The group began their set at approximately 4:15 p.m. in a field behind the church. They performed skiffle repertoire, such as "Cumberland Gap," "Maggie May," and "Railroad Bill," along with rock 'n' roll hits, such as "Be Bop A Lula" by Gene Vincent and the Blue Jeans, and "Come Go with Me" by the Del Vikings. As recalled by McCartney, Lennon was singing "Come Go with Me" when he arrived with Vaughan. Not being familiar with the song's lyrics, Lennon improvised words as he went along, adding colorful rhythm 'n' blues lines ("Down, down, down to the penitentiary").

Later that day, McCartney met Lennon backstage in the church hall. McCartney played Eddie Cochran's "Twenty Flight Rock," along with other numbers such as "Be Bop A Lula," for Lennon, and wrote down the lyrics of several songs. He showed Lennon how to play chords properly, as well as tune a guitar. Although Lennon was impressed that McCartney knew the lyrics of Cochran's song, he was more impressed with McCartney's musical abilities and invited him to join the Quarry Men one week later in order to strengthen the group. McCartney made his debut with the Quarry Men on 18 October 1957 at the New Clubmoor Hall in Liverpool. He fluffed a guitar solo when the group played "Guitar Boogie."

The two future Beatles quickly became close friends and formed a songwriting partnership. According to Lennon, McCartney was a rocker with interests in Broadway and vaudeville.[13] Lennon admired Buddy Holly, whom he considered as the first singer-songwriter to speak to his generation. In any event, Lennon and McCartney agreed to put both of their names on each of their songs, no matter who wrote most, if not all, of the song. Thus, one of the greatest songwriting teams in pop music history began.

After joining the Quarry Men, McCartney urged Lennon to allow George Harrison to join the group. Lennon was reluctant to accept Harrison, due to his age (he was almost fifteen), but relented because of the way Harrison played "Raunchy" on a bus ride home from a gig at Wilson Hall, Garston, on 6 February 1958.[14] In the summer of that same year, the Quarry Men cut their first record at Percy Phillips's studio at 53 Kensington, Liverpool. The A–side featured "That'll Be the Day" by Buddy Holly, with Lennon singing lead vocal, whereas the B–side included Harrison and McCartney's "In Spite of All the Danger."

Despite the various lineup changes in the Quarry Men and their disbanding as a group, McCartney, Lennon, and Harrison stayed together, continuing as a trio. Stuart Sutcliffe, Lennon's friend from the Liverpool College of Art, joined the group as a bass guitarist in January 1960. According to various sources, Sutcliffe could not play the bass guitar very well, and would often turn his back to the audience in order to hide that fact. McCartney complained about Sutcliffe's musical ability, considering him a hindrance to the band's chances of succeeding in show business. Pete Best of the Blackjacks joined the group as a drummer just in time for their first trip abroad to Hamburg in August 1960. The group called itself by several names during this period, such as Johnny and the Moondogs, the Beatals, the Beetles, or the Silver Beetles, before settling on the Beatles for their residency in Hamburg. Their insect name was inspired by, and possibly a homage to, Buddy Holly and the Crickets, as well as a pun on beat music.

Once in Hamburg, the Beatles started playing at the Indra Club. After the Indra closed, the group worked at the larger Kaiserkeller, moving to the Top Ten Club in October 1960. At the Kaiserkeller, the Beatles met Ringo Starr (Richard Starkey), who was playing drums for Rory Storm and the Hurricanes, a Liverpool band that was the club's featured act. At the Kaiserkeller, the two bands took turns playing for 12 hours straight. In late 1960, the Beatles had to leave Hamburg because the German authorities deported Harrison, who was too young at age 17 to be working after 10:00 p.m. each night. They revoked Lennon's work permit a few days later, and he returned to Liverpool. McCartney and Best were arrested for attempted arson—as a joke, they pinned a condom to a concrete wall at the Bambi Kino, their accommodations while playing at the Indra Club, and lit it on fire. They spent three hours in a local jail and were subsequently deported. Instead of leaving for Liverpool like the others, Sutcliffe remained in Hamburg to stay with his German girlfriend, Astrid Kircherr.

The 1960 residency in Hamburg was the beginning of a pivotal turning point for the Beatles. Because they had to play long sets, often taking drugs to help them get through the night, the group got immensely better, honing their musical skills both individually and as an ensemble. According to Harrison, it was in Hamburg that the Beatles especially jelled as a group:

> In my opinion[,] our peak for playing live was Hamburg. At the time we weren't so famous, and people who came to see us were drawn in simply by our music and whatever atmosphere we managed to create. We got *very* tight as a band there. We were at four different clubs altogether in Germany. Originally we played the Indra, and, when that shut, we went over to the Kaiserkeller and then, later on, the Top Ten. Back in England, all the bands were getting into wearing matching ties and handkerchiefs, and were doing little dance routines like the Shadows. We were definitely not into that, so we just kept doing whatever we felt like.[15]

After leaving Hamburg, the Beatles got back together in Liverpool and started to play again, working the Cavern Club for the first time in February 1961. Because of Sutcliffe's absence, McCartney started to play bass for the group, although Sutcliffe returned to Liverpool in January 1961 and actually appeared as bass guitarist with the Beatles at their Cavern Club debut on 9 February 1961. The Beatles returned to Hamburg in April and appeared at the Top Ten Club. They recorded an album with Tony Sheridan, a former regular on the British television series *Oh, Boy!* Besides backing Sheridan on several numbers, including "My Bonnie," the Beatles recorded "Ain't She Sweet," with Lennon on lead vocal, and "Cry for a Shadow," an instrumental credited to Harrison. Although reuniting with the Beatles at this time, Sutcliffe left the Beatles when the group returned to Liverpool in July 1961. He remained in Hamburg in order to pursue his art studies as well as to be with Astrid Kircherr. At this time, McCartney became the Beatles' permanent bass player.

After noticing customers requesting a recording of the Beatles' "My Bonnie" at his North End Music Store (N.E.M.S.) in Liverpool, as well as reading about the group in *The Mersey Beat*, a newspaper that he stocked at the store, Brian Epstein (1934–67) decided to visit the Cavern Club on 9 November 1961 during a lunchtime session to see the Beatles. Impressed by what he had heard, he later signed the Beatles to a management contract. Epstein cleaned up the Beatles' act, forbidding them to curse, drink, eat, or smoke on stage. Moreover, Epstein had the group shed their leather jackets and blue jeans for smartly tailored matching suits.

Besides securing numerous gigs, Epstein was determined to obtain a recording contract for the Beatles. On New Year's Day, 1962, the Beatles auditioned for Mike Smith of Decca Records in West Hampstead, London. Judging them unimpressive, Smith declined to offer them a recording contract. After being rejected by other record companies, along with playing many gigs including a stint in April at the Star Club in Hamburg, where they learned that Sutcliffe had died of a brain hemorrhage shortly before their arrival, the Beatles finally signed a recording contract with Parlophone Records, a division of EMI Records, on 9 May 1962. Although not impressed by the repertoire he heard when the Beatles auditioned, George Martin, a producer at Parlophone and a classically trained musician, was struck not only by their musical potential but also their immense personal charm. On 18 August 1962, Epstein fired Pete Best at McCartney and Harrison's request, because they were displeased with his drumming. (For his part, Lennon got along with Best.) Ringo Starr was hired immediately as the new drummer for the Beatles.

On 11 September 1962, the Beatles recorded "Love Me Do" as a single, with session drummer Andy White (instead of Starr) playing the drums. The B–side featured "P. S. I Love You." "Love Me Do" was released on 5 October 1962 and reached as high as No. 17 on the British pop charts. McCartney wrote most of the song in 1958, with Lennon contributing to the song's middle section.[16] According to McCartney, it was influenced by Buddy Holly.[17] Buoyed by the success of "Love Me Do," Martin asked the Beatles for another song to record as a single. They complied by offering a faster version of Lennon's "Please, Please Me." The song reached No. 1 on the British pop charts, ushering Beatlemania into the United Kingdom, and, ultimately, the entire world.

Because of the instantaneous success of "Please, Please Me," George Martin had the Beatles make an album of the same name on 11 February 1963 at Abbey Road Studios. The Beatles recorded what were essentially live performances on primitive two-track equipment. The songs included Lennon and McCartney originals, as well as cover songs from their stage act.[18] Further singles, such as "From Me to You" and "She Loves You," and the album *With the Beatles*, followed in 1963, solidifying the Beatles' stature with the British public. The Beatles quickly became popular, furthermore, in the rest of Europe. To ensure their worldwide success, they had to conquer America, which they did in 1964 through a series of performances on *The Ed Sullivan Show* in February and the release of several singles and two albums on the Capitol label, *Meet the Beatles* and *The Beatles' Second Album*. What followed from 1964 to 1970 was a spectacular musical success story, with the Beatles accumulating numerous No. 1 hits and staggering record sales.[19]

During their reign as pop icons in the 1960s, the Beatles grew in artistic stature. They improved greatly as musicians, turning away from their earlier, innocuous pop songs to music rivaling that of classical composers, an astonishing musical development, to say the least. They also became cultural spokesmen for the youth generation of the turbulent 1960s, speaking out against the Vietnam War and racism. In short, every Beatle activity, album, interview, public appearance, or press conference was frequently a cultural, media, or musical event.

As songwriters, Lennon and McCartney's collaborative efforts varied according to their circumstances. In 1963, they composed and arranged most new songs on tour buses or in hotel rooms between concert dates due to a hectic recording schedule. They collaborated fully on early songs such as "From Me to You," "Thank You Girl," "She Loves You," and "I Want to Hold Your Hand." But with more time for recording in 1964, Lennon and McCartney reverted to their earlier practice of composing their own songs, with the other typically contributing to the song's bridge. They often composed their songs at various residences in and outside London, such as 57 Wimpole Street (the London home of the parents of McCartney's girlfriend Jane Asher, where McCartney lived prior to 1966), 7 Cavendish Avenue (McCartney's London home beginning in 1966), or Kenwood (Lennon's country mansion in England). From 1965 onward, they frequently finished their songs during studio time.

As far as songwriting approaches were concerned, McCartney normally composed the music first and then added lyrics. For Lennon, it was usually the reverse. According to commonly held views regarding the two, Lennon was the master of imagery and words, whereas McCartney was the more sophisticated musician.[20] Lennon's songs evince, in other words, more intellectual substance than those by the sentimental McCartney. Lennon would encourage McCartney to polish his lyrics, whereas McCartney would help Lennon musically. Although there is a grain of truth to all of this, is it fair to McCartney? Consider his lyrics to "Yesterday" or "Blackbird"; surely they are not superficial.

Besides writing songs for the Beatles to record, McCartney played bass in the group, becoming a top rock 'n' roll bassist in the process as he performed on his iconic, cello-shaped Hoffner.[21] In early Beatle songs, McCartney would often play the roots and fifths of chords in dotted rhythms or repetitive arpeggio-based figures. In 1963, he began to play more intricate bass lines, incorporating more melodic motion than before as well as incorporating vertical open fifths to mark song divisions. Later, the bass lines got even more virtuosic as McCartney, freed from supporting a live group, would overdub the bass part onto its own track. In addition to his Hoffner bass, McCartney played other instruments on Beatle recordings, such as a Rickenbacker bass (beginning with *Rubber Soul*), an Epiphone Texas acoustic guitar, an Epiphone Casino electric guitar, and keyboard instruments.

McCartney and Lennon were the best singers in the Beatles. McCartney was a highly versatile singer. He could shout out rock 'n' roll numbers in the style of Little Richard, as well as sing ballads with the best of crooners. Lennon was equally adept at singing rock 'n' roll songs, although in a less abrasive style. He was clearly a more soulful singer than McCartney, possessing a euphonious falsetto. When the two Beatles sang duets, McCartney, who had a higher vocal range than Lennon, would often sing a descant to Lennon's melody. When McCartney sang the melody, Lennon sang a lower harmony part. For emphatic moments in their songs, they would sing in octaves, with McCartney taking the higher note. While their duet techniques stemmed from rockabilly artists such as the Everly Brothers or Buddy Holly (who over-dubbed his own backing vocal), McCartney and Lennon's three-part vocals with Harrison were influenced by the Jordanaires, the Coasters, Motown artists, and girl groups, such as the Shirelles, of the early 1960s.

During the 1960s, McCartney was involved with musical projects outside the Beatles. He wrote songs for Peter and Gordon, Billy J. Kramer and the Dakotas, Cilla Black, Mary Hopkin, and Badfinger. He composed the sound-track to the 1966 film *The Family Way*, starring Hayley Mills. McCartney also produced recording artists, such as Mary Hopkin, Jackie Lomax, the Bonzo Dog Doo-Dah Band, and Badfinger. He became interested in electronic music, especially that by Cage and Stockhausen, experimenting with tape loops that materialized on *Revolver*'s "Tomorrow Never Knows."

After serious romantic relationships with Liverpool flame Dorothy ("Dot") Rhone and the British actress Jane Asher, McCartney married the American photographer Linda Louise Eastman (1942–98) on 12 March 1969 in London. He met Eastman at a Georgie Fame and the Blue Flames concert at the Bag O' Nails Club in Soho, London on 15 May 1967.[22] Eastman was on assignment in London to take photographs of some of the city's major groups. On 19 May, McCartney and Eastman met again at a party launching the Beatles' *Sgt. Pepper's Lonely Hearts Club Band* album at Brian Epstein's home in Belgravia. After finally breaking it off with Asher in July 1968, McCartney pursued Eastman. After seeing Eastman in New York in May 1968 when he and Lennon were promoting the newly founded Apple Corps, McCartney contacted her in September, requesting that she come to London, which she did. They lived together for several months before they decided to get married. At the time of their marriage at a small civil ceremony at Marylebone Registry Office, Eastman was four months pregnant with their first daughter, Mary Anna. McCartney and Eastman were to have two more children together, Stella Nina and James Louis. McCartney adopted East-man's daughter Heather Louise from her first marriage to Joseph "Mel" See.

When the Beatles started, Lennon was the leader of the group. But that began to change in 1965 as McCartney began to assert himself within the group's dynamics. He matched Lennon song for song and began to be quite demanding with the other Beatles when it came to realizing his music in the studio. He was often critical of Harrison's guitar playing and could be equally harsh on Starr and his drumming. By 1967, McCartney dominated the group musically and even filled a business void left open by the death of Brian Epstein in August 1967. He was the driving force behind the Beatles' *Magical Mystery Tour* television special of 1967, and, according to Harrison, conceived of the film *Let It Be*.[23] Lennon became increasingly disillusioned with the Beatles, as by this time he was not consciously making any decisions and regarded recording songs with the group as just another nine-to-five job.

As a group, the Beatles experienced a slow, agonizing death. They ceased to function as a musical ensemble by 1968. During the recording of the *White*

Album (*The Beatles*), they often served as session players for each other's songs. Their increasing disenchantment with each other is typified by the filmed row between Harrison and McCartney during the rehearsals of *Let It Be*. Harrison and Starr quit temporarily in 1968–69, and Lennon permanently—although privately—on 20 September 1969. But it was McCartney who made the break both permanent and public. In his debut solo album *McCartney*, released on 17 April 1970, McCartney provided an insert with album copies that included a self-written interview. In the insert, McCartney announced his break with the Beatles, stating that he had a better time with his family. As he became the *de facto* leader of the group, McCartney was pitted against the other Beatles in business disagreements over Apple Corps. McCartney wanted his father-in-law, Lee Eastman, to manage the Beatles' affairs, while the others wanted Allen Klein. The others won out, although Eastman and his son John were appointed as the Beatles' lawyers to oversee Klein's activities. On 31 December 1970, McCartney filed suit to dissolve the Beatles' partnership, citing interference with the creative control of his musical projects by the group and others. On 9 January 1975, the Beatles & Co. was formally dissolved. Lawsuits by ex-Beatles against Klein, against each other, and EMI/Capitol continued until 1989.

WINGS, 1971–80

After Lennon announced that he was leaving the Beatles on 20 September 1969, McCartney and his family retired to his High Park Farm in Scotland the following October.[24] McCartney was bewildered, depressed, and angry not only over the breakup of the Beatles but also about his future as a recording artist. In short, he was suffering from a nervous breakdown. Could he make it as a musician after 12 years as a member of the world's most successful rock band? Yes, he could, according to Eastman. She was instrumental in giving McCartney the courage and strength to move on so that he could write songs and perform again.

McCartney also felt trapped by an unfair contract that obligated him to the now defunct Beatles. In July 1967, when Apple Corps was created, all four Beatles had signed an agreement that connected them financially for 10 years. Aside from songwriting royalties, all profits went into Apple, which the group jointly owned. Thus, all four Beatles would share in the royalties arising both from their work as a group and their solo albums. While still insisting that all things associated with the Beatles should be shared equally, McCartney wanted profits from his individual efforts to be his sole property, in addition to having complete artistic control over his work. Realizing that McCartney had composed the most commercially successful Beatle songs and would probably make the most commercially successful solo albums, Klein did not want to see McCartney dissolve his legal relationship with the Beatles, because

Lennon, Harrison, and Starr, as well as Klein, would lose their share of McCartney's potential earnings. But McCartney wanted out of the Beatles, hence he sued his fellow band members in court.

With Eastman's encouragement, McCartney began to record again. After returning from Scotland just before Christmas 1969, McCartney installed a Studer four-track tape recorder in his London residence on Cavendish Avenue. Without the benefit of a mixer or VU meters, McCartney began to record tracks for a solo album, the first of which was a song written in Scotland called "The Lovely Linda," which was done to test the machine. He finished many of the tracks at Abbey Road Studios No. 2 and Morgan Studios in Willesden. What resulted was McCartney's first solo album entitled *McCartney*. Aside from some backing vocals by Eastman, McCartney sang all the vocals and played all the instruments on the album.

McCartney found recording as a solo artist to be an exhilarating endeavor, similar to what he had experienced as a Beatle in the group's early days. Moreover, he wanted to form a new band, determining that there was life after the Beatles. He insisted that Eastman be a part of his new musical career by becoming a member of the band so that she and the children could be with him when the band was on tour. Despite her protests, she relented, and had to learn the piano under McCartney's tutelage. Although she did this for her family, it meant that she had to put her career as a photographer on hold.

McCartney's second album, *Ram*, was released in May 1971. He recorded it in New York between January and March 1971. Backing musicians included Dave Spinoza and Hugh McCracken on guitars, and Denny Seiwell, future member of Wings, on drums. McCartney also secured the services of the New York Philharmonic to play on the album. He worked intensively with Eastman on singing harmony parts in order to ensure that the album's vocal tracks sounded good. According to McCartney, he and Eastman cowrote some of the songs on *Ram*, which raised eyebrows everywhere, especially on the part of McCartney's publisher, who sued him.[25] Because of Eastman's hard work, the album was credited to both McCartney and Eastman.

After recording *Ram*, McCartney formed Wings in August 1971 with Denny Seiwell on drums; Denny Laine, former member of the Moody Blues, on guitar; McCartney on bass; and Eastman on keyboards.[26] In keeping with his back-to-basics approach that he was espousing as a Beatle during the filming of *Let It Be*, McCartney did not want to form a supergroup. Rehearsing at Rude Studio, a small four-track demo studio on McCartney's farm in Scotland, the fledgling band developed material for what would later constitute their first album, *Wings Wild Life*, at Abbey Road Studios. McCartney introduced the band to the press on 3 August 1971. He thought of the name Wings while in a hospital waiting room as his daughter Stella was being born by Caesarean section.

During the 1970s, Wings was extremely successful as a band. Despite several lineup changes, they rivaled the accomplishments of the Beatles, releasing

10 albums, receiving gold records, garnering 11 Grammy Award nominations, and playing to sold-out concerts. By 1980, Wings had sold more records than the Beatles. When they began, Wings played impromptu concerts at British universities and toured Europe in an open-air double-decker bus. For these early tours, McCartney recruited another guitar player, Henry McCullough, formerly of Joe Cocker's Grease Band. Wings eventually toured Europe, the United States, and Australia. In October 1972, McCartney and Wings recorded the theme song for the 1973 James Bond film, *Live and Let Die*, which showcased their versatility. In December 1973, Wings released the album *Band on the Run*, their most acclaimed work that won them two Grammy Awards. Recorded in Lagos, Nigeria, with McCartney, Eastman, and Laine serving as the album's musicians (McCullough and Seiwell had recently left the group), *Band on the Run* reached the top of the charts on both sides of the Atlantic and became Wings' first platinum disc. Their single, "Mull of Kintyre," a Scottish waltz featuring bagpipes, took the UK by storm in 1977. Written by McCartney and Laine, the song remained the UK's top-selling single until Band Aid recorded "Do They Know It's Christmas" in 1984.

Wings broke up in 1981 amid disagreements between McCartney and Laine over touring and the payment of salary to Laine for playing in the band, as well as royalties for songs he cowrote with McCartney. Laine wanted to continue touring, but McCartney did not, fearing that he would be the next Beatle murdered in the wake of John Lennon's death on 8 December 1980. Laine was likewise not satisfied with the salary McCartney paid him, or with the fact that he was not collecting what he believed to be proper songwriting royalties.

But for McCartney, the breakup actually began when he was arrested at Tokyo's Narita Airport on 16 January 1980 for possession of 7.7 ounces of marijuana in his luggage. He had finally received permission from Japanese authorities to tour that country, something denied him for Wings' 1975–76 world tour due to his previous drug convictions. McCartney's arrest and subsequent release meant that the Japanese tour had to be canceled. MPL productions, McCartney's company, also canceled tours of other countries scheduled for that year. The cancellations were a costly affair not only for McCartney but also for the other members of Wings, who resented him for the loss of substantial potential earnings. As a result, Wings began to disintegrate. Reflecting on those events years later, McCartney remarked that Wings was finished at the time. He felt that the band had "sort of lost its charm. It wasn't fun anymore and the bust had definitely sort of cemented that."[27]

To compound matters, McCartney and his band mates were going their separate ways in 1980. In May, McCartney released *McCartney II*, an album in which he played all the instruments and did most of the vocals (Eastman provided some backing vocals). Laine signed a new record deal and vented his anger against McCartney's drug bust through a single called "Japanese

Tears," a song he recorded with former Wings members Henry McCullough and Denny Seiwell. Furthermore, he and Steve Holly (Wings's drummer at the time) went on tour with Laine's wife Jo Jo, Mike Piggot, and Andy Richards (of the Alex Harvey Band). Things came to a head with the murder of Lennon in December. As he began to receive death threats against him and his family, McCartney decided not to tour any more. As a result, Laine quit the group in April 1981 because he wanted to play concerts again, initiating the official breakup of the band. McCartney informed band members Steve Holly and Laurence Juber (Wings's lead guitarist at the time) by telephone that Wings had folded. McCartney was working on a new album entitled *Tug of War* with his old producer George Martin beginning in late 1980. He explained to Holly and Juber that the band was now defunct and that his forthcoming album, on the advice of Martin, would be a solo project.[28]

COLLABORATIONS AND AN ORATORIO, 1981–96

The murder of John Lennon motivated McCartney to collaborate with George Harrison and Ringo Starr in 1981 on Harrison's tribute to Lennon, "All Those Years Ago." The first of numerous collaborations with various artists during the 1980s and 1990s, McCartney contributed backing vocals to the song. Yet, despite the sorrow McCartney felt at the loss of Lennon, which spurred him to work on "All Those Years Ago," his relationship with Lennon had changed over the years. The arguments they had over the management of Apple, the barbs they traded in the press and in songs such as McCartney's "Too Many People" (*Ram*, 1971), as well as Lennon's "How Do You Sleep" (*Imagine*, 1971), along with the divisive influence of Yoko Ono, produced a rift that the two could never really repair. Even if they avoided talking about the financial mess at Apple on the phone or during McCartney's visits to Lennon's apartment in New York, underpinning any cordial conversation about family life was a bitter musical rivalry and a dislike McCartney had for Ono.[29] But regardless of the rancor between them, they were actually fond of each other, although they were reluctant to communicate those feelings to each other when Lennon was alive.

During their years together as Beatles, McCartney condescended to Harrison, criticizing him in the studio for his solo guitar work on McCartney's songs. Moreover, according to Harrison, McCartney began to resent his emergence as a songwriter, which meant that he deserved more songs on Beatle albums.[30] In spite of being McCartney's original mate in the Beatles and lifelong "little brother," Harrison did not get along with McCartney. He did not care for McCartney's superior attitude during and after their years as Beatles. But in the final analysis, they ultimately cared for each other, as seen by McCartney's visit to Harrison a few weeks before his death in 2001 when he held Harrison's hand for a couple of hours, and McCartney's attendance and participation at special tribute concerts in 2002 at the Empire Theatre in Liverpool and the Royal Albert Hall in London.

In contrast, McCartney got along very well with Starr. He contributed two songs, "Private Property" and "Attention," to Starr's 1981 album, *Stop and Smell the Roses.* On both songs, McCartney played bass and piano and sang backing vocals.

McCartney continued to collaborate with other musical artists in the wake of Wings' breakup by inviting some famous musicians to play and sing with him on his 1982 album, *Tug of War.* Recording part of the album on the island of Montserrat, McCartney was joined in the studio by the likes of Ringo Starr, Stanley Clarke, Denny Laine, Stevie Wonder, Carl Perkins, Steve Gadd, and Eric Stewart. His most famous collaboration on the album was with Stevie Wonder on "Ebony and Ivory," his song about racial harmony. McCartney envisioned the song as a duet with an African-American singer, and asked Wonder to record the song with him. Besides their recording of the vocals, McCartney played piano and bass, while Wonder played drums and synthesizer.

In the early 1980s, McCartney worked with Michael Jackson on three duets. Having recorded McCartney's song "Girlfriend" for his album *Off the Wall* (1979), Jackson wrote a song entitled "This Girl Is Mine" and contacted McCartney to see if he might be interested in recording the song with him as a duet. McCartney agreed. Between recording sessions for *Tug of War,* McCartney recorded "This Girl Is Mine" with Jackson in Los Angeles, adding finishing touches to the song, which earned him a songwriting co-credit.[31] The song was included on Jackson's 1982 *Thriller* album, which became one of the greatest selling albums of all time. In early 1981, Jackson went to London in order to write some songs with McCartney. Out of this collaboration came the duets "Say, Say, Say" and "The Man." Although written quickly, "Say, Say, Say" took a long time to record, with final overdubbing taking place in 1983. It and "The Man" were included on McCartney's 1983 album, *Pipes of Peace.*

McCartney worked with other artists on songs from his feature film, *Give My Regards to Broad Street.* Two years in the making, and initially financed by McCartney, the film was released in 1984.[32] It was a flop at the box office, and critics panned the film. But the film's songs featured McCartney, joined by Eastman, playing with musicians such as George Martin on piano, Ringo Starr on drums, John Paul Jones on bass, and Dave Edmunds and Chris Spedding on guitar. Starr and his wife, former Bond girl Barbara Bach, costarred with McCartney and Eastman in the film. Their presence, however, could not save the film from its inane script and expensive music videos.

After *Give My Regards to Broad Street,* McCartney continued to find new musical partners with whom to create and record music. For his 1986 album *Press to Play,* he teamed up with 10cc guitarist Eric Stewart to write six of the album's songs. In 1987, McCartney asked Elvis Costello if he would like to write songs with him, to which Costello agreed. Some of the songs from their collaboration wound up on McCartney's 1989 album, *Flowers in the Dirt.* In Costello, McCartney found a songwriting partner who challenged him creatively, something he had not experienced since the days of John Lennon. Yet, McCartney found himself at odds with Costello when it came to producing *Flowers in the Dirt.* Costello was, in a word, too avant-garde for McCartney's commercial musical tastes, making McCartney seek other producers with which to work.

In 1988, the Royal Liverpool Philharmonic Orchestra commissioned McCartney to compose a work to celebrate its sesquicentennial. With the help of British conductor Carl Davis, McCartney wrote his first major classical work, the *Liverpool Oratorio.* It was an ambitious musical project for McCartney. Composed in the tradition of English choral music, the *Liverpool Oratorio* features a semi-autobiographical text set to music composed primarily by McCartney but realized by Davis. The Royal Liverpool Philharmonic Orchestra premiered the 95-minute work on 28 June 1991 at Liverpool's Anglican Cathedral. EMI Classics recorded the premiere and issued it in the UK and US in October 1991.[33]

McCartney reunited with Harrison and Starr in the early 1990s to work on *The Beatles Anthology,* an audio-video history of the band. While the project began before the group broke up, nothing of any substance materialized during the 1970s and most of the 1980s.[34] But in 1989, the surviving ex-Beatles rekindled their interest in the project and approached several top directors about working with them on it. They decided to work on the project by themselves through the auspices of Apple, securing Geoff Wonfor as director. Besides three double-CD sets of previously unreleased material and a 10-hour video documentary, McCartney's collaboration with Harrison and Starr yielded the first new Beatles single in 25 years, "Free as a Bird," which was included on the *Anthology I* CD-set released in 1995. Apple Corps approached Yoko Ono, Lennon's widow, in order to see if there were any rough homemade demos by Lennon in her possession that could serve as the basis of a new single. Ono complied by giving them four songs, one of which was "Free as a Bird," composed by Lennon in 1977. McCartney, Harrison, and Starr added new vocal tracks and instrumentation to the song, pretending that Lennon was away on vacation. They did the same with Lennon's "Real Love," composed by Lennon in the late 1970s. That Beatles single was included on the *Anthology II* CD-set released in 1996.

SOLO WORK AND MORE CLASSICAL MUSIC, 1997–2007

Beginning in 1997, McCartney released an unprecedented series of critically acclaimed solo albums. He issued *Flaming Pie* in 1997, considered by critics to be his best album since *Tug of War* (1982). After the death of his wife Linda Eastman due to breast cancer in April 1998, McCartney explored his rock 'n' roll roots by releasing a collection of 1950s-style songs called *Run Devil Run* in 1999, which reaffirmed his credentials as a rocker. That same year saw him inducted into the Rock and Roll Hall of Fame as a solo artist. In May 2001, McCartney released *Wingspan: Hits and History*, a compilation of hits by Wings, to coincide with the documentary *Wingspan: An Intimate Portrait*, which featured McCartney being interviewed by his daughter Mary throughout the film.[35] The album included songs recorded before and after McCartney's association with Wings.

In November 2001, McCartney released *Driving Rain*. He recorded the album at Henson Recording Studio in Los Angeles in two weeks in order to keep things fresh. Assisting McCartney were Rusty Anderson on guitar, Gabe Dixon on keyboards, and Abe Laboriel, Jr., on drums. He penned two of the songs, "Spinning on an Axis" and "Back in the Sunshine Again," with his son James. McCartney went on tour in 2002 with a new band composed of Anderson and Brian Ray on guitars, Paul "Wix" Wickens on keyboards, and Laboriel on drums. The tour culminated with a concert in Red Square in 2003. Two years later, McCartney released his twentieth studio album, the Grammy-nominated *Chaos and Creation in the Back Yard*, about which critics raved. In 2007, McCartney issued his twenty-first album, *Memory Almost Full*.

McCartney continued to explore classical music throughout the late 1990s and first decade of the twenty-first century. In 1997, McCartney released his second large-scale classical work, *Standing Stone: A Symphonic Poem*. To help celebrate EMI's hundredth anniversary and its close relationship with McCartney, Richard Lyttleton, president of EMI Classics, commissioned McCartney to compose *Standing Stone*. McCartney spent four years composing the music without the help of a full-time collaborator, although he had several musicians assist him with the project's realization. In 1999, McCartney released *Working Classical*, a collection of songs inspired by his wife, Linda Eastman. The album blended McCartney's pop and classical music interests. Finally, in 2006, McCartney released his fourth classical album with the oratorio, *Ecce Cor Meum* (*Behold My Heart*). After a visit to Magdalen College, the University of Oxford, Oxford, England, with Eastman in 1997, McCartney received a commission from Anthony Smith, President of Magdalen College, to compose an oratorio similar to Handel's *Messiah* that would celebrate the College's recently opened chapel. The work was recorded at the Abbey Road Studios in March 2006, and premiered at the Royal Albert Hall in London on 3 November 2006.

SCOPE AND ORGANIZATION OF THIS BOOK

Paul McCartney is regarded as the most successful composer, singer/songwriter, and musician in popular music history. Since leaving the Beatles in

1970, McCartney has been very active as a performer and recording artist. As reflected by albums such as *Driving Rain, Chaos and Creation in the Backyard, Ecce Cor Meum,* and *Memory Almost Full,* McCartney continues to compose and record in the twenty-first century, embracing different musical styles, most likely for years to come.

Although scholars have examined McCartney's music as a member of the Beatles, they have neglected his solo music.[36] They have done relatively little work analyzing the elements of his musical language, or the ways in which he integrates music and text into a unified song. The present volume intends to rectify that situation.

In *The Words and Music of Paul McCartney: The Solo Years,* I present a broad view of McCartney's solo music, beginning with his debut album *McCartney* (1970) and encompassing his work up to *Memory Almost Full* (2007), and consider its impact on popular music and culture. I offer a portrait of a deeply personal artist whose music continues to speak to generations of people. Although McCartney's days as a Beatle have informed his solo music, I will demonstrate that he has successfully transcended his musical past in the albums he has released since 1970. While I will focus on both his popular and classical music, I will not examine, due to the volume's scope, McCartney's electronic music activities, music for films (except for *Live and Let Die, Give My Regards to Broad Street,* and *Spies Like Us*), and albums recorded and produced under pseudonyms (e.g., the Fireman). In addition, I will only examine what I consider to be his most significant singles, which can be found as bonus tracks on CDs.[37]

The Words and Music of Paul McCartney considers McCartney's solo music in a chronological fashion. It examines his individual songs along with the albums from which they emerge. The book will also include any personal information about McCartney that has any direct bearing on the listening experience, as well as the cultural and musical scenes that may have influenced his songwriting. As for his classical music, the approach taken in this book requires a basic familiarity with musical terms associated with choral and instrumental music.

The discussions in this book about McCartney's popular and classical music presupposes a basic knowledge of melody, harmony, rhythm, texture, timbre, and form. Besides the detail I provide in my discussions about McCartney's works for the musically trained reader, I include information about chord structure, form, keys, melody, and scales in the glossary that I hope will assist the reader in grasping the material. In sum, I strive to enhance the reader's listening experience of McCartney's music by providing perspectives that prompt him or her to make informed judgments about McCartney's creative work.

In order to facilitate my discussions of McCartney's music, I encourage the reader, whenever possible (especially through the auspices of a library), to listen to each song or classical work with sheet music publication or musical score in hand.[38] MPL Communications (McCartney's publishing company), in association with Hal Leonard Corporation, has published piano-vocal-guitar songbooks of most of McCartney's solo albums. Although not containing entirely accurate transcriptions of the songs, they do include tunes and piano parts that relate to McCartney's recordings. MPL Communications has also collaborated with Faber Music to publish scores of most of McCartney's classical music.

In *The Words and Music of Paul McCartney*, I tell the story of McCartney's solo music album by album in seven chapters. Chapter 1 examines McCartney's first two solo albums, *McCartney* and *Ram*, in the aftermath of the Beatles' breakup. Chapters 2 and 3 continue to chart McCartney's solo career in the 1970s by considering his work with Wings, beginning with *Wings Wild Life* and ending with *Back to the Egg*. In Chapter 4, the book considers McCartney's music of the 1980s, particularly his collaborations with other artists, such as: Stevie Wonder, Michael Jackson, Eric Stewart, and Elvis Costello. The chapter also looks at *McCartney II* and his music for two films, *Give My Regards to Broad Street* and *Spies Like Us*.

Chapter 5 looks at McCartney's forays into classical music in the 1990s by examining *The Liverpool Oratorio* and *Standing Stone*. It also considers McCartney's work with Harrison and Starr on *The Beatles Anthology* project, which resulted in "Free as a Bird" and "Real Love," along with the albums *Off the Ground* and *Flaming Pie*, the latter considered to be his most Beatles-influenced work. Chapter 6 focuses on four of McCartney's albums issued during the first decade of the twenty-first century: (1) *Driving Rain*, (2) his critically acclaimed *Chaos and Creation in the Backyard*, (3) *Ecce Cor Meum*, and (4) *Memory Almost Full*. In Chapter 7, I close my discussion of McCartney and his music by exploring his stature as a pop music icon.

To conclude the book, I include a glossary and a selected discography/videography, as well as a selected bibliography. As mentioned above, the glossary surveys musical concepts that will help the reader understand the book's discussions about McCartney's music. The selected discography/videography lists a sampling of McCartney's albums, films, and videos since leaving the Beatles. The selected bibliography includes sources of both McCartney's Beatle and solo work.

The Remaking of a Beatle: Paul McCartney as Solo Artist, 1970–71

McCartney (1970)

Paul McCartney released his debut solo album entitled *McCartney* on 17 April 1970. Work on the album began in December 1969 when he was still a member of the Beatles.[1] McCartney regarded his solo project as an escape from the acrimonious disputes he was having with Lennon, Harrison, and Starr over the management of Apple. Keeping a low profile in order to prevent Apple and Allen Klein from knowing of the album's existence, McCartney started to record the album's songs in his London home on Cavendish Avenue. He used a Studer 4-track tape recorder (borrowed from EMI) and one microphone. He also worked without the benefit of a mixer or VU meters. McCartney finished the songs begun at home, as well as recorded other songs for the album, at Abbey Road Studios No. 2 and Morgan Studios in Willesden. Aside from some vocal contributions from his wife, Linda Eastman, McCartney was a veritable one-man band in his debut as a solo artist. One week before the album's release, McCartney informed the world through a press release that he and the other Beatles were going their separate ways.

In comparison with the artistically polished *Abbey Road*, the Beatles' last album released in 1969, *McCartney* is a big disappointment, suggesting, in the minds of McCartney's critics, that without John Lennon as a sounding board, his solo work would never attain the stature of his work as a Beatle. The album is rough and unpolished in content, containing tracks of questionable quality, many of which are either reworked unfinished numbers or simply improvised. But McCartney loved the spontaneity and rough edge of the album and decided to release it, never envisaging it as a continuation of his work as a Beatle.

The album opens with a 45-second fragment entitled "The Lovely Linda," dedicated to Linda Eastman. McCartney used this unfinished number to test his recording equipment. Based on the commentary he provided for the album, McCartney stated that the song was a "trailer to the full song, which will be recorded in the future."[2] And indeed it was. McCartney reworked the song and included it on *Paul McCartney's Working Classical* in 1999.

Written in Scotland, "The Lovely Linda" is played in the key of A major, although tuned high to sound closer to B♭. It consists of four vocal phrases, arranged in two antecedent-consequent pairs. The melody starts on E, the dominant of A, and descends in each of the song's four phrases. To balance each antecedent ending on a lower E, McCartney ends each consequent on an A. McCartney recorded the vocal and acoustic guitar accompaniment on the first track. On the other tracks, he added another acoustic guitar part, hand slaps on a book, and bass guitar.

McCartney wrote "That Would Be Something," the album's next track, likewise in Scotland. He recorded the tune at his London home and mixed it later at Abbey Road Studios. On the song, McCartney sings, provides percussive vocal sounds, and plays acoustic and electric guitars, bass, tom-tom, and cymbal. The song opens with a catchy guitar riff in F major based on the song's vocal line, played by McCartney via a capo in E major with guitar strings tuned to an E-major chord (E–B–E–G♯–B–E).[3] After the riff is sounded at the song's beginning, the bass and then vocal join the musical texture.

The text of the song may refer to McCartney's relationship with Linda Eastman, who, according to John Blaney, is symbolically cleansed by the rain and "becomes one with nature."[4] McCartney sings the text, "That would be something . . . to meet you in the falling rain, mama," repeatedly throughout the song. He achieves contrast by setting the first part of the text ("That would be something . . . ") to a jerky musical motif, following it with a more flowing melodic line on "to meet you in the falling rain, mama."

The third track on *McCartney*, an instrumental number called "Valentine's Day," was ad-libbed at McCartney's Cavendish Avenue home. For this instrumental, McCartney layered parts onto the multitrack tape of his Studer tape recorder, beginning with drums, proceeding to acoustic and electric guitars and then to bass. In using this layering procedure, McCartney was revisiting a recording practice begun on the *White Album* when he recorded backing tracks for his songs without the assistance of the other Beatles. It allowed him to explore his creativity freely, building up a song on multitrack tape without knowing to where it would lead. McCartney completed the final mix of "Valentine's Day" at Abbey Road Studios No. 2 on 22 February 1970.

McCartney begins "Valentine's Day" with an acoustic guitar riff on the notes C–D–D and A–G–A, with drums in the background. The riff is supported by open-fifth sonorities—power chords, in the vocabulary of guitarists (C5–D5–D5, A5–G5–A5). McCartney then improvises a solo on electric guitar—and adds a bass part—as he plays rhythm guitar on the acoustic. As the tempo quickens, the music increases in intensity, culminating in a cadenza for electric guitar, before fading out with electric guitar, bass, and drums.

In January 1969, McCartney performed an unfinished version of "Every Night" while rehearsing at Twickenham Studios during the filming of *Let It Be*. He completed the song's lyrics while vacationing in Greece later that year, recording and mixing the song at Abbey Road Studios on 22 and 24 February 1970 in order to include it on *McCartney*. "Every Night" includes a double-tracked vocal part, acoustic guitar, bass, and drums. Like "The Lovely Linda" and "That Would Be Something," "Every Night" was inspired by McCartney's relationship with Linda Eastman.

Unlike the three previous tracks, "Every Night" exhibits a more tightly knit musical structure. Set in E major, the song consists of an intro, two verses, and a bridge, which fades out the last time it is sung.[5] Each verse consists of three sections, with the first section composed of two three-measure phrases and the last two sections of separate four-measure phrases, each parsed into two-measure units. In the first section, McCartney sounds an E7 harmony for two measures, followed by an E7sus4 in the third measure, generated by the melodic A that concludes the first vocal phrase. That phrase and its harmonies are then repeated. Because they suggest a secondary dominant seventh chord, V7/IV, thereby throwing the key of E major into doubt at the beginning of the song, the E7 and E7sus4 harmonies heighten the sense of uncertainty faced by the protagonist. What will he do every night? McCartney accentuates the protagonist's answer by sounding an E–F♯m7–B7–E harmonic progression (I–ii7–V7–I) that clarifies the key of E major in the verse's third section. Tonight, he opts for domesticity (over less desirable options) by wanting to be with his love and inspiration, Linda Eastman.

McCartney composed the next track on the album, the instrumental "Hot as Sun," in 1958 or 1959. It makes a brief appearance during the filming of *Let It Be* when McCartney improvises a few lines in a humorous Hawaiian style. McCartney never developed the song for the Beatles. He recorded the instrumental and added the "middle eight" (bridge in a 32-bar form) at Morgan Studios. On the song, which lasts 1 minute and 28 seconds, McCartney plays acoustic guitar, electric guitar, rhythm guitar, bass, organ, drums, bongos, and maracas.

"Hot as Sun" segues into two unrelated pieces, "Glasses" and "Suicide." "Glasses" consists of 48 seconds of multi-tracked wineglass sounds. It is followed by a nine-second snippet of the chorus of "Suicide," which McCartney originally intended for Frank Sinatra. McCartney has described "Suicide" as a horrible, cabaret-like song that he wrote before the Beatles became famous. During McCartney's Beatle days, Sinatra actually contacted McCartney and requested that he write a song for him. McCartney complied by sending him a demo of "Suicide." Having heard the song, Sinatra promptly rejected it, thinking that McCartney was "having him on." McCartney eventually premiered "Suicide" on the BBC's *Michael Parkinson Show* on 2 December 1999. The show was broadcast on 3 December on BBC One.[6]

"Hot as Sun" is set in G major. The song's three verses feature McCartney playing a series of ascending and descending sixths on the guitar that are decorated by upper- and lower-neighbor embellishments (e.g., B–G/C–A/B–G). Each verse ends with a half cadence on V, a D-major chord, creating a sense that more is to come. In the bridge, McCartney plays a harmonic progression (IV–I–IV–V) in broken-chord style on the organ that begins with IV, a C-major chord, to set up the retransitional dominant that directs the music back to the verse. As the third verse ends, the bridge comes back— spliced in rather clumsily, sounding a D-major chord. The song fades out while the next song, "Glasses," emerges. Following that, McCartney splices in the chorus of "Suicide," an aural snippet in which he sings while accompanying himself on the piano in F major.

McCartney wrote "Junk" in March 1968 while attending the Maharishi's camp in Rishikesh, India, to learn transcendental meditation. In May, he completed a demo of the song at George Harrison's home in Esher, southwest of London. Despite the fact that it was completed in time for the *White Album* in 1968, "Junk" was shelved. During the filming of *Let It Be*, McCartney went through a version of "Junk" in January 1970 at Twickenham Studios; however, the Beatles never recorded a formal studio version of the song. Ultimately, "Junk" was not issued until its inclusion on *McCartney* in April 1970. McCartney recorded the vocal of the song, plus parts for two acoustic guitars and bass, at his Cavendish Avenue home in London. Later, he added backup vocals, bass drum, snare drum with brushes, and a small xylophone part at Morgan Studios in Willesden.

"Junk" is a sentimental triple-time waltz in A major.[7] Each verse begins, however, in F♯ minor before moving to A major. Such tonal ambiguity recalls McCartney's Beatle song, "And I Love Her," from 1964. In the beginning of that song, a conflict of priority arises between C♯ minor and E major as the verse emphasizes the former key, whereas the refrain ends in the latter. In the two phrases that constitute each verse of "Junk," the first phrase begins with a key-defining i–V7–i (F♯m–C♯7–F♯m) harmonic progression in F♯ minor. It then ends on a Dmaj7, a chord that prepares the key of A major in the second phrase through its membership in both keys (VI7 in F♯ minor, IV7 in A major). In the second phrase, A major is established by a plagal progression (IV–I) involving that Dmaj7 chord. After being sounded for two measures, it progresses to an A chord that is prolonged by the upper-neighbor note embellishments of an Asus4, 9 chord.

In the first two verses of "Junk," the melody accentuates the tonal ambiguity suggested by its chordal support. In the first phrase, the melody affirms the tonality of F♯ minor by descending, with some melodic embellishments, from

C# to F#, articulating a key-defining structural descent in F# minor via scale degrees $\hat{5}$–$\hat{4}$–$\hat{3}$–$\hat{1}$. In the second phrase, two melodic gestures (F#–G#–A–B, F#–A) still emphasize F# in the first two measures. Acting as a large-scale upper neighbor to the phrase's last note, F# finally resolves to E, clarifying the tonality of A major. Finally, in subsequent verses of "Junk," despite the wordless melodic embellishments added to the first phrase, the melodic structure as described above is left unchanged.

Situated between the verses of "Junk" are two phrases that comprise the song's contrasting bridge. Gone is the tonal ambiguity of the verses; instead, through both melody and harmony, the bridge articulates A major. The melody begins on a D and descends stepwise to a G# before resolving to an A decorated by its upper-neighbor note B. The harmonic support starts with a Dm7, a chord (iv7) borrowed from the key of A minor that points to McCartney's penchant for modal mixture in his songs. The harmonic support then establishes A major through E7 and A chords in the third and fourth measures of each phrase. Finally, reinforcing the bridge's role as an element of contrast in the song is the absence of dotted and syncopated rhythms in the vocal part, as opposed to those found in the song's verses, and the faster harmonic rhythm found in the chordal support.

Since the five verses are essentially identical to each other musically, "Junk" exhibits an AABAABA form. In the last section, the voice drops out in order to let the guitar end the song with melodic riffs based on the harmonic structure of the verse. Through this formal structure, McCartney narrates a story about buying junk found in a shop. The sign in the shop window says "buy," while the junk asks the question, "Why?" But ultimately, the junk serves as memories for McCartney and Eastman.

"Singalong Junk" is an instrumental version of "Junk." It is the eleventh track on the album. When he recorded "Junk" at his London home, McCartney taped two versions, without and with vocals, respectively, before adding more parts at Morgan Studios. Take one was "Singalong Junk," whereas take two was "Junk." For "Singalong Junk," McCartney laid down guitar, bass, and piano parts at home, adding electric guitar, bass drum, sizzle cymbal, and string sounds from a Mellotron at Morgan. Although longer than "Junk," "Singalong Junk" essentially follows the form of its vocal counterpart. Acoustic guitar and piano take their turns with the melody of each verse, while the electric guitar plays the melody of the bridge. But why did McCartney include this track on the album? The most likely answer is that he did not have enough material, so he had to pad it.

"Man We Was Lonely," the seventh track on the album, is a song that focuses on McCartney's emotional pain arising from the breakup of the Beatles. The opening lyrics depict his anguish at the dissolution of the only band that he had known up to that time. It was devastating experience to be alienated from band mates with whom he had shared so much during the last 13 years. But McCartney somehow remained upbeat in spite of all the turmoil. Through the song's refrain, "But now we're fine all the while," McCartney affirms, rather defiantly to John Lennon and Yoko Ono, that he, with the help of his wife Linda Eastman, had weathered a furious storm.

McCartney wrote "Man We Was Lonely" in bed at his London home, shortly before he completed the album.[8] He finished the song on 25 February 1970 at Abbey Road Studios after doing 12 takes, overdubs, and mixing in a 7-hour session. On the song, McCartney sings the melody while his wife sings the harmony a third above in the verse or answers him antiphonally in the bridge. He also plays electric guitar, bass, and bass drum. McCartney even achieves a steel-guitar-like sound on the track by playing a Fender Telecaster with a drum peg.[9]

"Man We Was Lonely" is in A major.[10] McCartney begins the song with an 18-measure intro that features not only the steel-guitar sound of the Fender Telecaster but also a plagal progression enhanced by modal mixture (I–IV–iv–I), a harmonic technique characteristic of his compositional style. Beginning with an A13, the music cycles through D, D-minor, and A chords, with the D-minor chord borrowed from A minor. Complementing this harmonic progression is a series of ascending melodic gestures that culminate with appoggiaturas resolving down by step on the downbeats of every even measure.

After the intro, verse and bridge alternate. The verse consists of a 16-measure parallel period, with the first phrase sounding tonic and subdominant chords, A and D, before concluding with a half cadence on an E7 chord. The second phrase repeats the chordal sequence of the first but ends with the tonic chord on A. The bridge modulates to the key of E minor, heightening the contrast between bridge and verse. It consists of two phrases, the first eight measures in length, the second extended to twelve measures through the prolongation of the closing tonic chord, now E major. That tonic harmony is reinterpreted as a retransitional dominant in order to lead back into the verse. After a succession of verses and bridges, the song concludes with the music of the intro now used as an outro.

"Oo You," the eighth track on the CD, opened the second side of the original vinyl album. McCartney recorded the first three tracks of the song as an instrumental at his London home with the idea that it might one day become a song. He wrote the lyrics to "Oo You" one day after lunch, just before he left for Morgan Studios to complete the song. That afternoon McCartney added vocals and made overdubs involving electric guitar, cowbell, tambourine, and aerosol spray (panned hard right).[11] While mixing the song, he used tape echo to manipulate guitar feedback from one channel to another at each repetition of the song's bridge.

"Oo You" is an upbeat rock song in G. The nonsensical lyrics center around descriptions of a woman and her persona. After he taps off four beats on the hi-hat, McCartney plays a bluesy electric-guitar riff that is doubled an octave lower by the bass. After repeating the riff with the guitar part double-tracked, McCartney accompanies himself with thirds on the guitar as he sings the vocal. Harmonically, the verses are based on a G chord alternating with a C chord, whereas the bridge takes that same harmonic pattern but ends with the retransitional dominant chord on D. Overall, the song seems underdeveloped, a veritable "throwaway," with an intro–verse–bridge pattern that is stated three times with little musical variety.

McCartney improvised the next track, the instrumental "Momma Miss America," at his London home. Initially, "Momma Miss America" consisted of two pieces, but according to McCartney's commentary of the album's songs, the two pieces were joined together accidentally (and rather clumsily) by an edit that McCartney retained. At the beginning of the track, someone announces the original title of the song by saying, "Rock 'n' Roll Springtime, take one." Each piece is marked by introductions played on the drums, with the second piece beginning at ca. 1:57.

Both parts of "Momma Miss America" are based on three-chord blues progressions featuring tonic, subdominant, and dominant harmonies, the first in A minor and the second in G major. McCartney devised the instrumental's harmonic structure before adding the melody. That being said, the second part of "Momma Miss America" is more dynamic melodically than the first because of its predominant electric guitar solo where McCartney plays guitar riffs based on a G minor pentatonic scale, all enhanced by frequent string bending. Yet, in the final analysis, this number is another "throwaway" that should have never made it onto the album.

McCartney started "Teddy Boy" in India in 1968, only to complete it in Scotland and London. He recorded the song with the other Beatles during the *Get Back* sessions on 24 and 28 January 1969 at Apple Studios, London. Because it did not meet McCartney's standards, this group version of the song was scrapped from the *Let It Be* film and remained unreleased until it appeared on the *Anthology 3* CD released in October 1996.[12] McCartney recorded a solo version of "Teddy Boy" for his debut album, beginning it at his Cavendish Avenue home and then overdubbing it at Morgan Studios. On the song, McCartney plays guitar and bass and is joined on harmony vocals by Linda Eastman on the chorus.

"Teddy Boy" is in the key of D major. McCartney opens the song with a four-measure intro on the acoustic guitar. He strums an open-position D chord on every beat, with a quick A chord (minus the C♯) thrown in on the offbeat before the next measure. In the first part of the verse, McCartney plays a harmonic progression in D major that moves structurally from the tonic to the dominant: D, A, Am, Em, G, and A (I–V–v–ii–IV–V). His use of a minor dominant following a major one in the verse's middle illustrates yet again his penchant for modal mixture in order to generate colorful harmonic effects. McCartney uses the penultimate G chord as a lower-neighbor embellishment to the final A chord in order to highlight the half cadence in D. He then repeats this two-chord succession a third higher, but this time with sevenths added to each chord (B7–C♯7), in order to modulate to F♯ major. The rest of the verse features the opening chord progression now transposed to the new key.

The chorus is a parallel period that features descending-fifth progressions involving secondary dominants. The first part of the chorus moves from F♯ (V/vi), to B7 (V7/ii), to E (V/V), and to a half cadence on A (V). The second half of the chorus uses the same progression but reaches closure through an authentic cadence on D (I). McCartney closes the song with an outro consisting of a repetition of the first verse followed by an instrumental coda that ends in F♯ major.

McCartney wrote "Maybe I'm Amazed" in London at the piano. The song was finished on 22 February 1970 at Abbey Road Studios. Its instrumentation includes piano, organ, solo guitar, backing guitars, bass, and drums. McCartney sings lead vocal with Linda Eastman joining him on backup vocals. McCartney made a promotional film of the song that was produced by Charlie Jenkins and directed by David Putnam. The film featured Eastman's photos of McCartney, herself, and her daughter, Heather. The film was shown on London Weekend Television and *The Ed Sullivan Show* on 19 April 1970.[13]

"Maybe I'm Amazed" is clearly the best song on the album. It deals with McCartney's disenchantment with the dissolution of the Beatles and Eastman's role in helping him regain his confidence in order to begin anew as a solo artist. At the outset of the song, McCartney accentuates his personal insecurities musically by vacillating between the keys of D and C major. He begins by playing an intro on the piano consisting of a chord progression in D major that culminates with a half cadence (D, Dm, Em7, and A7 [I–i–ii7–V7]). The expectation of D major is thwarted by a deceptive progression to a B♭-major chord as McCartney begins to sing the song's first verse. Acting as a pivot chord (♭VI in D, ♭VII in C), this B♭-major chord facilitates a modulation to C major when the verse begins.

Each verse consists of two parallel periods set to the same basic chord progression. The first period begins with B♭, F, C, and G chords in the antecedent, followed by B♭, F, and C chords in the consequent. A chromatic scale connects the first period to the second. Because it functions as ♭VII in C major, the B♭-major chord lends a diatonic mixolydian flavor to the verse. The second period differs harmonically from the first by an effective use of modal mixture in its consequent. McCartney uses mixture chords from C minor, A♭, and E♭ major to enhance the expression of the line, "And maybe I'm amazed at the way I really need you."

The bridge of "Maybe I'm Amazed" is in D major and consists of two phrases. Besides key, McCartney distinguishes bridge from verse by prolonging the tonic chord via a plagal progression (I–IV–I). He intensifies the bridge harmonically through an inner line that descends primarily by half steps (D–C♯–C♮–B–A), producing D, Dmaj7, D7, G, and D chords as a result. More significantly, the static (that is, unchanging) qualities of the bridge may underscore McCartney's realization that Eastman "may[ ]be ... the only woman who could ever help [him]." In order to return to each verse by means of a retransitional dominant, McCartney appends the song's intro, coupled with a wordless melisma, after the G chord of the bridge's second phrase. This move also enhances the coherence of the song through the consistent reintroduction of its intro.

"Kreen-Akore" is the last track on *McCartney*, and given its experimental qualities, an unusual way to close a debut solo album. According to the album's commentary, McCartney saw a television documentary about the Kreen-Akore Indians of Brazil and the pressures placed upon them to adapt to European ways.[14] Inspired by the program, McCartney began to record himself playing drums at Morgan Studios in order to depict the Indians on their hunt. He eventually structured the track into two sections, with the first initially featuring drums and then guitar, organ, and piano (0:00–1:54). Near the end of the section, McCartney and Eastman mimic animal noises (via tape manipulation) and even use a guitar case to simulate an animal stampede. The second section (1:55–4:14) begins with harmonies sung by McCartney and Eastman, followed by more drumming, overdubbed breathing, organ, and lead guitars in harmony. "Kreen-Akore" is in B♭, with the guitar riffs drawn from a B♭-minor pentatonic scale.

With the release of his solo debut album, McCartney wanted to prove to the musical world that he could be successful as a singer-songwriter without the Beatles. In terms of album sales, he was; in terms of critical reception, he was not.[15] Critics could not reconcile the album's homespun production values with the virtuosity of *Abbey Road*. The album, in short, sounded hastily put together and incomplete. Nonetheless, *McCartney* surprisingly stands the test of time. Two songs from the album, "Momma Miss America" and "Sing-along Junk," were included on the 1996 film *Jerry Maguire* and fare rather well with the rest of the movie's soundtrack.

RAM (1971)

In late 1970, McCartney was ready to record his second album. He and his family arrived in New York City on 3 January 1971 to begin work on what was to become *Ram*. Instead of playing all of the instruments himself as he did on his first album, McCartney wanted to enlist the aid of studio musicians to play guitar and drums on this new project. Upon arriving in New York City, McCartney held auditions for selected musicians. At the end of the tryouts, he secured the services of guitarist Dave Spinoza (one of New York's top session guitarists) and drummer Denny Seiwell (a future member of *Wings*). Later, McCartney replaced Spinoza with guitarist Hugh McCracken.[16]

McCartney recorded most of *Ram* at A & R Studios between January and March 1971, going to Columbia Studios for further overdubs and Sound

Recorders, Los Angeles for final mixing. In May, the album was released. When recording *Ram*, McCartney would sing his parts and would play either guitar or piano. He did not play bass, preferring to overdub the instrument later. On three of *Ram*'s songs, "Uncle Albert/Admiral Halsey," "Long Haired Lady," and "The Back Seat of My Car," McCartney enlisted the aid of the New York Philharmonic to play orchestral parts.

McCartney insisted that Linda Eastman be heavily involved with *Ram*. She sang harmonies on the album's songs and, by all accounts, received a baptism by fire due to McCartney's perfectionist bent. McCartney also claimed that he and Eastman cowrote some of the songs on *Ram*, which was met with skepticism on the part of reviewers and a lawsuit from Sir Lew Grade of ATV and Northern Songs. Most people regarded this as a sham, because Eastman was clearly not in John Lennon's league as a song collaborator. But in the final analysis, Eastman's work earned her an official co-credit on the album.

In *Ram*, McCartney included references to his deteriorating relationships with the other Beatles, particularly John Lennon. On the back of the album's cover is a photograph of two beetles fornicating, an obvious vulgar reference to what McCartney believed the others were doing to him. In the introduction to the album's first song, "Too Many People," McCartney sings "Piss off, cake," an epithet directed at Lennon. According to Blaney, "3 Legs" and "Smile Away" also contain oblique references to McCartney's disenchantment with his fellow band mates and Apple.[17] Naturally, the other Beatles responded, particularly Lennon. Through a postcard of him holding a pig by the ears inserted inside his 1971 album *Imagine*, Lennon satirized *Ram*'s cover of McCartney holding a ram by the horns. More significantly, Lennon included a track on *Imagine* entitled "How Do You Sleep" (George Harrison played slide guitar on the song) that characterized all of McCartney's songs, except "Yesterday," as "muzak." He felt compelled to write the song because of the insults he perceived McCartney made in "Too Many People" and "Dear Boy."[18]

The acerbically tinged "Too Many People" opens *Ram*. It reflects McCartney's view of Lennon as a self-righteous hypocrite. Besides the "Piss off, cake" (not "Piece of cake") of the introduction, McCartney took two swipes at both Lennon and his wife Yoko Ono.[19] Because he had had enough of what he considered Lennon and Ono's hypocrisy in which they would say one thing in public while doing the opposite in private, he inserted the line, "Too many people preaching practices," into the song. McCartney lashed out at Ono specifically in the original version of the line, "Yoko took your lucky break and broke it in two," which was changed later to "You took your lucky break and broke it in two."

In the instrumental intro of "Too Many People," McCartney displays his fondness for using modal mixture by alternating the tonic chord on G (I) with its minor subdominant on C (iv). The verse features a typical mixolydian-based rock progression composed of F (♭VII), C (IV), D7 (V7), and G (I) chords. The bridge recalls the intro through its use of tonic and modally altered subdominant chords: G (I), G7 (V7/IV), C (IV), and Cm (iv). This connection between bridge and intro allows McCartney to append the actual intro after the bridge as a means not only to return to each verse but also enhance the coherence of the song, a compositional strategy he used in "Maybe I'm Amazed."

McCartney makes room for lead guitar solos in the middle and end of the song. In both instances, he departs from the chord progressions of either the song's verse or bridge. In the middle of the song, the guitar solo is supported by a diatonic harmonic progression in G Major that ends on the dominant, facilitating a return to the verse: Am (ii), Em (vi), G (I), and D (V). At the song's end, the music modulates to C major, fading out on a repeated C7 chord.

Although Blaney notes that "3 Legs" alludes to McCartney's relationships with the other Beatles, neither he nor anyone else has attempted to show how the text's metaphors could be interpreted in that light. The statement that McCartney's dog has three legs but cannot run may refer not only to Lennon, Harrison, and Starr but also to his resolve that they will not get away with treating him unfairly in the lawsuits associated with Apple. In the line, "Well, when . . . I fly above the crowd," and others, such as his acknowledgment that he could be knocked down by a feather, but such treatment will not be accepted, McCartney suggests that he will do better both musically and monetarily than the other three, and will not tolerate any financial interference or musical disparagement of his work. In a word, he no longer needs them.

"3 Legs" is a bluesy number in the key of A major. The verses follow a standard 12-bar blues harmonic progression involving I–IV–V7 chords: (1) bars 1–4, A–D–A (I–IV–I); (2) bars 5–8, D–A (IV–I); and (3) bars 9–12, E7–D–A–E7 (V7–IV–I–V7). The bridge is more static harmonically than the verse as it constantly sounds an A-major chord. In the last verse, the music departs from a strict 12-bar blues by alternating A and D chords (I–IV) before progressing to an E7 chord (V7).

The message of "Ram On" is to press on and be positive in the here and now. It builds upon the symbolism inherent in the album's title of moving forward with confidence and strength. "Ram On" is a short song, almost a jingle, that encourages everyone to take a chance and love somebody without hesitation. Although it opens with a florid piano part, "Ram On" features the ukelele, an instrument made famous by George Formby, whose work the Beatles admired.[20] The uke underscores the directness of the message. But the music belies the straightforward qualities of the lyrics. McCartney accompanies his singing by playing chord progressions in Db and C major. For most of the verse, he alternates Dbmaj7 (I7) and Bbm (vi) chords, only to alternate C (I) and F (IV) chords at the verse's end. Eastman reinforces the Dbmaj7 and Bbm chords through multitracked sustained harmonies, while McCartney accentuates the C and F chords with an electric piano part.

"Ram On" lasts 2:30, fading out before it is finished. It returns on the second side of the original vinyl LP (before "The Backseat of My Car"), beginning where it left off and lasting only 0:56. As Blaney has noted, McCartney was fond of reprising a theme to suggest the appearance of coherence and continuity.[21] In this final part of the song, the texture becomes increasingly more complex before the song abruptly ends. After that, Mc'Cartney suddenly starts singing "Who's that coming 'round the bend?" as the track fades out, a phrase drawn from the song "Big Barn Red" from *Red Rose Speedway* of 1973.

McCartney and Eastman cowrote "Dear Boy." The song focuses on the relationship between the two, and how Eastman helped McCartney to move beyond the breakup of the Beatles. According to McCartney, however, certain passages in the autobiographical "Dear Boy" were actually directed at Eastman's ex-husband Melvin See instead of John Lennon.[22]

"Dear Boy" is set in the key of A minor. McCartney employs a threefold structure for each verse. The first two parts establish A minor through a diatonic harmonic progression that emphasizes motion from i (Am) to V7 (E7). The third part of the verse departs from the minor mode aspects of the first two parts by suggesting the Aeolian mode on A through its lack of the leading tone G♯: F (VI)–C (III)–G (VII)–Am7 (i7). As McCartney sings the second and following verses, Eastman provides a slower countermelody enhanced by multitracking and reverb.

The bridge is more adventurous harmonically, suggesting the key of C major before abruptly turning to the Aeolian mode on A. During the bridge, McCartney underscores Eastman's role as a loving and stable figure in his life by singing "but her love came through and brought me 'round, got me up and about." In fact, the words "brought me 'round, got me up" are supported by two iterations of a cadential $^6_4$ chord (C/G) moving to V (G) in C major, suggesting a note of optimism.

The next track on the album, "Uncle Albert/Admiral Halsey," was McCartney's first number one single in the US after he left the Beatles. McCartney credited Eastman as a cowriter. "Uncle Albert/Admiral Halsey" is reminiscent of the long medley that closes *Abbey Road* (from "You Never Give Me Your Money" to "The End") as it is constructed from several unfinished song fragments, patched together by McCartney and enhanced by the participation of the New York Philharmonic Orchestra.[23] The first part of the song was inspired by McCartney's boyhood memories of his Uncle Albert Kendall, who would read passages from the Bible after he got drunk. According to McCartney, the line "We're so sorry, Uncle Albert," represents an apology to the older generation for the way his generation has done things.[24] On the other hand, the Admiral Halsey character in the second part of the song is an authoritarian figure that should be ignored.

"Uncle Albert/Admiral Halsey" is a quintessential example of McCartney's style of urbane pop. In keeping with the names of its two title characters, the song is divided into two large sections, with each section containing smaller parts. The "Uncle Albert" section is in the key of G major enhanced by modal mixture. As McCartney sings the opening vocal line, Am7/D (V11) and D (V) chords provide harmonic support. As McCartney finishes, these chords yield to a harmonic sequence composed of Gm7 (i7), C (IV), C♯ (♯IV), and D (V) chords. Following this half cadence on D is an instrumental interlude that alternates Gm7 and C chords, which prolong the minor tonic, before the same Gm7–D sequence from the verse's end is repeated. The next two subsections repeat the music of the first, the only essential difference being that in the third subsection, McCartney speaks the vocal line.

The "Admiral Halsey" section is in the key of C major and is divided into four parts. More upbeat in tempo, the music of this section begins with an instrumental intro that suggests an Aeolian framework on A with its alternation of Am (i) and C (III) chords that cadence on an Em chord (v). C major is clearly established when Eastman sings "Hands across the water ... " to a harmonic accompaniment of C (I), Am (vi), Dm (ii), G7 (V7), and C (I) chords. The next subsection repeats the music of the first, but this time McCartney sings "Admiral Halsey notified me ... " during the aforementioned Aeolian passage.

Instead of the threefold repetition of each subsection found in the "Uncle Albert" section, resulting in an A–A^1–A^2 structure, McCartney arranges the second half of the song into an A–A^1–B–A structure by including a faster contrasting subsection in its midst. The melodic lines of this part are supported by basic I–V7–I harmonies in C major, C, G7, and C chords. Following this subsection, McCartney repeats the opening subsection of "Admiral Halsey." The song ends with an outro based on the B subsection.

"Smile Away" examines, according to Blaney, the hypocrisy of McCartney's former band mates and Allen Klein. But as with "3 Legs," neither Blaney nor anyone else has attempted to interpret the song's text in relation to McCartney and his adversaries. I view the song's ambiguous metaphors as reflecting, at best, a general disdain on the part of McCartney for the other Beatles and possibly Klein. To convey that message in this song, McCartney reverses roles by assuming the part of the friend on the street who observes how McCartney's feet, breath, and teeth stink, which are really metaphors for the actions the other Beatles and Klein had taken against McCartney. All of this is portrayed in a blues-based rock song in the key of E. The verses of "Smile Away" alternate dominant and subdominant chords on B (V) and A (IV), respectively, with a passing B♭ chord (♭V) thrown in to connect the two harmonies. The chorus features the tonic chord on E (I) alternating with the subdominant chord on A (IV).

The next track on *Ram*, "Heart of the Country," reflects the domestic bliss McCartney experienced with his family on his Scottish farm ca. 1969–70. He viewed this time as a refuge from the pressures of fame and fortune. As a result, McCartney became more in tune with nature, which helped his emotional well-being and, consequently, his ability to better deal with the dissolution of the Beatles and Apple's business problems. For this song, McCartney produced a 16mm promotional film that is now available on the DVD collection *The McCartney Years.*[25]

Reflecting his spiritual renewal, "Heart of the Country" is an upbeat country rock song that has McCartney scatting during the bridge. The song is in the key of B♭ major, but probably played by McCartney on the guitar in G major via a capo on the third fret. "Heart of the Country" includes six verses that close with the refrain "in the heart of the country." The first part of each verse consists of a B♭–Dm/A–Gm chordal progression (I–iii–vi). The second part features essentially the same harmonic progression except that Dm/A has now been changed into a D7 chord, a secondary dominant (V7/vi) that intensifies the concluding Gm chord of each verse.

Instead of focusing on a typical subdominant chord (E♭), the bridge emphasizes the raised supertonic chord (II) on C by its alternation of G7 (V7/II) and C9 (II9) chords.[26] McCartney follows his vocal with a scat that is doubled by his acoustic guitar, but with no chordal accompaniment (tacet). At the end of the scat, McCartney sounds a G–C–C/E–F–G chordal progression that bolsters the emphasis on C at the end of the bridge. After the sixth verse, the song ends ambiguously with an incomplete rendition of the bridge, closing on a C9 chord.

According to John Blaney, children's names for milk and Leiber and Stoller's "Love Potion No. 9" may have inspired McCartney to write "Monkberry Moon Delight," as the songwriter indicates: "When my kids were young they used to call milk 'monk' for whatever reason that kids do—I think it's magical the way . . . kids can develop better names for things than the real ones. . . . So, monk was always milk, and monkberry moon delight was a fantasy drink, rather like 'Love Potion No. 9'."[27] According to Bill Harry, "Monkberry Moon Delight" may have been "inspired by Screamin' Jay Hawkins's [recording of] 'Love Potion No. 9'."[28] Hawkins even released "Monkberry Moon Delight" as a single in 1973 (Queen Bee 1313).

"Monkberry Moon Delight" is probably the most Beatlesque song on *Ram* because of its surrealistic imagery where lyrics do not make any sense. It is in the key of C minor and features a simple harmonic scheme in keeping with its expressive intentions. McCartney supports his raucous singing in each verse with Cm, Gm7, and G7 chords (i–v7–V7). In the chorus where Eastman takes a more active role on the vocals, McCartney supports their singing with Cm and Fm chords that eventually give way to an A♭7–G7–Cm harmonic succession, with the A♭7 functioning as a Ger+6, a chromatic dominant preparation. Overall, the vocals, harmonic language, and instrumentation of the song project a circus-like atmosphere.

"Eat at Home" is yet another song by McCartney, co-credited to Eastman, that celebrates the domestic bliss he shared with his wife in the aftermath of the breakup of the Beatles. It is a three-chord rock song in the key of A major that uses I, IV, and V harmonies. In each verse, McCartney begins by alternating A (I) and D (IV) chords before eventually moving to an E (V) chord at the verse's climax, returning to an A chord at the verse's end for closure. He includes a turnaround consisting of A, G (♭VII, or IV/IV), and D chords to prepare the next section of the song. McCartney structures the bridge harmonically by sounding E, D, and A chords in its first half. He returns to the E chord in the bridge's second half before moving to yet another turnaround that moves ultimately to the bridge's retransitional dominant on E.

McCartney joined "Long Haired Lady" with "Love Is Long" to produce the longest track (at 6:04) on *Ram*.[29] Like other songs of this period, McCartney wrote these compositions for Eastman. As some critics have noted, both songs feature unimaginative lyrics, no doubt the result of the absence of John Lennon in McCartney's musical life. McCartney refers to Eastman sentimentally as his "sweet little lass," "long haired lady, " or "sweet delectable baby" in "Long Haired Lady," and belabors the phrase "love is long" in "Love Is Long."[30]

From a structural point of view, "Long Haired Lady"/"Love Is Long" is cast in an ABCBCDAD form in G major, with the D sections devoted to the "Love Is Long" text. In the A sections, McCartney and Eastman engage in a dialogue in which Eastman asks McCartney whether or not he truly loves her. McCartney attempts to reassure Eastman that he has "been meaning to talk to [her] about it for some time," and that she is, rather uninspiringly, his "sweet little lass" and "long haired lady." The A sections are based on a three-chord harmonic scheme featuring tonic, subdominant, and dominant chords typical of folk and rock music. McCartney alternates tonic and subdominant chords on G and C, respectively, before moving to the dominant on D7, followed by C7, C, and G harmonies to end the section.

The B and C sections constitute the verses and chorus, respectively, of the track. In each verse, McCartney notes how fortunate he is to have such a wonderful woman like Eastman interested in him. After each verse, McCartney sings a bland chorus, "Long haired lady." Musically, McCartney expands the harmonic palette of the song by using an incomplete progression in the verse that begins with mixture chords, F (♭VII) and B♭ (♭III), and ends with dominant-to-tonic harmonies, D7 to G.[31] In the chorus, McCartney continues to expand the song's harmonic palette by alternating a Cm chord, the minor subdominant, with a G7 chord, the tonic harmony with minor seventh.

The melody of "Love Is Long" is supported by a double-plagal progression composed of G, F, C, and G chords. Used by the Beatles, this progression consists of "two successive perfect fourths in roots moving to the tonic, ♭VII–IV–I."[32] In "Love Is Long," the double-plagal progression (I–♭VII–IV–I) is stated four times, lending a static musical quality to the already static lyrics of the section.

Following the reprise of "Ram On" is "The Backseat of My Car," which closes *Ram*. McCartney must have composed the song before January 1969, because on 14 January, he was seen rehearsing it during the filming of *Let It Be* at Twickenham Studios.[33] For some reason, it was shelved at the time and, like other songs written during this period, resurrected when McCartney departed the Beatles. On *Ram*, McCartney credited Eastman as a cowriter of the song.

According to McCartney, "The Backseat of My Car" is the "ultimate teenage song," a "kind of meet-the-parents song."[34] And obviously, the "backseat" references are sexual in nature. But the song is far from a car song about teenagers; rather, it is rather grand in scope, enhanced by the musical presence of the New York Philharmonic. Instead of following a typical AABA format, "The Backseat of My Car" is cast in a more sophisticated structural mold, namely an ABAB(inst.)A(inst.[orchestra]/vocal)BACABACB(outro [inst.]) form in the key of B♭ major.[35] The A sections constitute the song's verses, each one concluding with the refrain, "Sitting in the back seat of my car." McCartney begins each verse with an incomplete progression consisting of Cm(7) and F7 chords, supertonic and dominant harmonies, respectively, that eventually settle on the tonic harmony B♭ at the end of the refrain.

The B sections comprise the song's chorus. The lyrics focus on the protagonist's desire for adventure by his insistence on "looking for a ride" or "strolling around." The chorus is set to a static accompaniment consisting of a tonic harmony on B♭ prolonged by a neighboring motion to a subtonic harmony on A♭, all over a B♭ pedal point. The two C sections are distinguished by both a new tonal center on C and Dorian framework. The line, "Ah, we believe that we can't be wrong," concludes on a Cm chord preceded by E♭ and B♭ chords, a III–VII–i progression in C Dorian. In the section's second rendition where the line is repeated several times, McCartney departs from the Dorian framework by moving to E♭ major before the instrumental outro enters and fades out as the song ends.

In 1993, *Ram* was reissued as a part of *The Paul McCartney Collection*, containing "Another Day" and "Oh Woman, Oh Why" (the B–side of "Another Day") as bonus tracks. In the following paragraphs, I shall discuss "Another Day," the more consequential of the two songs.

Although played during the filming of *Let It Be* in 1969, McCartney recorded "Another Day" during the *Ram* sessions in New York City in 1971.[36] He sang lead and played guitar and bass on the track. In addition to Eastman on backing vocals, McCartney employed the services of McCracken or Spinoza on guitar, Seiwell on drums, and the New York Philharmonic playing orchestral parts. With "Another Day," McCartney was attempting to develop a truly individual musical sound that had little connection with the Beatles.

As with McCartney's "Eleanor Rigby," "Another Day" is a commentary about social alienation. It narrates a story about the tedium experienced by a woman who goes through her daily routine of preparing to go to work, working at her office, and being with the "man of her dreams" in the evening, who leaves the next day. She is a part of the rat race, with no sense of individuality. Indeed, even "Prince Charming" cannot take her away from her dreary life.

"Another Day" is in G major. In the song's first verse, the narrator describes the woman's routine of bathing and getting dressed for work, all supported by stock progressions in G major and ending with the refrain, "It's just another day." The second verse details the woman's day at the office, concluding with the first chorus in a strongly affirmed G major. The bridge focuses on the woman's sadness arising from her way of life, which even her lover cannot dispel. McCartney brings out the woman's angst-filled mindset by modulating to the key of E minor and changing the music's metric structure to a waltz-like triple time. He establishes E minor primarily by using an E-minor chord as an initiating and closing harmony in the bridge's phrases (Em–Cmaj9(7)–A9/C♯–Cmaj7–Em). Finally, after the repetition of various sections of the song, "Another Day" repeats the first verse, as if to underscore the fact that the woman is starting yet another cycle of her tedious routine.

Ram closes the beginning chapter of McCartney's musical career as a solo artist. As Ian Peel notes, the album exhibits the "influence of Brian Wilson . . . from the production on 'The Backseat of My Car' and the vocals on 'Dear Boy' to the vibes on 'Uncle Albert.' "[37] But *Ram* reflects, more importantly, McCartney's increasing preoccupation with the fact that he was on his own, having left the only band he ever knew, hard feelings and all. That being said, there was more pressure on him to produce consistently superior lyrics and music, a challenge that he sometimes did not meet. Of all the Beatles, McCartney was the most gifted musically. There was no question that he could churn out commercial hit after hit as a popular solo artist, which he did with Wings. In one sense, he had to go through the 1970s with Wings in order to prove that he could be successful without the Beatles. But in a more significant sense, this was but one leg of a long journey as a solo artist, a journey that would take him to heights almost 40 years later that no one could imagine in 1971.

Paul McCartney and Wings, 1971–74

Regarding his motivation behind forming Wings in 1971, McCartney stated the following:

> I didn't really want to keep going [on] as a solo artist, just me and a guitar, so it became obvious that I had to get a band together. Johnny Cash had just come back, and he had a band and was touring. Linda and I talked it through and it was like, "Yeah, but let's not put together a supergroup, let's go back to square one."[1]

Thus, McCartney put a band together. From the *Ram* sessions, McCartney secured the services of Denny Seiwell on drums. After guitarist Hugh McCracken declined his offer to join the band, McCartney invited guitarist and singer Denny Laine to become a member. McCartney knew Laine from Laine's days with the Moody Blues and liked the way he sang "Go Now." Laine accepted the invitation. Thus with McCartney on bass and Eastman on keyboards, Wings was born. The newly formed band began to rehearse on McCartney's farm in Scotland.

WINGS WILD LIFE (1971)

Inspired by Bob Dylan's idea to record an album in a short amount of time in order to capture the creative spontaneity of a live performance, McCartney and his new band recorded the music for their debut album, *Wings Wild Life*, in two weeks.[2] Released in December 1971, *Wings Wild Life* generally garnered negative reviews, especially for the haste with which it was recorded. However, it did relatively well on the charts on both sides of the Atlantic, receiving gold record status in the US.[3] According to McCartney, he and Eastman penned every song except "Love Is Strange."

"Mumbo," the opening track on the album, is a high-energy rocker recorded on the first take. It actually begins while the band is playing, with McCartney saying to engineer Tony Clarke, "Take it, Tony!" The song features a series of nonsense words that mirrors the track's title (in other words, mumbo jumbo). Set in the key of F major, "Mumbo" has a simple harmonic structure, with the verses alternating F and B♭ chords, while the chorus stays on an F chord. Two distinct guitar riffs are heard during the verses. They are played separately at first, then one after the other, and then finally simultaneously as the song fades out, in order to lend an air of coherence to the song.

According to McCartney, the next track, "Bip Bop," was the weakest song he had ever written in his life.[4] It is in the key of E major and cast in a form that includes only verse and refrain.[5] The harmonic setting of each verse uses the stereotypical blues progression involving tonic (I), subdominant (IV), and dominant (V7) harmonies. In between verses is an instrumental passage that provides the only musical contrast of the song. After moving through B7, A, and E chords to conclude each verse, McCartney plays G, A, B, C, and D chords that provide harmonic contrast through modal mixture—the G, C, and D chords are harmonies borrowed from the key of E minor (♭III, ♭VI, and ♭VII). The C and D chords provide, in particular, an effective coloristic lead-in to the tonic chord of each verse, a ♭VI–♭VII–I progression reminiscent of harmonic sequences found in "P. S. I Love You" (1962), "With a Little Help From My Friends" (1967), and "Lady Madonna" (1968) from McCartney's Beatle days.

"Love Is Strange" is the only song on the album not composed by McCartney. Written and recorded by the husband-and-wife duo of Mickey Baker and Sylvia Vanderpool in 1957, the song became a hit for the Everly Brothers when they released it as a single in 1965. McCartney's reggae-influenced recording of "Love Is Strange" on *Wings Wild Life* emerged from the trip he took with his family to Jamaica in 1971. McCartney and Eastman were clearly taken with the reggae music they experienced while in that island country. Upon returning to the UK, Wings developed a reggae-inspired instrumental that coincidentally could accompany the melody of "Love Is Strange," hence the instrumental and song were combined to make for a creative arrangement of a pop standard.

On the surface, the album's title track, "Wild Life," is a song about either animal rights or saving the planet. According to McCartney, he was inspired to write the song after a visit to a game park in Ambosali, near Nairobi, Kenya, in November 1966. He remembered the game park as a place "where the animals have the right of way over you."[6] But "Wild Life" might suggest an even subtler message. Citing John Mendelssohn's review of the song in *Rolling*

Stone, John Blaney writes that the song may be a critique of left-wing activism.[7] McCartney might have been parodying Lennon's political critique through the screaming he employed in his vocal, which is reminiscent of Lennon's primal screaming in his *Plastic Ono Band* album (1970). Indeed, McCartney's critique of left-wing activism may even be seen in the line, "You're breathing a lot of political nonsense in the air."

After opening with an introduction in C major, "Wild Life" is cast in C minor. It features a descending four-measure C–B♭–F bass line that is repeated throughout the song. These notes are harmonized, respectively, with Cm, Gm, and F9 chords. Above the bass line and chords float McCartney's vocalizations. This melodic/harmonic drone is reminiscent of a passacaglia, a form associated with classical music in which a bass line and an associated set of harmonies is repeated incessantly with melodic variations sounding above.

"Some People Never Know" opened the B–side of the original *Wings Wild Life* album. The ballad dates from the summer of 1969, when McCartney and Eastman vacationed in Barbados.[8] Its tender lyrics explore McCartney's relationship with Eastman through the metaphor of people oblivious to what true love is. "Some People Never Know" is a lengthy number (6:36), featuring McCartney on lead vocal and Eastman singing harmony, accompanied by acoustic guitar, bass, keyboards, and drums.

"Some People Never Know" uses an expanded version of the standard AABA form of pop music. The enhanced structure arises from the repetition of the introduction, as well as the song's verse/refrain (A) and bridge (B), after the initial AABA: Intro/A/Intro/A/Intro/B/A(inst.)/ Intro/B/A/ Intro/B(humming)/A/Coda(intro/perc.). Set in the key of A major, the song opens with an introduction dominated by the acoustic guitar. The introduction is expanded during the song, especially in the coda, where it eventually dissolves into a passage for percussion as the song ends.

The A sections comprise the verses and refrain of the song. In each verse, McCartney focuses on some aspect of his love for Eastman: (1) In verse 1, he refers to the amount of faith Eastman has in him; (2) in verse 2, he mentions how far he is from Eastman, and how he would like to come home to her; and (3) in verse 4, he declares how Eastman outshines all others when it comes to true love. All of these declarations contrast with the image of the refrain in which "some people [will] never know" the depth of his love for his wife. McCartney sets these images musically by singing a descending, primarily stepwise melodic line that begins on E and ends on A. He harmonizes the line in turn with a series of chords that progress mainly by descending steps, E–D–C♯m–Bm–A–G♯m–F♯m–E–D–A. The melodic and harmonic closure on A afforded by the last three notes and chords (E–D–A) accentuates the negative imagery of the song's refrain, serving as a creative foil to the musical materials that support the song's more positive imagery.

In the B section that constitutes the song's bridge, McCartney mentions how some people maintain that love is a lie. He may be one of them, but asks Eastman to turn his wrong into a right. McCartney underscores the textual contrast of the bridge musically by alternating C#m and F#m chords. This harmonic succession eventually moves to a retransitional dominant on E via a series of harmonies that includes a Dm chord. This mixture sonority (iv) highlights the rhetorical question asked by McCartney of anyone being right all of the time.

"I Am Your Singer" is yet another song about McCartney's relationship with Eastman. It describes their bond in terms of the reciprocity shared between singer and song. The song is cast in a conventional AABA(inst.)BA form, with a recorder solo in the middle. McCartney and Eastman alternate on the vocals, backed by guitar, bass, recorders, and drums.

While its form may be straightforward, the song's harmonic setting is not. "I Am Your Singer" features chromatic chords in the A and B sections. McCartney uses Gm, F# (a chromatic passing chord), Fm, and Eb chords to accompany the melody of each A section. With Eb established as a tonic via its position as the closing melodic note and chord of the A sections, McCartney then moves to the key of Bb major for the B sections. This modulation to the key of the dominant enhances the song's main message of the two lovers flying away, singing their love songs for each other. McCartney returns to Eb major at the end of the B sections by traversing though a series of chords that include two chromatic harmonies, Bbm and Abm (Eb–Bbm–Cm–Abm–Fm9), before repeating part of a previously heard chord succession (F#, Fm, and Eb) in order to attain harmonic closure on Eb.

After an instrumental version of "Bip Bop" entitled "Bip Bop Link," the next track on *Wings Wild Life* is "Tomorrow." The song is again directed to Eastman. Using the metaphor of getting away for a picnic, the lyrics of "Tomorrow" celebrate McCartney's newfound optimism and self-confidence that Eastman helped to foster.

"Tomorrow" is in the key of D major and set in an AABABA form plus coda. The A section can be parsed into a 3 + 2 + 3 phrase structure ending with a strong key-defining harmonic progression consisting of Em7 (ii7), A7 (V7), and D (I) chords. The B section can be parsed into a 4 + 4 + 4 phrase structure. In the first eight measures, a Bm chord alternates with an E7, which functions as raised supertonic (II7) in D. In the last four measures, a harmonic surprise is thrown in as C, G, and A chords are sounded to accentuate the text, "Tomorrow, when we both abandon sorrow." This sequence of chords is a bVII–IV–V harmonic succession, with the last chord, a climactic retransitional dominant, supporting McCartney's sustained high A.

The coda of "Tomorrow" reiterates the idea of the protagonist's love not letting him down tomorrow, which suggests that McCartney still relied heavily on Eastman for support. To draw attention to this idea, McCartney uses G–Gm–D chord sequences at first, inserting A7 chords after each

G-based chord later in the coda. In addition to this use of modal mixture, McCartney employs a slower tempo for the coda, as well as moving from duplet eighths to triplets in the coda's first section, to draw attention to the significance of his dependence on Eastman.

McCartney wrote "Dear Friend" for John Lennon as a gesture of reconciliation. He recorded it in 1971 as a part of the *Ram* sessions. McCartney was tired of Lennon's public criticisms of him. But instead of writing a song criticizing Lennon in an obvious tit-for-tat ploy, McCartney composed a sensitive song that reflected his thoughts about his former partner. Through the song's lyrics, McCartney wanted to send a message to Lennon that the public bickering must stop. But underneath the surface of this plea is a sense of nostalgia on McCartney's part for the happier times he experienced with Lennon in the past.

"Dear Friend" is in the key of C minor and consists only of verses. Its instrumentation features McCartney accompanying his vocals on the piano, Seiwell playing drums, and other instruments, such as an alto saxophone and oboe, joining in later in the song. Based on the harmonic setting of its verses, "Dear Friend" is reminiscent of a lament from classical music, which reinforces the thesis that rather than being about a cease-and-desist plea to Lennon regarding public feuding, McCartney missed the good times he experienced with Lennon in the past. Like laments in classical music, "Dear Friend" is in the minor mode and features a structural bass line moving down by step, namely C–B♭–A♭. McCartney harmonizes these bass notes, respectively, with Cm, Cm7, and A♭ chords. But instead of eventually concluding on a G, the dominant of C minor, as is typical of classical laments, McCartney has the bass line move to an F—C minor's subdominant—and then to a C to conclude the verse. Harmonically, this motion from F to C, with Fm, Fm6, and Cm chords sounding above, is part of a plagal cadence that adds poignancy to the song's message of regret.

"Mumbo Link" closes *Wings Wild Life*. Like "Bip Bop Link," it was unnamed on the original LP, to be identified only when *Wings Wild Life* was released as a CD in 1988. It is a recording of a brief jam session. Its inclusion, along with that of "Bip Bop Link," may be McCartney's attempt to develop a more coherent album, instead of one composed of individual songs, by reprising earlier music.

When reissued as a part of *The Paul McCartney Collection* in 1993, *Wings Wild Life* included four singles as bonus tracks, "Give Ireland Back to the Irish" and "Mary Had a Little Lamb," along with their B–sides, "Little Woman Love" and "Mama's Little Girl." Wings recorded these songs in 1972. Of the four tracks, "Give Ireland Back to the Irish" is the most consequential, a subject to which I shall now turn.

McCartney wrote "Give Ireland Back to the Irish" in response to the events on "Bloody Sunday," 30 January 1972, in which British soldiers fired on Catholic protestors, killing 13 of them, during a demonstration in

Londonderry, Northern Ireland. McCartney stated, "It was so shocking. I wasn't really into protest songs—John had done that—but this time I felt that I had to write something, to use my art to protest."[9] The song was released and subsequently banned by ATV, the BBC, GPO, ITV, and Radio Luxembourg. But "Give Ireland Back to the Irish" reached the top of the charts in Ireland and Spain.

"Give Ireland Back to the Irish" is a rocker in D major that is cast in an ABCAABCAA form with intro and outro. After a two-chord intro, the song opens with the chorus, followed by a verse and bridge. This pattern of chorus/verse/bridge is then repeated but with the addition of a guitar solo after the chorus. The song concludes with two statements of the chorus and an outro. In the chorus, McCartney strongly pleads for the British to hand over Northern Ireland in order to avoid future bloodshed ("Don't make them have to take it away"). He structures the chorus as a parallel period using tonic, subdominant, and dominant harmonies (D–G–D–A, D–G–D–A–D).

From a textual point of view, verse and bridge form thematic poles that take the British to task for their occupation of Northern Ireland. While acknowledging the greatness of Britain in verse 1, in the following bridge, McCartney asks the British people if they would tolerate Irish soldiers stopping them on their way to work. While he applauds Great Britain's stance on the need for all people to be free in verse 2, McCartney then identifies with the plight of the Irish in Northern Ireland by referring to an Irishman who looks like him, invoking, in other words, his Irish ancestry. In bridge 2, McCartney sings about this person, who, like the British, "dreams of God and country," but is feeling bad, sitting in a prison. Should this person tolerate this situation? asks McCartney.

Through the use of D (I), Em (ii), G (IV), and D (I) chords, McCartney employs plagal progressions (I–IV–I), which suggest stability, to highlight the praise he offers to the British people. But in each bridge, where McCartney castigates the British, the harmonic language is more chromatic and thus unstable. The first phrase of each bridge is supported by Bm7, E, Gm, and D chords, a vi7–II–iv–I harmonic progression. The second phrase of each bridge begins harmonically like the first, but replaces the Gm chord with a major one before culminating with the retransitional dominant chord on A.

In 2001, McCartney wanted to include "Give Ireland Back to the Irish" on his two-CD compilation, *Wingspan: Paul McCartney: Hits and History*.[10] EMI wanted the track pulled due to a terrorist incident in London earlier in the year where a number of people were killed by a bomb. Although he believed that Northern Ireland should be given back to Ireland, he agreed to EMI's request, stating that the inclusion of the song in the compilation could be seen as a tacit approval of the IRA and its use of violence to achieve its political goals.

RED ROSE SPEEDWAY (1973)

Paul McCartney and Wings recorded *Red Rose Speedway*, their second album, between March and October 1972 and released it in the spring of 1973. McCartney credited Linda Eastman as a cowriter on all of the album's songs. Originally conceived as a double album, with contributions from Eastman and Denny Laine, McCartney ultimately opted to release a less expensive and more commercial single album, upon the recommendation, according to guitarist Henry McCullough, of McCartney's business advisors.[11] While more polished than *Wild Life*, their debut album, Wings was still searching for a definitive musical sound in *Red Rose Speedway*. As a result, the album is uneven in content, with the best track being "My Love."

"Big Barn Red" opens *Red Rose Speedway*. It consists of a series of lyrics that seem strung together, with no obvious attempt to make them cohere. The song's form matches its rambling lyrics, with an ABCB^{1}A(inst.)B formal design. Accordingly, "Big Barn Red" is clearly freer in structure than other songs by McCartney. Set in the key of F major, "Big Barn Red" uses blues inflections in the forms of ♭$\hat{3}$, the lowered third scale degree A♭, and ♭$\hat{7}$, the lowered seventh scale degree E♭, in its melody. In the A section, McCartney sings four phrases, of which the first three are harmonized by F9 and F chords. In the last phrase, he replaces the expected F9 with an E♭–B♭7–B♭ chordal succession before cadencing on an F in the melody that is supported by the song's tonic chord.

Although employing a new theme, the B section uses the same basic chordal succession that closed the A section, E♭–B♭–F. The C section features fragmented melodic gestures accompanied by F and F9 chords. What follows next is a variant of the B section. Unlike its single iteration in each phrase of B, an A♭–F melodic gesture (filled in with a passing tone G) is reiterated three times in each phrase of B^1, supported by an F tonic harmony throughout, all lending a sense of anticipation that a previously heard section is about to return.

According to McCartney, Linda Eastman inspired "My Love": "I sat down at a piano ... [and] I was thinking about Linda[,] and the song came."[12] Released in the spring of 1973, "My Love" topped the charts in the US for four weeks in April–May 1973, becoming Wings' first No. 1 single. It is an outstanding song highlighted by equally outstanding ensemble playing. Recorded live in the studio with a full orchestra, "My Love" features a sublime solo played by guitarist Henry McCullough that almost did not make it onto the recording. McCartney elaborates:

> We had an interesting moment on the *My Love* session. Instead of piecing it together and overdubbing [it,] I wanted to record it live with an orchestra. Everyone was ready in Abbey Road [S]tudio [T]wo, we knew exactly what we would be doing, and then just before the take Henry came over and whispered

in my ear, "Do you mind if I try something different on the solo?" I had to make one of those decisions—to stick with what we'd rehearsed or to run with his new idea. At the risk of messing the thing up[,] I went with his idea and he pulled a great new solo out of left field.[13]

"My Love" is in F major and follows a standard AABAA form with outro. The A sections consist of a verse/refrain with chorus. The lyrics of each verse convey a sense of instability through distance ("And when I go away/I know my heart can stay with my love") or material emptiness ("And when the cupboard's bare/I'll still find something there with my love"). McCartney accentuates this instability musically by accompanying the F–major-oriented melody of each verse with chords that do not suggest that key. The melody of each verse's first three lines suggests F major through the strategic use of F and C. McCartney accompanies the first two lines with a B♭maj7–Am7 chord succession. He then supports the third line with D9 and Gm7 chords, a harmonic progression that tonicizes Gm (V9/ii–ii7). For the refrain, which turns the listener's attention to the emotional security offered to the protagonist by his lover ("And my love does it good"), McCartney goes even further a field by sounding B♭maj7, Am7, and Bm7♭5 chords, heightening the contrast between the instability of each verse/refrain with the stability of the chorus.

In the chorus, McCartney establishes F major through a plagal progression (I–IV–I) composed of F, Gm7, B♭, and F chords (I–ii7–IV–I) in order to further underscore the protagonist's emotional stability resulting from his relationship. In the song's bridge, the protagonist celebrates his relationship, which is also represented by key-defining progressions in F major. In the outro, which is based on the bridge, the music affirms the love shared between the protagonist and his lover one last time by affirming F major through an authentic cadence (B♭–C7–F [IV–V7–I]).

McCartney recorded "Get on the Right Thing" during the *Ram* sessions in 1971. The song featured McCartney on lead vocals and bass, Eastman on backup vocals, Dave Spinoza on lead guitar, and Denny Seiwell on drums. Through its lyrics, "Get on the Right Thing" conveys a message of discernment and self-awareness in the midst of life. But the images found in the song's lyrics do not match the sophistication of its musical setting. "Get on the Right Thing" is in the key of E major. It opens with an introduction that builds tension via E, F♯, G, F♯, F, and E chords sounding above a pedal point on E. The verses repeat part of the intro's chord progression before suggesting G major with Em, A, D, and G chords (vi/♭III–V/V/♭III–V/♭III–♭III, respectively). This flirtation with G major is followed by a return to E major with the appearance of the dominant chord B at the end of each verse. The harmonic structure of the chorus dispenses with the chromaticism of the verses. It is situated solidly in E major via tonic, subdominant, and dominant harmonies on E, A, and B, respectively, as the title line is repeated as a part of a call-and-response pattern.

In an interview with Geoffrey Giuliano, Denny Laine commented on McCartney's equivocal opinion about "Get on the Right Thing," which may help explain the uneven quality of songs found on *Red Rose Speedway*:

> He never really thought [that the song] was finished. He did it in New York during the *Ram* sessions. He never wanted to use it on anything. He didn't think the lead vocals were any good. He just laid the vocal down at the end of the day and really didn't know all of the words. I used to say, "But it's great. I love it. If you change the vocal though, it won't be as strong." And eventually he put it on *Red Rose Speedway*.[14]

The next track on the album, "[Only] One More Kiss," is a country-inspired shuffle in G major. The lyrics address the typical country music theme of reconciliation after quarreling. The song begins with its chorus, establishing G major through an incomplete progression composed of Bm, Em, Bm, B♭m (a chromatic passing chord), Am7, D7, and G chords, followed by a key-affirming G–D–G chord succession without vocals. The song's verses feature basic chord progressions in G major, with one secondary dominant, an E7 chord (V7/ii) that moves to its intended Am harmony (ii), thrown in for harmonic variety as the verse cadences on the dominant (D7).

As with "Get on the Right Thing," McCartney recorded "Little Lamb Dragonfly" during the *Ram* sessions, with Hugh McCracken playing guitar. As Bill Harry notes, the song may have actually been inspired by the death of one of McCartney's sheep on his Scottish farm, but there is no other corroboration for that assertion.[15] McCartney originally planned to use "Little Lamb Dragonfly" as a part of his *Rupert the Bear* film project but abandoned the idea.[16] For some reason, he decided to revisit the song for *Red Rose Speedway*.

Like other songs on the album, the music of "Little Lamb Dragonfly" is more sophisticated than its lyrics. But we must not be too harsh on the song's childlike text, since "Little Lamb Dragonfly" was initially intended for McCartney's *Rupert the Bear* film. That being said, the song is both clever and complex from musical perspectives. It is in ternary form, A–B–A¹, with the A¹ section an abbreviation of the initial A. The A section comprises the "Little Lamb" part of the song, oscillating between the keys of D and C major. The B section consists of the "Dragonfly" segment of the song and is in the key of E major. The A¹ section recapitulates part of the A section. The "Little Lamb" section begins with an introduction in D major that quickly moves to C major then back to D major via a Bm chord when the vocal enters. After an authentic cadence in D major via G, A7, and D chords (IV–V7–I), the music moves to C major, at which point McCartney sings a predominantly repeated-note "la–la–la" chorus that is supported by the same chords in C major that characterized the introduction.

After two measures of an E chord, which facilitates a direct modulation to the key of E major, the "Dragonfly" section begins. The harmonic language is diatonic, except for: (1) an E7–A–Amaj7–Em/G chord succession involving a tonicization of A major, the subdominant of E major, and mode mixture involving the minor tonic; along with (2) an Em7–A7–D chord succession tonicizing D major, the subtonic scale degree, a harmonic progression drawn from the "Little Lamb" section. Before the third verse of the "Dragonfly" section, McCartney repeats music from the "Little Lamb" section in order to foster an element of structural coherence. Finally, the end of the "Dragonfly" section culminates with a B7 chord, the dominant of E major, before moving ultimately to C major through D major for the truncated recapitulation of the "Little Lamb" section and its "la–la–la" chorus.

In "Single Pigeon," Wings switched instruments when recording the track. McCartney sang lead vocal and played piano, Laine played drums, and Seiwell played bass. Eastman added backing vocals and McCullough played acoustic guitar, with brass joining in later in the song. Wings recorded "Single Pigeon" at Olympic Studios. It is a short, cabaret-like song that is reminiscent of McCartney's "Rocky Raccoon" or "Honey Pie" from the *White Album* released in 1968. In the song, McCartney befriends a lonely pigeon and a seagull in a self-pitying way.

Although situated in the key of B♭ major, "Single Pigeon" does not suggest that key until the bridge when the harmonic setting emphasizes B♭ and B♭maj7 chords. At that moment, the tonal stability afforded by these B♭ chords highlights McCartney's identification with his avian friends ("I'm a lot like you"). The verses are more tonally ambiguous, suggesting B♭ major only at their end through a half cadence on an F chord. The song actually closes with that half cadence through the repetition of the opening line, suggesting the lack of resolution in the song's story.

"When the Night" is a love song that vacillates between the relative keys of A minor and C major, two keys that share the same key signature. The song features McCartney on lead vocal with the other members of Wings providing harmony vocals. Moreover, McCartney plays piano, Eastman electric bass piano, Laine and McCullough acoustic guitars, and Seiwell drums. "When the Night" is probably the weakest song on *Red Rose Speedway*. It contains lyrics that are simply unimaginative and pointless, such as "Well, the night is beautiful and mellow," or "That the night was marvelous and yellow." The harmonic setting is not that creative either, although in the song's verses and bridge (which emphasizes F major, C major's subdominant, before settling on a retransitional G7 dominant harmony), McCartney uses a signature F–Fm modally mixed chordal succession (IV–iv) in order to enhance the song's harmonic sound.

The next track, "Loup (1st Indian on the Moon)," is an instrumental number that has all of the members of Wings singing a chant in A minor. As for the song's instrumentation, McCartney plays bass and Moog synthesizer,

Eastman organ, Laine and McCullough electric guitars, and Seiwell drums. As described by John Blaney, "Loup (1st Indian on the Moon)" sounds like a "bad Pink Floyd outtake" that "plods along aimlessly."[17] The song is restricted to tonic and dominant chords in A minor, Am and E7, during the singing of the chant. There is some harmonic variety after that, as the E7 chord is changed to an Em7, during the middle part of the song where there are only instruments playing. But when all is said and done, the song is uninspired, suffering from a lack of balance between its parts and too much echo.

"Medley," an 11-minute and 26-second collection of four songs, closes *Red Rose Speedway*. It is an attempt to imitate the magic of *Abbey Road*'s McCartney-inspired medley. Unfortunately, while in certain respects creative, "Medley" does not rise to the level of excellence found on *Abbey Road*. Instead of a collection of songs that compares favorably with nineteenth-century classical music song cycles, such as Robert Schumann's *Dichterliebe*, as *Abbey Road* does, "Medley" comes off sounding like four individual song fragments strung together in a haphazard fashion.

The vaudevillian-flavored "Hold Me Tight" opens "Medley." After beginning in the key of A major, the song is characterized harmonically by a chromatic succession, A–B♭–Bm7–C–C#dim–D, that gives way to a circle-of-fifths progression, G–C–F–B♭–E♭–A♭–D♭–C#(F#)–B–E, in which McCartney repeats the line, "Hold me tight, hugga me right," over and over again. (For this writer, McCartney's "Hold Me Tight" from 1963's *With the Beatles* album is superior to this later musical namesake.) Since "Hold Me Tight" ends on its dominant E, it segues smoothly into "Lazy Dynamite," which is in the key of E major.

"Lazy Dynamite" refers metaphorically to the love that needs to be coaxed out from the protagonist's muse. The song opens with the chorus in which McCartney sings the title line four times (a formula drawn from "Hold Me Tight") over a plagal progression involving E, A, Am, and E chords (I–IV–iv–I). Like the chorus, the verses are not that harmonically adventurous either, with their G#m–A–B–A–E chord successions. The closing chords of the outro are, conversely, more harmonically adventurous. They include a use of modal mixture reminiscent of McCartney's "Lady Madonna" in which mixture chords emerge from harmonies progressing in ascending parallel motion (E–F#–B–*G–A–B–C*–E [I–V/V–V–♭*III–IV–V–*♭*VI*–I]). Finally, only McCartney (piano, Mellotron, and bass), Laine (harmonica), McCullough (electric guitar), and possibly Seiwell (drums) play instruments on "Lazy Dynamite."

The closing tonic harmony on E of "Lazy Dynamite" is reinterpreted as a dominant in a V–IV–I transitional passage (E–D–A) played on the guitar that establishes the key of A major for the next song, "Hands of Love." As Blaney notes, the Beatles used a similar approach to connect "Mean Mr. Mustard" with "Polythene Pam" on *Abbey Road*, which was accomplished with "more panache," according to Blaney, than on *Red Rose Speedway*.[18] But in "Hands of Love," this E–D–A progression has a quasi-motivic status through its consistent use as a harmonic/rhythmic marker for the ends of some of the phrases in the song.

Like "Hold Me Tight," "Hands of Love" is a song that recalls the pop music of the 1920s and 1930s. Although McCartney sings lead vocal, Eastman has a prominent harmony part, which reflects, on a musical level, their identification with the song's lyrics about falling in love. The song's verses and bridge follow stereotypical harmonic patterns and key relationships. The harmonic structure of the verses follows a key-defining progression of A, B7, E(7), and A chords (I–V7/V–V[7]–I). As expected, the bridge temporarily tonicizes D major, A major's subdominant, by turning the last chord of the verse, A, into a secondary dominant, A7, that sets up the move to D major. After tonicizing D, the bridge moves to its retransitional dominant E by preceding it with A and B7 chords (IV–V7/V), which support an ascending melodic sequence in the vocal line. Finally, the song closes with a harmonic cliché involving a German augmented-sixth chord, F7 (E♭ respelled as D♯), moving to a dominant harmony, E7, followed by the tonic on A.

McCartney wrote "Power Cut," the final song of "Medley," during the British miners' strike in 1972.[19] During the following year in Britain, there were power shortages throughout the country due to the introduction of a three-day workweek. In the lyrics of "Power Cut," McCartney refers to the power shortages people were experiencing, but does not make any political statements about their plight or the industrial unrest prevalent at the time. Instead, he emphasizes how much he adores his love, repeating the line "Baby, I love you so" once too often, turning the song into a highly sentimental conclusion to both "Medley" and the album.

"Power Cut" emerges from a cross-fade with "Hands of Love." It is in A major and features a prolongation of the tonic harmony A via McCartney's signature chord succession involving modal mixture (I–IV–iv–I), namely, A–D–Dm–A chords, all over an A pedal point.

In order to highlight its place as the climactic song of "Medley," McCartney recapitulates motifs from the three previous songs in the guitar solos at the end of "Power Cut," first individually then in combination. Initially, motifs from "Lazy Dynamite," "Hands of Love," and "Hold Me Tight" are sounded successively. Then, "Lazy Dynamite" and "Hands of Love" are sounded simultaneously as "Power Cut" fades out.

Red Rose Speedway included four singles as bonus tracks when it was reissued as a part of *The Paul McCartney Collection* in 1993: (1) "Hi, Hi, Hi," (2) "C Moon" (the B–side of "Hi, Hi, Hi"), (3) "The Mess" (the B–side of "My Love"), and (4) "I Lie Around" (the B–side of "Live and Let Die," with lead vocal by Denny Laine). Wings recorded these singles between 1972 and 1973. In the following paragraphs, I shall discuss "Hi, Hi, Hi" and "C Moon."

"Hi, Hi, Hi" did much to dispel the image of Wings as a squeaky-clean band.[20] Cowritten by Linda Eastman, "Hi, Hi, Hi" is a hard-rock boogie song banned from radio play by the BBC for its sexually suggestive lyrics, not for any drug references implied by the song's title.[21] The BBC took exception to various lines, such as "I want you to lie on the bed, get you ready for my body gun." However, "body gun" is not in the song, "polygon" is ("get you ready for my polygon"). Apparently, Northern Songs sent incorrect lyrics to radio stations with the far more sexually suggestive "body gun" as a part of the textual package. Although he used "polygon" to tone down the sexual innuendo of the line, McCartney believed "body gun" was a better choice of words.

"Hi, Hi, Hi" is in E major and consists of an intro, two verses, two statements of a chorus, an instrumental interlude, and an outro that speeds up, heightening the song's naughty message. It is a three-chord blues-based song, with B and E chords alternating for most of the verse and chorus, with an A–E chordal succession introduced later to add harmonic variety before each section reaches tonal closure.

While "Hi, Hi, Hi" did much to enhance Wings' newly found rebellious image, "C Moon" did much to reverse it, reinforcing the idea that their music was essentially pleasant, middle-class entertainment. Ironically, because it was the B–side of the banned "Hi, Hi, Hi," "C Moon" received much airplay in Britain.

From a musical point of view, "C Moon" is a reggae-inspired composition, reggae being one of cowriter Linda Eastman's favorite musical genres. Textually, it has a connection to Sam the Sham and the Pharaohs' song, "Wooly Bully." McCartney explains:

> There's a line in that [song] that says "Let's not be L7"—and at the time everyone was saying[,] "What's L7 mean?" Well, L7, it was explained at the time, means a square—put L and 7 together and you get a square. So I thought of the idea of getting a C and a crescent moon together to get the opposite of a square. So "C Moon" means "Cool."[22]

Set in the key of C major, "C Moon" consists of two large sections composed of five verses juxtaposed with a contrasting bridge. The melody of each verse features an ascending C-major triad, beginning on G and ending on E, that is chopped up by rests. The melody concludes with a D–E neighboring motion. The straightforward melodic structure of each verse is complemented by an equally uncomplicated harmonic scheme. McCartney harmonizes the triadically based melody with C, E, Am, F, C, G, C chords, producing a I–V/vi–vi–IV–I–V–I harmonic progression.

Compared to the repeated "C Moons" in the verses, the bridge contains lyrics that are more substantial. In the first set of lyrics, McCartney wonders why people misunderstand him, but in the final analysis, he should not "[fill his] head with gloom." In the second set of lyrics, McCartney sings about the troubles of two hypothetical lovers Bobby and Patty, which may or may not refer to him and his wife. The melody of the bridge uses a descending idea that is sequenced a step lower before cadencing on a G, producing a 2 + 2 + 3 phrase structure. After this melodic unit is repeated, McCartney inserts a two-measure climactic outburst, "What's it all to you / about?" Composed of a D moving up to G, it pushes the music back to each verse. As with the verses, McCartney uses a straightforward harmonic scheme in the bridge. He harmonizes the first two melodic units with Dm, C, G, and Gm chords (ii–I–V–v), while the bridge's concluding outburst is set to an Am7–D7–G progression (vi7–V7/V–V) that forcefully draws attention to the bridge's retransitional dominant. Finally, "C Moon," like "Single Pigeon," has Wings switching instruments, with McCartney singing lead vocal and playing piano and marimba, Eastman singing harmony vocals and playing tambourine, Laine playing bass, McCullough drums, and Seiwell a cornet solo.

LIVE AND LET DIE (1973)

In 1972, United Artists contacted McCartney about composing the theme song for their upcoming James Bond movie, *Live and Let Die*. McCartney agreed and set out to write and record the song:

> I read the *Live and Let Die* book on a Saturday, got the feel of it, and on . . . Sunday sat down at the piano and wrote the music. Linda and I dug around with the words for a bit, then I asked George Martin if he'd produce it, and we recorded it with Wings [in October 1972 during the *Red Rose Speedway* sessions], all mixed all proper, as you hear it [on] the film.[23]

George Martin went to Ocho Rios in order to present the newly recorded title song to Harry Saltzman, the producer of *Live and Let Die*.[24] After listening to the record and thinking it was a demo, Saltzman asked Martin who would sing the real track, perhaps Shirley Bassey or Thelma Houston? Aghast, Martin informed Saltzman that it was not a demo but a finished track, and that an ex-Beatle, the world's top recording star, would be singing his Bond film's theme song. Saltzman agreed that McCartney should sing the song, and Wings' recording of "Live and Let Die" was included in the movie. As a result, approximately 60 million Bond fans worldwide became acquainted with the rock group Wings.

With "Live and Let Die," McCartney excelled as a composer and Wings as a band. "Live and Let Die" is symphonic rock at its best, a collection of freewheeling musical ideas that not only expresses the atmospheric nature of the film's subject matter but also is in keeping with the character of previous Bond theme songs. "Live and Let Die" begins in the key of G major and can be parsed into eight sections. The first section, which I shall label verse 1, begins in an unpretentious manner with McCartney singing ("When you were young and your heart was an open book...") accompanied by piano chords. He articulates three phrases, with each phrase moving from the tonic harmony on G to the dominant harmony on D. The total effect of the first section is that of asking one colossal question, which McCartney, accompanied by enormous chords in the orchestra, answers in the next section, which I shall label chorus 1. As McCartney repeats the line "Live and let die," the orchestra plays a series of *fortissimo* chords over a G pedal point: G7, C/G, Gdim, G7, and C/G. It is only in the third section where the orchestra plays a dynamic riff, which functions as an orchestral ritornello (an orchestral refrain in classical music) in the song, that we get a sense of the tonic G, minor in this case over another G pedal point.

In the fourth section, McCartney introduces a quirky, almost incongruous reggae break, perhaps at the instigation of Eastman. The section culminates on a high C in the melody supported by an F chord before the orchestral ritornello comes back, which reignites the song's frenetic energy. The sixth section repeats the first, but with the exception of a solo cello playing the first phrase of the vocal line. Chorus 2, the song's seventh section, and the orchestral ritornello, the song's last section, follow verse 2. Functioning as an energetic outro, the orchestral ritornello heightens the song's dynamic drive before it culminates on an unexpected E♭m chord at the song's end.

BAND ON THE RUN (1973)

Recorded in Lagos, Nigeria, from September to October 1973 and released two months later, *Band on the Run* was a hugely successful album for McCartney and Wings, topping the charts on both sides of the Atlantic. Besides being the first Wings album to go platinum in both the UK (1975) and the US (1974), *Band on the Run* made history by becoming the first LP to reach the number one spot in *Billboard* magazine's record charts on three different occasions.[25] It was, in short, one of the best-selling albums of the 1970s. Unlike *Wings Wild Life* or *Red Rose Speedway*, critics praised *Band on the Run*, with *Rolling Stone* magazine declaring it Album of the Year for 1974.[26] In a review of the album for *Rolling Stone* in that same year, Jon Landau declared it the most successful album to date (with the exception of John Lennon's *Plastic Ono Band* [1970]) by any of the former Beatles.[27] In 1975, it won Grammy Awards for Best Contemporary/Pop Vocal and Best Engineered Album in recognition of the contributions of sound engineer Geoff Emerick, who had worked on *Revolver*, *Sgt Pepper's Lonely Hearts Club Band*, and *Abbey Road*.[28]

Making *Band on the Run* was problematic for McCartney. After completing "Live and Let Die," McCartney wanted to record his next album in an EMI studio abroad. He chose the one located in Lagos, Nigeria, because he loved African music and thought it would be a great experience to record in what he perceived to be an exotic locale. Unfortunately, that was not the case: "I thought Lagos was going to be gorgeous but I'd overlooked the realities of going to somewhere like that—the studio wasn't built properly and it was . . . monsoon season. Again, though, out of adversity came something good."[29]

Compounding McCartney's problems were the departures of guitarist Henry McCullough and drummer Denny Seiwell from Wings just before McCartney, Eastman, and Laine left for Lagos. If that were not enough, while in Lagos, McCartney and Eastman were mugged. Although the robbers took their camera, cassettes (which contained demos of *Band on the Run*), jewelry, and money, McCartney and Eastman were lucky to escape with their lives. McCartney also suffered from a bronchial spasm because he smoked too much, and was accused of stealing African music by a top local musician, Fela Ransome-Kuti. All of these events contributed to an inauspicious start for this new Wings album. Nevertheless, McCartney, Eastman, and Laine were determined to produce a great LP. Mark Lewisohn describes their recording procedures:

> The recording of most tracks began with Paul playing drums and Denny the rhythm guitar, laying down the song's foundation. From here, by a process of layering, and with Linda adding keyboards, each song slowly took shape. No mean lead guitarist, Paul played most of these parts. Losing the two band members had galvanised Paul, Linda[,] and Denny, fostering a "we'll show yer" attitude and a survival instinct that might not otherwise have been present.[30]

Band on the Run opens with its title track. The song weaves a narrative around the quest for personal freedom, inspired by an offhand remark by George Harrison about Apple's financial difficulties during a company business meeting.[31] Likening the difficulties to serving time in prison, Harrison supposedly lamented, "If we ever get out of here." Accordingly, "Band on the Run" is a song about escaping the ugly realities of life that, for one reason or another, keep us from a better place.

"Band on the Run" is a multi-sectional song, and combined with its story line, is almost operatic in quality. It contains 13 sections (A(inst.)AB(inst.) BC(inst.)DEDEE(inst.)EDE), with the first four sections a prelude to the last nine. This 4 + 9 grouping is reinforced additionally by key relationships, with the first part of the song set in D major, and the longer second part in C major. In the first part of "Band on the Run," McCartney explores the angst associated with captivity. He begins the song with an instrumental intro that flows seamlessly into verse 1, where he sings about being stuck inside four walls, seemingly forever, not permitted to see someone nice again like his love. Tonic and subdominant harmonies accompany McCartney's melody, namely Dmaj7, Dmaj9(no 3rd), and G6 chords. At the end of the verse, McCartney underscores the poignancy of missing his loved one by substituting a Gm6 for the G6, an expressive change of harmonic color arising from modal mixture.

The third section is an instrumental introduction to the fourth, verse 2. At this point in the song, things get gloomier as McCartney sings about wanting to get out of captivity, and what he would do if that were to happen. He reinforces the depressing tone of his lyrics by sounding Am and Bm chords, replacing the brightness of the key of D major with a more foreboding A minor. However, with the onset of escape, things change as an instrumental fanfare in C major featuring power chords on D and C ushers in the second part of the song, where C and Fmaj7 chords consistently alternate.

At this point, "Band on the Run" proceeds through a series of verses and choruses, with an instrumental interlude inserted for musical variety. In each verse and chorus, McCartney advances the narrative of escaping from the despair of his own making by using the metaphor of a band on the run, full of determination and hope. Despite such negative characters as the jailer man, sailor Sam, people in the town, and the county judge, who doggedly search for the band and attempt to rail them back into captivity, that band escapes to a better place, thereby achieving the deliverance for which they (that is, McCartney) have hoped. In order to represent this optimistic tone through stable musical materials, the verses emphasize the tonic harmony C through plagal progressions (C–Fmaj7/C) before concluding on an Em chord. The choruses likewise emphasize the tonic harmony C through the same plagal progressions, although G, C, Em, C, and Am chords are inserted at the beginnings of these sections to expand their harmonic palette. The song concludes in chorus 4 with an Em–G–C chord succession (iii–V–I), cementing the deliverance achieved by the band.

McCartney wrote "Jet," the next track on *Band on the Run*, which he released as a single, after being inspired by a black Labrador puppy that he and Eastman owned.[32] This runt of the litter matured and eventually became pregnant, giving birth to its own litter of puppies, one named Jet, another named Golden Molasses.[33] One would expect that the song's lyrics would tell a story about the adventures of these pets, but they do not. The lyrics are, to wit, nonsensical, as evinced by the line, "I thought the major was a lady suffragette," which has little to do with dogs.

The music of "Jet" makes up for any deficiencies in its lyrics. The song is in the key of A major and features a series of verses and choruses that are intertwined with two statements of a bridge and a synthesizer solo, all framed by an intro and outro. At the beginning of the intro, McCartney reiterates Bm, D6, and C♯m7 chords that do not signal a clear A-major tonality. He clarifies the intro's tonal ambiguity by moving to an A chord near the end of the intro where he shouts "Jet!" on a high A. In each verse, McCartney continues to emphasize A major by supporting his triplet-laced pentatonic melody with A, D/A, and A chords that prolong the tonic harmony. But in order to heighten the element of contrast in the song, he returns to the harmonic ambiguity of the intro in each chorus, sounding the same three opening chords before moving to a more stable tonic harmony on A. Finally, following a statement of the fifth and last chorus, the outro enters with the same chords of the intro. The song concludes with one last statement of its opening phrase on the saxophone (performed by Howie Casey, McCartney's friend from his Liverpool days), coming to rest on an E over a final A chord.

"Bluebird" probably dates from 1970–71, if not before, as evidenced by McCartney's and Eastman's singing the song on a live radio interview in New York City in 1971.[34] In "Bluebird," a confident McCartney sings about the transcendent freedom that only the power of love provides. The bluebird of the song symbolizes that love. The protagonist informs his lover that through his magic kiss as a bluebird, she, too, can become one. When both lovers become bluebirds, they obtain absolute freedom, symbolized by their flying away together through the air and across the sea, living in the trees on a desert island and being able to fly in the breeze.

"Bluebird" is played in the key of F major (although sounding in E♭ major because the guitars are tuned a whole step lower).[35] It consists of a series of alternating verses and choruses that are varied structurally by three statements of a bridge and an outro that repeats the text and music of the bridge. In each verse, McCartney uses the same incomplete progression composed of Am, Gm, and C chords (iii–ii–V–ii–V) to accompany the melody. He contrasts the harmonic instability of each verse with the harmonic stability of each chorus by emphasizing the tonic triad through an Fmaj7 alternating with its subdominant, B♭ (I7–IV). The harmonic schemes of verse and chorus strongly suggest that the text of each verse raises a question, only to be answered by each chorus through its exclamations of being a bluebird. For each statement of the bridge, McCartney moves to the relative key of D minor, incorporating two phrases that are supported harmonically by a strong, classically oriented pattern composed of Dm, Dm/C, Em7, and A7 chords, a $i–i_2^4–ii7–V7$ progression. While the first phrase ends with a half cadence on A (via an A7 chord), the second phrase is extended so that it ends with an authentic cadence on F (via an Fmaj7), whose appearance is delayed by the subdominant harmony B♭. Thus, in this bridge, there is no retransitional dominant.

Despite its key of A minor, "Mrs. Vanderbilt," the next track on the album, is a carefree and insouciant song. It has an unusual formal design, with an A (intro)BCDDED[1](refrain)CE(inst.)D[1](refrain)CDED[1](refrain)C structure. The instrumental intro presents the harmonic materials that are to dominate the song, an Am–Em(7)–E7–Am chordal succession (i–v[7]–V7–i). It is used in all sections save for the last part of D, D[1], and E. The B section has McCartney singing, almost chattering, about living in a tent in the middle of the jungle and not caring about material things nor the passage of time.[36] The C section that follows, "Ho, Hey, Ho," is the song's chorus. In the D sections, McCartney admonishes us not to worry if our light goes out, or if we miss our bus, or if our pile (probably of money) is decreasing as he sings an ascending and descending melodic line that is sequenced down a step. He concludes the D sections with a refrain, which is supported by key-defining E and Am chords (V–i), that asks the song's two key questions, "What's the use of worrying?" and "What's the use of anything?" The E sections constitute the song's bridge. Initially, the bridge moves to the relative key of C major via a Dm–G–C–Em chordal progression (ii–V–I–iii), but then settles back into A minor as McCartney incorporates a varied form of the refrain that closed the D sections, which I label D^1. In addition to using E–Am harmonic motions, McCartney concludes D^1 by singing the climactic word, "anything," to a B–A–A melodic line, supported by Dm6 and Am chords.

Many critics have characterized "Let Me Roll It" as Lennon-esque in quality.[37] With its earthy guitar riff, tape echo, sparse texture, and strong rhythm section, "Let Me Roll It" resembles Lennon's grittier songs, such as "Yer Blues" from the Beatles *White Album*, or "Cold Turkey" recorded with the Plastic Ono Band. McCartney comments on the origin of the song and its connection with his former musical collaborator:

> I wrote ["Let Me Roll It"] in Scotland one day . . . . We took it off to Lagos and put down a backing track with Linda playing organ, me playing drums[,] and Denny playing guitar. Then we overdubbed the big guitars you can hear . . . through it, going through a PA amp, not a guitar amp. . . . [That riff is] great . . . to play, and whenever we played it live, it goes down great. We'd play it on two guitars, and people saw it later as a kind of John pastiche, . . . [w]hich I don't mind. ["Let Me Roll It"] could have been a Beatles song.[38]

"Let Me Roll It" is in the key of E major and features a clear verse/refrain–chorus structure with instrumental interludes, preceded and concluded, respectively, by an instrumental intro and outro.[39] The intro begins with an alternation of A and F#m chords, an ascending third progression involving subdominant and submediant triads (IV–vi). The music then settles into E major with E and A chords alternating, the A harmony decorated by an upper-voice melodic roulade that moves to a B at the top of the E chord (D–C#–B–A–B). The repeated E–A motions prolong the tonic harmony E via its subdominant A (I–IV). The guitar riff then enters over this prolongation of tonic harmony, but an F#m chord, a supertonic triad, has now replaced the A chord.

The text of the song is earthy and straightforward, paralleling the song's distinctive guitar hook. In the refrain of each verse, the protagonist compares his heart to a wheel, offering to roll it to his lover in each chorus. The harmonic schemes of the verse, refrain, chorus, and outro follow precedents established in the intro. In each verse, E and F#m chords alternate, prolonging the tonic harmony. The refrain sounds A and F#m chords, concluding with one on E. In each chorus, A and E chords alternate, prolonging the tonic harmony. The outro closes with the guitar riff played over alternating E and F♯m chords, fading out as the song ends.

While on vacation with Wings in Marrakesh in early 1973, McCartney noticed a house name-plate with the word "Mamounia" on it, which means "safe haven" in Arabic.[40] Inspired by the positive connotations of the word, he wrote "Mamunia" while in that Moroccan city. The song has the distinction of being the first song recorded in Lagos for the *Band on the Run* album.

"Mamunia" is another typical example of McCartney's style of pop music. The song is in the key of A major and from a formal standpoint, proceeds intro(inst.)–chorus–interlude(inst.)–chorus–verse–verse–chorus–verse–verse–bridge–verse–chorus–interlude(inst.)–chorus. After the intro, the song opens with McCartney, backed up vocally by Eastman and Laine, singing "Mamunia." The vocal line consists of one long phrase that can be parsed into two four-measure units. It features a bouncy, syncopated idea—reflecting the breezy, upbeat nature of the song—that is repeated several times before it closes melodically with a B–A ($\hat{2}$–$\hat{1}$) motion. Harmonically, the chorus begins with a prolongation of the tonic harmony via A, Amaj7, A6, A, D, and A chords. The tonic harmony then moves to E and A chords, a V–I harmonic motion that supports the closing B–A melodic movement above. Supporting the chorus's harmonic scheme is a diatonic contrapuntal line played by an acoustic guitar that moves downward by step from one A to another an octave lower. The A, Amaj7, and A6 chords of the scheme arise from the line's first three notes, A–G♯–F♯.

In order to bring out the textual differences between chorus and verses, McCartney employs a different key and a slower-moving vocal line in the latter sections. He uses rain as a metaphor for the cloudy times in a person's life throughout the verses. Do not complain, urges McCartney, for while it rains on everyone, focus on a sunny disposition, one's safe haven or "mamunia" in times of trouble. The verses are in the key of C major, which is in a chromatic-mediant (or -third) relationship with the chorus's key of A major (the roots of the tonic triads of C and A are a third apart; the C of the C chord and the C♯ of the A chord are chromatically related). That combined with the slower-moving melody of the verses, which is enhanced by creative background vocals, underscores the differences in imagery between verses and chorus. The bridge of "Mamunia" is based on the verses, altered to end on a G7 chord, the retransitional dominant. Finally, optimism wins out as the song concludes with the chorus, enhanced by a synthesizer obbligato.

"No Words" is the only song on *Band on the Run* not credited to McCartney and Eastman. Denny Laine and McCartney collaborated on the song, with Laine starting the song and McCartney finishing it. On the recording, McCartney, Eastman, and Laine sing the melody in unison, with McCartney taking a vocal solo, and, according to Mark Lewisohn, roadies Ian Horn and Trevor Jones providing backing vocals.[41] The instrumental accompaniment consists of McCartney on guitar, bass, and drums; Laine on guitar; and brass and strings scored by Tony Visconti, husband of Mary Hopkin, Welsh singer and McCartney protégée, who became famous for her 1968 hit, "Those Were the Days."

The formal structure of "No Words" exhibits an AABAAB form, enclosed by an instrumental intro and outro. Cast in A major, the A sections constitute the song's verses. They are essentially identical to one another, revealing an asymmetrical 4 + 3 phrase structure that imparts a sense of urgency regarding the protagonist's views about his lover's constancy. The B section, the song's chorus, presents the song's title line and thereby main thought, "No words for my love," a reflection, perhaps, of the protagonist's one-sided relationship. The chorus moves to E major and is preceded and followed, respectively, by its own intro and outro. The intro begins with E, C#7, and F#m chords, a I–V7/ii–ii progression that sets up a B9 dominant harmony when the vocals enter. After sounding an A chord, the chorus settles on an E, now functioning as a retransitional dominant. As this chord is reached, the B section's outro begins, sounding the same chords as its intro. After the first B section is heard, the third A section follows. Focusing on the burning love deep inside the protagonist's lover, the melody of this section is based on the first three notes, C#–D–E, of the first two A sections, using faster note values. After the last chorus, the song moves to its outro, a guitar solo played over Bm and E chords, a ii–V progression in A major. Because it emphasizes the dominant harmony on E, the outro's open-ended nature underscores the uncertainty of the protagonist's situation.

Because it was released as a single in October/November 1973 and reached No. 10 on the American charts, Capitol record executives included "Helen Wheels" on the American version of *Band on the Run* after "No Words" (the song was not included on the British version of the album). Since it was included on the twenty-fifth anniversary edition of *Band on the Run* (1999) that is the basis of this chapter's discussion, I shall comment on "Helen Wheels" here.[42]

McCartney's Land Rover, christened Helen Wheels, inspired both the title and content of the song.[43] According to McCartney, his Land Rover was a reliable vehicle that transported him and his family around Scotland. Indeed, the Land Rover's name, Helen Wheels, may be a pun related to the vehicle's dynamic qualities: in the chorus, McCartney sings "Helen, hell on wheels." An homage to the road, "Helen Wheels" details a road trip from McCartney's Scottish farm to London, describing stops along the way in Glasgow, Carlisle, Kendal, Liverpool, and Birmingham. Musically, the song contains an intro, alternating verses and choruses, and an outro. It is static from both melodic and harmonic perspectives, with the melody hovering primarily around C#, E, and F#, and the harmony stuck on an A chord, with brief excursions to an E5–A5 harmonic succession, suggesting a cadential V–I motion, to support the chorus's last line about how McCartney's vehicle will never be taken away.

While on vacation with his wife in Jamaica in 1973, McCartney wrote "Picasso's Last Words (Drink to Me)" during a visit with actor Dustin Hoffman.[44] McCartney and Eastman were staying in a house near Montego Bay and read in *The Daily Gleaner*, a local newspaper, that Hoffman and Steve McQueen were in Jamaica filming the movie *Papillon* (1973). Since Hoffman was staying in a place nearby, along the coast, McCartney and Eastman thought it would be a great idea to meet him by getting together for dinner. Thus, Eastman telephoned Hoffman's wife Annie and made the arrangements.

During the visit with the Hoffmans, McCartney and Hoffman talked about songwriting. McCartney compared songwriting to acting, informing Hoffman that just as he could instantly assume the role of a character as an actor, McCartney could write a song. Hoffman was intrigued by the idea, and when McCartney and Eastman returned to the Hoffmans' residence a few days later, Hoffman asked McCartney if he could compose a song on any subject, to which McCartney said yes. Hoffman then showed him an article from *Time* magazine (23 April 1973) about Pablo Picasso in which the painter supposedly said to his friends, "Drink to me, drink to my health, you know I can't drink anymore." Picasso painted some more, and then went to bed around 3:00 a.m. The next morning, he was dead.

Since he had his guitar with him, McCartney began composing, singing and strumming chords that were to eventually become "Picasso's Last Words (Drink to Me)." Hoffman became ecstatic, leaping out of his chair, and informing his wife that McCartney was doing it, writing a song right before his eyes (and ears). McCartney was touched by Hoffman's appreciation.

Inspired by Picasso's painting style, McCartney arranged "Picasso's Last Words (Drink to Me)" as a musical collage, a collection of disparate musical elements and events. As befits its subject, "Picasso's Last Words" sounds at first like a drinking song that one would encounter at a pub or tavern. Formally, the song begins verse–chorus–bridge–chorus in the key of G major. In the verse and bridge, McCartney tells the story of Picasso's final journey as noted in the *Time* magazine article. The chorus features Picasso's last words ("Drink to me . . . "). Structurally, the verse is cast as a contrasting period, two phrases that are melodically different and punctuated, respectively, by half and authentic cadences. The chorus is structured, conversely, as a parallel period, with two phrases that are melodically similar but still punctuated, respectively, by half and authentic cadences. The bridge consists of one long phrase that culminates with a retransitional dominant on D.

After the second statement of the chorus, the song moves through several sections of music, beginning with a 1920s-style interlude that features a clarinet solo with instrumental accompaniment, heard over a French dialogue. The interlude starts in A♭ major before moving to B♭ by means of a sequencing of the musical materials. It then segues into a reprise of "Jet" in the key of G, which in turn moves to a restatement of the song's chorus and bridge, which is laden with disco-inspired strings arranged by Tony Visconti.

The music then moves to another statement of the chorus, this time in the key of C major. This chorus recaptures the drinking spirit of the song's beginning, as the vocals and background noises sound as if they were emanating from a bar.

As if to structure this part of the song, the 1920s-style interlude is repeated, complete with French dialogue. After a brief transition based on the interlude, the C-major version of the chorus reappears, but is cut off abruptly as McCartney, Eastman, and Laine sing the "Ho, Hey, Ho" chorus from "Mrs. Vanderbilt" in the key of G as the song fades out. During the chorus, McCartney doubles the vocal line two octaves lower with his bass guitar while Ginger Baker provides a rhythmic accompaniment with various percussion instruments.

"Nineteen Hundred and Eighty-Five" is the last track on *Band on the Run*. It is a dynamic, optimistic song characterized by a hard-driving piano part and forceful, broken-octave bass lines reminiscent of disco. Addressing the album's emphasis on the need of escaping to a better place, the lyrics of "Nineteen Hundred and Eighty-Five" describe metaphorically how the protagonist has gained true artistic freedom by winning the heart of his love. Nothing else will suffice in throwing off the shackles that have restricted him.

The sparseness of the lyrics is compensated for by the music's intricate nature. "Nineteen Hundred and Eighty-Five" begins in the key of C minor with an energetic, piano-dominated introduction. The music then proceeds through various vocal and instrumental sections. Repeated notes in the melody and the alternation of Eb and Cm chords, III–i harmonic movements, in the harmony characterize the song's verses. McCartney links the song's chorus with its verses motivically by taking the three notes that end both of the verse's phrases—F–Eb–C—to generate the chorus's first two ideas. He then follows these ideas by a phrase related to those found in the verses.

After the first verse and chorus, McCartney inserts an instrumental interlude driven by a descending, stepwise bass line in C minor, C–Bb–Ab–G, harmonized, respectively, by Cm, Cm/Bb, Abmaj7, and G7 chords. The bridge that follows suggests Ab major, particularly from a harmonic perspective, as seen by its use of a Dbm6 chord, iv in Ab. The wordless melody of the bridge moves to verse 2, which is in turn followed by another statement of the chorus. This cycle of bridge, verse, and chorus is repeated, but this time with verse 1 replacing verse 2. The song continues to its outro, which consists of the previously heard instrumental interlude, bolstered by the addition of other instruments, followed by a reprise of the chorus from "Band on the Run," now in C major and fading out as the album comes to a close. By recapping the album's title song, McCartney suggests that the quest for personal freedom is never-ending, as themes from the album's songs resurface regularly in an artist's life.

Band on the Run is Wings' finest album. Unlike *McCartney, Ram, Wings Wild Life,* or *Red Rose Speedway,* all of the songs on *Band on the Run* are fully developed and polished numbers. The album does not contain song fragments, improvised numbers, or throwaways. The songs are linked together by an overarching theme of a desire for personal freedom. In forming Wings, McCartney wanted to have the freedom to experiment with the sound and style of his new band. In that quest, he realized some things would work and others would not. In the final analysis though, he wanted Wings to be Wings. He did not want them to be compared to the Beatles, because he thought that such a comparison not only was unfair but, more importantly, artistically stifling.

Paul McCartney and Wings, 1975–80

As *Band on the Run* enjoyed phenomenal success in 1974, Paul McCartney realized that in order for Wings to tour again, he had to replace guitarist Henry McCullough and drummer Denny Seiwell, who had left the band in 1973. Accordingly, McCartney hired Jimmy McCulloch and Geoff Britton as the group's new lead guitarist and drummer, respectively.[1] McCulloch was a guitar prodigy who distinguished himself on Thunderclap Newman's song, "Something in the Air," from 1969. McCartney remembered that record, which hit No. 1 in the UK pop charts, and, impressed by McCulloch's playing, asked him to join Wings, to which McCulloch said yes. As for Britton, McCartney auditioned numerous drummers at the Albery Theatre, St. Martin's Lane in London in April 1974. Britton applied and was allowed to audition. After being invited back for two more auditions, Britton ultimately won the job, as he impressed McCartney with his solid rock-and-roll drumming. He also impressed his future boss with his black belt in karate.

With his lineup intact, McCartney and Wings went to Nashville in June 1974 not only to work at jelling as a band but also to record some new songs. They eventually went into the studio and cut several tracks, including "Junior's Farm" and "Sally G." But Britton ultimately left the band for both personal and professional reasons.[2] He did not get along with either Denny Laine or Jimmy McCulloch. After playing on some initial tracks of what was to become *Venus and Mars* at Abbey Road Studios and then following the band to New Orleans in January 1975 to record the rest of the album at Sea Saint Studios, Britton quit Wings after it was apparent that the sessions were not working. On the advice of Tony Dorsey, who arranged brass for *Venus and*

Mars, McCartney replaced Britton with Joe English. After recording the basic tracks for *Venus and Mars* in New Orleans, Wings went to Los Angeles for mixing sessions at Wally Heider Studios. Except for "Medicine Jar" and "Crossroads," McCartney wrote all of the album's songs, crediting Eastman as a cowriter.

VENUS AND MARS (1975)

Venus and Mars, the long-awaited follow-up to *Band on the Run*, was released in May 1975.[3] From a commercial standpoint, the album was an unqualified success, reaching the top of the charts on both sides of the Atlantic. From an artistic standpoint, the album garnered mixed reviews.[4] For this writer, although *Venus and Mars* contains an attractive mix of songs that is painstakingly produced, with superior solo work and brass arrangements, it does not match the structural breadth, emotion, or unity of *Band on the Run*.

"Venus and Mars," the album's title track, opens the LP. From the outset, people thought that both the title of the album and first track referred to Eastman and McCartney, respectively. McCartney denied the association or any allegorical relationship deriving from the named Roman gods. Rather, for McCartney, the song could be about a friend who is into astrology or a woman who greets people by asking them what their sign is.[5] In any event, "Venus and Mars" functions as a prelude to the following track, "Rock Show," from both textual and musical perspectives. The lyrics of the song's single verse describe someone sitting in a sports arena waiting for a show to begin. Near the end of the song, the protagonist's good friend, who is into astrology, states that Venus and Mars are "alright tonight." Cast in the key of D major, the music begins with an instrumental intro that features a melody played by a recorder supported by D, Am, Em, Em7, A7sus4, and A7 chords. After an opening phrase in D mixolydian, the song turns to those same melodic and harmonic materials from the intro, but this time both McCartney and the recorder articulate the melody. After the lyrics end with the aforementioned "alright tonight," the song continues with an instrumental outro composed of primary triads D, G, and A, colored by a mixture chord, F6. The outro concludes with a vigorous guitar riff that ends on an E supported by an A chord. The music moves immediately into "Rock Show."

McCartney obviously wrote the upbeat "Rock Show" for the upcoming 1975–76 Wings World Tour. By exploring different rhyming possibilities for the song's chorus (for example, "long hair at the Madison Square"), he was able to mention different concert venues in Amsterdam, New York, and Los Angeles. Musically, "Rock Show" is in the key of A major and has a basic structure of intro(inst.)–verse–verse–chorus–verse(inst.)–bridge–chorus–interlude (spoken)–verse–chorus–chorus(repeated)–outro(repeated vamp). After the instrumental intro, McCartney begins to tell the story of the rock show in the first two verses, with references to "Silly Willy with the Philly Band" in verse 1 and a guitar that looks like one used by Jimmy Page of Led Zeppelin. He anchors the verses harmonically with tonic and dominant harmonies on A and E, respectively, reserving the subdominant harmony on D for the chorus, where he rattles off a litany of those previously mentioned concert venues.

After the instrumental solo that constitutes verse 3, the song's bridge enters. Over a static D chord, McCartney advances the song's story line. The lights are dimmed as the audience anticipates the appearance of the band. As you (the concertgoer) get a glimpse of one of the guitars behind the amplifiers, you are able to obtain an ounce of marijuana (presumably) to get high on as the show finally begins. As the bridge ends, the music moves from the aforementioned D chord to the retransitional dominant on E via its dominant B7 (V7/V). After another statement of the chorus, McCartney includes a spoken interlude with allusions to glam rock ("In my green metal suit"). The harmonic language is static at this point as it sits on an A chord. Monotony is relieved by the inclusion of some chromatic chord successions as the interlude builds to a climax.

After the interlude, verse 4 continues the narrative as McCartney comments on the loudness of the concert through a reference to decibel meters. The song then moves to several repetitions of the chorus, which suggest that the song will end with some big bang. But McCartney throws in a surprise as the chorus segues into an outro introduced by a piano vamp involving A, D, and G chords (I–IV–♭VII). Other instruments join in as McCartney talks about getting ready for the rock show.

The next track on the album, "Love in Song," was one of three songs from the LP that were recorded at Abbey Road Studios. Initially, it was released as the B–side of the single, "Listen to What the Man Said." On the track, McCartney plays his newly acquired stand-up bass used by Bill Black on Elvis Presley's RCA recording of "Heartbreak Hotel" (1956).[6]

The lyrics of "Love in Song" evoke a gentle sadness that is out of character with other contemporaneous love songs by McCartney. The G Aeolian setting contributes to the song's melancholic tinge. After an intro played on a 12-string guitar, McCartney sings two verses followed each time by the song's refrain. In verse 1, the lyrics center on the protagonist crying out to love, whereas in verse 2, by contrast, the tone is more cheerful as the protagonist revels in the security of being loved. Each verse features a Gm7–Gm9/6–Cm7–Gm7 chordal succession, while the refrain, "Love in Song," is singled out by a modal shift to a G7 chord (B♭ has become B♮).

In the bridge, the protagonist recalls happier times. The harmonic language underscores this nostalgic turn with the addition of major-based chords (Gm–E♭–Dm7–F7–Gm–F7–Gm) into the song. After this point, "Love in Song" moves to further statements of the verse/refrain and bridge before concluding. McCartney still plays with the idea of juxtaposing contrasting thoughts in successive verses when he sets off verse 3 against verse 4: the former verse deals with sorrow arising from misunderstanding, whereas the latter reaffirms the security of being loved.

With "You Gave Me the Answer," McCartney revisits the music that he heard growing up as a child in Liverpool. By listening to BBC radio and his father's piano playing, he became familiar with popular music of the 1930s and 1940s, particularly Hollywood musicals featuring Fred Astaire. "You Gave Me the Answer" pays homage to this type of music. One might question, however, the inclusion of this song on a rock album in an era of disco and glam rock. In response, this is the same McCartney who wrote "When I'm Sixty-Four" (1967) and "Honey Pie" (1968), two songs that were included on the Beatle albums *Sgt. Pepper's Lonely Hearts Club Band* and the *White Album*, respectively. But more significantly, this is the same McCartney who would write and record "Mull of Kintyre," a sentimental Scottish ballad complete with bagpipes, in 1979, at the height of punk rock. Thus, far from being a questionable inclusion on *Venus and Mars*, "You Gave Me the Answer" is completely in keeping with McCartney's musical predilections.

In keeping with its style, the form of "You Gave Me the Answer" follows a straightforward AABA with an introduction and interlude. The song is in the key of D major and has the light, bouncy feel of a Fred Astaire song. Indeed, as one listens to the track and its 1930s-style text, one could easily imagine Astaire singing and dancing as he is trying to woo Ginger Rogers. The A sections feature McCartney mimicking Astaire's singing style, accompanied by chordal successions moving up and down (primarily) by seconds: D–Em–F#m–G–C–G–F#m–F–Em–D. The B section incorporates a chromatic chordal ascent from B♭ to D, perhaps to reinforce, via a return to the tonic chord D, the textual idea of the protagonist returning to an idyllic state of love, expressed metaphorically by a return to familiar places where the cobwebs blow away, and by ridding one's self of superficial airs and graces.

An interlude in G major based on the A section provides an instrumental break in which, conceivably, the protagonists of the song dance (McCartney even asks, "Shall we dance?"). The interlude is scored to evoke the instrumental sound of a 1930s musical. In the last A section, the protagonist comments upon his love's unaffected manners. While the aristocracy would never accept her, she would win them over by inviting them to her home for a cup of tea. The section winds down by repeating the words, "You seem to like," and its accompanying Em chord, three times in order to emphasize its textual and musical resolution: "me" and its accompanying tonic harmony on D (decorated by the subdominant harmony G).

Inspired by Marvel Comics, the song "Magneto and Titanium Man" is about heroes and villains. McCartney composed the song while on vacation in Jamaica.[7] Every Saturday, he and his family would go to the supermarket at which time there would be a new batch of comic books. Despite having thought he was over them at age 11, McCartney began to buy comic books again, reading them and loving the drawings. As John Blaney has noted, one can draw parallels between McCartney's comic-book inspired "Magneto and Titanium Man" and John Lennon's "Being for the Benefit of Mister Kite," a song whose lyrics were taken from a circus poster.[8] However, Lennon's song is more sophisticated than McCartney's, as seen by its key scheme and electronic music effects.

"Magneto and Titanium Man" is played in the key of D major, although tuned low to sound in D♭. It features a prominent shuffle rhythm that lends a relaxed atmosphere to the song, suggesting comparisons with the music of the rock group Queen. In a clear verse–chorus–bridge structure, the song spins a tale about how Magneto, Titanium Man, and the Crimson Dynamo inform the song's main character that his love is going to be involved in a bank robbery on Main Street. All four then get in a car and drive to the bank, where the protagonist discovers that his love is actually the law and the three comic book characters were lying to him, perhaps intending to rob the bank themselves. The harmonic language supports the casual tone of the song through its use of D major's three basic chords. In each verse and chorus ("You was involved in a robbery"), D and G chords (I–IV) predominate, while in the bridge ("Well, there she were and to my despair"), A and G chords (V–IV) alternate. At the climax of the song where the protagonist discovers the identity of his love, the music of the bridge shifts back to D and G chords, with a C chord added into the mix, producing the typical I–♭VII–IV progression in rock.

As with all of McCartney's love songs at the time, "Letting Go" centers on his wife, Linda Eastman. While cataloguing Eastman's attractive attributes as a person and pop star, McCartney realizes that he has to let her go for her own benefit. This was a difficult decision for someone who insisted that his wife play and sing in a band with him. Eastman sacrificed her own career as a photographer in order to support her husband's. Moreover, as a member of Wings, she had to tolerate criticism about her musical abilities. Yet, in spite of it all, during the 1975–76 Wings World Tour, McCartney noticed that Eastman "had answered all her critics."[9] She was on top of her game, playing and singing well. Thus, "Letting Go" may be a bittersweet realization for McCartney that he had to give his wife more personal space than he had done in the past. In the final analysis, "letting go" only bolstered an already strong marriage.

"Letting Go" begins in the key of A minor and ends in C minor. An intro and outro frame a simple verse–chorus structure that includes an instrumental interlude and verse. The text swings back and forth between descriptions of Eastman's qualities in the song's three verses, and the notion of letting go in the song's four choruses. McCartney accentuates these differences harmonically by using a relatively brighter sound with a major subdominant in the verses (Am–D7sus4–D7), as opposed to a relatively darker sound with a minor subdominant in the choruses (Dm7–Am). In the interlude, horns play a riff based on the harmonic scheme of the preceding chorus (2). After the guitar solo and chorus 3, the music modulates up a third to C minor in verse 3, which is in a chromatic-mediant relationship with the song's initial key of A minor. After one last statement of the chorus (4), "Letting Go" fades out with an outro for horns that is based on the interlude.

As with *Ram*, *Wings Wild Life*, and *Band on the Run*, McCartney included a reprise of an earlier track in an attempt to make the *Venus and Mars* album cohere. "Venus and Mars (Reprise)" differs from its counterpart chiefly through the addition of two different verses. In the first verse, the protagonist refers to the sports arena he is in as a great cathedral and talks again with his good friend who is into astrology. In the second verse, he mentions meeting another good friend, who not only has told him what her zodiac sign is but also encourages him to reach out for the stars. Both good friends declare, "Venus and Mars are alright tonight."

The next two tracks on *Venus and Mars*, "Spirits of Ancient Egypt" and "Medicine Jar," are the album's weakest songs. Although McCartney wrote "Spirits of Ancient Egypt," Denny Laine sang lead on the song. Lead guitarist Jimmy McCulloch and Colin Allen, formerly of Stone the Crows, wrote "Medicine Jar." As John Blaney has noted, McCartney always projected the public image of Wings as a complete band and cohesive unit. In other words, its other members were not simply backup musicians.[10] McCartney encouraged the others to contribute in one fashion or another to each album's songs. In particular, he was open to having the others have Wings record their material (if good enough).

The text of "Spirits of Ancient Egypt" ranges from the mundane, as exemplified by the refrain, "You're my baby and I love you," to the surreal, such as the line, "I can drive a Cadillac across the Irish Sea." The song is in the key of E major and set stylistically as a blues-flavored rocker. Its form consists of a simple verse/refrain–chorus structure. The verses begin and end with the refrain, which consists of the line, "You're my baby, and I love you," or variations of it, such as "I'm your baby—Do you love me?" The refrain consists of two bluesy motifs, D–E–G–E, and B–D–E–E, accompanied by the tonic chord E. In the interior of each verse, the harmonic support moves back and forth between tonic and subdominant harmonies, E–A–E(7)–A, making the entire section a prolongation of the tonic as the E chord is ultimately decorated by the A chord. But this static harmonic sound is relieved by the modal mixture of the song's chorus, "Spirits of Ancient Egypt." Here, McCartney borrows C and D chords from E minor as he colors the text at first by alternating C and E chords (♭VI–I), moving later onto D and E chords (♭VII–I).

(Since McCartney did not write "Medicine Jar," Jimmy McCulloch's song about drug abuse, I will not comment on it in this book. Accordingly, I will move onto one of the best songs on *Venus and Mars*, McCartney's "Call Me Back Again.")

the B–side of "Coming Up"), and (3) "My Carnival" (the
Like Us"). Interestingly, the smash Top 10 hit "Junior's
ncluded as a bonus track on the reissue of *Venus and Mars*,
um in *The Paul McCartney Collection* thereafter (it was, how-
the McCartney compilations, *All the Best!*, and, of course,
ce it was recorded in Nashville in 1974 and is therefore con-
ith the songs on *Venus and Mars*, I shall discuss "Junior's

rote "Junior's Farm" in Lebanon, Tennessee, at the country
e "Curly" Putnam, who wrote "Green, Green Grass of
D–I–V–O–R–C–E" (made famous by Tammy Wynette).[15]
ted Putnam's place for a couple of weeks, and he and Wings
cCulloch on guitar and Geoff Britton on drums) rehearsed in
rder to improve their sound as a band. Inspired by the time
ham's estate, as well as Bob Dylan's song, "Ain't Gonna Work
arm No More," McCartney composed "Junior's Farm,"
r with his new lineup in Nashville.

rm" clearly demonstrates that Wings could rock with the best
a hard-driving fantasy rock song in G major, with an intro and
lose a verse–chorus structure, and an outstanding guitar solo
. After an instrumental intro, McCartney narrates the story of
" in a formal pattern characterized by a sequence of two verses
In the first two verses, he describes how he got out of a poker
ick of time, and in an encounter with an Eskimo, a sea lion
ady to go." As a result of these experiences, in chorus 1 he
eryone he is with to go to "Junior's Farm" and hide out.
with the song's hard-edged rock style, repeated notes character-
y of the verses, with drop-offs in pitch occurring at the ends of
harmonic setting of the verses is equally sparse in content. In
lines of each verse, the tonic chord G, decorated by a brief C/
roughout, only to move to F and Em chords in the third line.
rus, things do not change much. Repeated notes and drop-offs in
nds of phrases still characterize the melody. The harmonic lan-
asizes the tonic chord G through neighboring motions to the
ord F, I–♭VII–I motions reminiscent of the opening of the
Hard Day's Night."
us 1, McCulloch takes his solo. Thereafter follow verses 3–4 and
verse 3, McCartney asks why are prices rising in a grocery store,
se 4, he repeats the poker story of verse 1. In chorus 2, he again
everyone to hide out at "Junior's Farm." The rest of the song
orus 3–interlude–outro. Interestingly, the outro breaks away from
and harmonic style of the song's verses and choruses by interject-
omplex musical materials. McCartney accompanies the outro's
h an Em–D–Em–D–C–Bm–Am7 chord succession, a series of root

McCartney started "Call Me Back Again" while staying at the Beverly Hills
Hotel in 1974, and finished the lyrics of the song while in New Orleans a year
later.[11] It is a soulful, New Orleans-style ballad, complete with an outstanding
vocal delivered by McCartney and terrific horn parts arranged by Tony Dorsey. Although its lyrics at first glance speak to unrequited love, "Call Me Back
Again" may be a response to the question of a Beatles reunion that the press
pestered McCartney with during the 1970s. On the documentary *Wingspan:
An Intimate Portrait*, McCartney recites a short, Muhammad-Ali style poem
he wrote at the time that conveyed his feelings about the matter:

The Beatles split in '69, and since then they've been doing fine . . . .[12]

After McCartney recites the poem, the documentary intersperses the Wings
performance of "Call Me Back Again" at the Seattle Kingdome in 1976 with
his explanation of the poem. Accordingly, "Call Me Back Again" may be
directed to those in the press and public who were constantly inquiring about
a Beatles reunion. Through the song's lyrics, McCartney may be delivering
the message that the Beatles had no interest in a reunion, especially as
reflected by the chorus: "But I ain't never no no no no never heard you [a
reunion] calling me."

"Call Me Back Again" is in the key of F major, though the rhythm guitar
parts are played in D major, capoed up three frets to sound in F. In keeping
with its soulful style, the song is in 12/8 time, with triplet figures abounding
in its accompaniment. It proceeds verse–chorus–verse(guitar solo)–chorus–
verse–chorus, framed by an intro and outro. The intro sets the mood of the
song, beginning and ending with a forceful C–Dm–F chordal exclamation
(V–vi–I) that not only defines the song's key but also returns at times to punc-
tuate the end of the chorus. The intro also includes the same chords—F, Dm,
E♭9, F—that characterize each verse. The lyrics do not cover much territory
and are repetitive. Both of the sung verses describe a long-term relationship
between the protagonist and his love in which he declares how earlier in their
relationship, calling her brought him joy. But as stated in the chorus, things
have changed; she never calls him anymore, thereby prompting the protagonist to plead for her to contact him.

The vocal line of the verses is angular in construction—descending and
ascending from a high F, sounding above a I–vi–♭VII9–I (F–Dm–E♭9–F) harmonic progression. (Here and in the latter part of the chorus, E♭9, the subtonic chord, substitutes for the dominant on C.) Although the melody of
the chorus is not as expansive as that found in the verses, it lies in a higher
range, hovering around a high F to C, consequently intensifying the protagonist's message. The chorus's harmonic support, however, is more varied than
that found in the verses. The first part of the chorus (which could be considered a pre-chorus by some) features a harmonic succession involving mixture

chords, B♭–A♭–F–E♭–C, cadencing on an augmented dominant chord on C (IV–♭III–I–♭VII–V–V+). The rest of the chorus lays out a series of harmonies that recall those found in the verses, F–G7–E♭9–F–E♭9–F (I–V7/V–♭VII9–I–♭VII9–I). In the outro, which is based on the last two measures of the chorus, McCartney shines as a bluesy vocal soloist, ad-libbing as the music fades out.

"Listen to What the Man Said" is the most popular track on *Venus and Mars*. The song is another great example of McCartney-style pop, a buoyant and optimistic song about love where words and music are wedded together. It was issued as a single in May 1975 and did well on the charts. Dave Mason and Tom Scott joined the new Wings lineup on guitar and soprano sax, respectively. While Mason added some guitar parts to the song, Scott improvised a fabulous solo as well as obbligato parts that greatly enhanced the number.

After some talking by Dr. John, "Listen to What the Man Said" opens with an eight-measure, guitar-dominated intro, joined in the fifth measure by a short sax riff. The intro returns throughout the song as an instrumental refrain (albeit with some variation), appearing after each verse and chorus. In the first two verses, McCartney advances an optimistic view of love, stating that despite its possible downside, such as love being blind or causing tragedy through the separation of a soldier from his sweetheart, it wins out in the end. Although the song is in G major, the verses do not provide any hint of that key in its two phrases. The first phrase opens with a prolongation of a Bm triad through a Bm/D–Cmaj7–Bm7 chordal succession (iii6–IV7–iii7), which then moves to an E chord (V/ii) at the end of the phrase. The second phrase begins with an Am chord (ii) and then ascends stepwise through Bm (iii) and Cmaj7 chords (IV7).

It is only in the chorus that the key of G major is affirmed. Interestingly, so is the song's main thought: the protagonist affirms his belief in love and that it will blossom, according to "what the man said," "the man" being God or any number of things. In a word, McCartney is advising everyone to stick with the basics of life, which for him means focusing on love. In keeping with the nature of the text's thought, the chorus is static harmonically, as the tonic harmony G is decorated and ultimately prolonged by its subdominant harmony C. In the first section of the chorus, C6/D and G chords alternate, moving to Gmaj7 and G7 chords that take the chorus to its middle section, which sits on a C chord. The last section of the chorus returns to the harmonic scheme of the first but with some variation, as Gmaj7 chords sometimes replace G chords.

The outro functions as a coda, rounding off the song and bringing it to a decisive close. It is even more static harmonically than the chorus, sounding G-based chords, along with a D and C6 chord, over a G–D bass pattern. The music then slows down and segues into a section that now includes

strings along with another s⌐
set the stage for the song's cl⌐

"Treat Her Gently/Lone⌐
What the Man Said." The tr⌐
McCartney efforts, are not⌐
related units, with the second⌐
ics focus on the mental, physi⌐
people in their old age, especi⌐
D major and evince a relaxed,⌐
Gently." McCartney sings ab⌐
and senile woman tenderly an⌐
simple, with piano, bass, and dr⌐
in the track by guitar, strings, a⌐
harmony A (decorated by G/A⌐
find another way," seem open-⌐
not be true. After that, the mus⌐
after which both songs are repea⌐

"Lonely Old People" focuses c⌐
a nursing home. It is more develo⌐
contains two verses and a chorus. ⌐
chords harmonizing its first line, v⌐
The chorus becomes more intens⌐
series of chords, which speaks to⌐
the first series, the A#dim7 is use⌐
chord, a coloristic sonority that sha⌐
cedes or follows it (in this instance,⌐
A#dim7–F#m–Bm–G–D. In the sec⌐
dary leading-tone seventh, vii°7/vi:⌐
(essentially, an A9 with a D instead⌐
highlight the fragile nature of the t⌐
while sitting in a park, are out of bre⌐
a game. The chorus concludes with th⌐
bility suggesting that the protagonist⌐
light years.

The last track on *Venus and Mars*,⌐
arrangement of Tony Hatch's theme⌐
soap opera that was on the air from 1⌐
People," McCartney intended "Crossr⌐
ting in the park and not being asked to⌐
and watch the soap *Crossroads*, a fav⌐
McCartney did not compose "Crossroad⌐

Venus and Mars included three singles⌐
as a part of *The Paul McCartney Collecti*⌐
Gang" (theme from the British televisio⌐

Box/Odd Sox"⌐
B-side of "Spies⌐
Farm" was not i⌐
or any Wings alb⌐
ever, included o⌐
Wingspan[14]). Si⌐
temporaneous ⌐
Farm" here.

McCartney w⌐
estate of Claud⌐
Home" and "⌐
McCartney ren⌐
(with Jimmy M⌐
the garage in o⌐
he spent at Put⌐
on Maggie's ⌐
recording it lat⌐

"Junior's Fa⌐
of bands. It is⌐
outro that en⌐
by McCulloch⌐
"Junior's Farr⌐
and a chorus.⌐
game in the ⌐
appeared, "r⌐
encourages e⌐

In keeping⌐
ize the melo⌐
phrases. The⌐
the first two⌐
G, sounds th⌐

In the cho⌐
pitch at the⌐
guage emph⌐
subtonic ch⌐
Beatles' "A⌐

After cho⌐
chorus 2. In⌐
while in ver⌐
encourages⌐
proceeds ch⌐
the melodic⌐
ing more ⌐
melody wit⌐

movements by descending seconds (vi–V–vi–V–IV–iii–ii7) before ending the song with G major's primary chords C, D, and G (IV–V–I).

WINGS AT THE SPEED OF SOUND (1976)

Compared to *Band on the Run* or *Venus and Mars*, *Wings at the Speed of Sound* is an artistic disappointment. There are no standout songs on the album, nor any overriding concept to link the numbers. It is also the most democratically conceived Wings album to date, which led some critics to disparage its quality. Since he felt uncomfortable being the star attraction in what he regarded as a band of equals, McCartney allowed everyone to sing a solo on *Wings at the Speed of Sound*. In addition, he made space on the LP for songs by Jimmy McCulloch and Denny Laine and permitted the horn section to develop their own parts for "Silly Love Songs." However, McCartney's band mates were not as talented as John Lennon or George Harrison, hence his attempt to display their talent did not enhance the album in a substantive way. Yet, to be fair, *Wings at the Speed of Sound* does contain solid tracks that evidently pleased the US public in 1976: the LP was that year's third most successful album, coming behind *Frampton Comes Alive* and *Fleetwood Mac*.[16]

"Let 'Em In" opens *Wings at the Speed of Sound*. It was the second song (after "Silly Love Songs") from the album to be released as a single. It went gold and was a smash Top 10 hit during the summer of 1976. McCartney originally composed "Let 'Em In" for Ringo Starr to record on his album, *Ringo's Rotogravure* (1976), but McCartney decided to record it himself.[17] (As a substitute for "Let 'Em In," Starr received and recorded McCartney's "Pure Gold.")

The song centers on a list of people waiting outside McCartney's door who parade into his home after being allowed entrance to a party he is throwing.[18] He rattles off several names, drawing primarily from people he knew: (1) Brother John (Lennon), (2) Phil and Don (Everly), (3) Brother Michael (McCartney), (4) Uncle Ernie (a character played by Ringo Starr in the Who's rock opera *Tommy*), and (5) his paternal Auntie Gin.

"Let 'Em In" is in the key of B♭ major and features a verse–bridge structure that is framed by an intro and outro, and varied by instrumental interludes. The song begins with the Westminster carillon in D major: F♯–D–E–A, A–E–F♯–D, followed by a piano-dominated intro that lays out the harmonic framework of the verses to follow. In verses 1–2, McCartney sings the song's well-known lyrics about hearing somebody knocking at the door and ringing a bell. He asks someone at the party to let them in. The melody of each verse consists of short figures dominated by repeated notes. The verses' harmonic setting emphasizes the tonic harmony B♭ through a B♭maj7–B♭6–B♭maj7–B♭6–F7/B♭–E♭/B♭–B♭maj7–B♭6 chordal succession. A B♭ pedal point sounds throughout the verses, reinforcing the static effect of the harmonic setting. Although essentially repeating the music of the intro, the instrumental interlude that ensues introduces an anapest (short–short–long) percussion riff, along with ascending/descending stepwise lines at its end, that will return in the song to add a sense of drive to later verses and the outro.

In bridge 1, McCartney articulates the names of the people outside his door. He distinguishes bridge 1 from verses 1–2 musically through modal mixture by alternating Fm (v) and B♭ (I) chords. After finishing his catalogue of names to this chordal accompaniment, McCartney asks someone inside to open the door and let these people in. The music accentuates this moment by moving from an Fm chord to a brighter F–Fmaj7–F7–F6–F chordal sequence, which supports an F–E–E♭–D–C upper line in the melody.

The rest of the song consists of a trombone solo based on verse 1, bridge 2, verses 3–4, bridge 3, verse 5, and an outro. Verses 3–5 repeat verse 1, except for vocal ad libs, and the interlude's anapest percussion riff and ascending/descending stepwise lines, added in verse 4. Bridges 2–3 repeat bridge 1, except for textual changes involving "Brother Michael" to "Uncle Ernie" in bridge 1 and "Auntie Gin" to "Uncle Ian" in bridge 2, and the addition of horn licks in both. The outro is based on the harmonic structure of verse 1. After beginning with B♭maj7 and B♭6 chords, the outro proceeds to the F7/B♭–E♭/B♭–B♭maj7–B♭6 chordal sequence that closes the verse. As this sequence is repeated three times, the anapest percussion riff and the ascending/descending stepwise lines from the song's interlude join the musical texture. The song appears to fade out but suddenly comes back in without losing a beat, ending on a B♭maj7 chord.

Wings recorded "The Note You Never Wrote" first for *Wings at the Speed of Sound* in September 1975. Although McCartney composed the ballad, he gave it to Denny Laine to sing. The song's text narrates a dreamlike, surreal tale about a note in a bottle that washes ashore. The protagonist finds the bottle, reads the note, and realizes that it is from his love, one that she never wrote to him. Somehow, the mayor of Baltimore enters the scene. The protagonist will not vote for the mayor, neither will he allow the mayor to get a quotation from his lover's note. Finally, the protagonist is arrested on the shore because of the government papers he possesses. As he is taken in, he reads his lover's note.

While the verse–chorus structure of "The Note You Never Wrote" may be simple, its melodic/harmonic content is not. The song as a whole is not in a major or minor key; rather, it has different tonal focuses, a strategy in keeping with the meandering lyrics. McCartney sets the song's three verses in E phrygian. The melody suggests an emphasis on E because of the strategic placement of B and E as beginning and ending notes in its phrases. The harmonic accompaniment defines an E phrygian framework for the melody through an alternation of Em and Fmaj7 chords, two harmonies that function as i and II7 in that mode. Near the end of the verse, the music moves from Em and E+ chords to cadence on a chord on A. Although complicating the verses' harmonic setting, the move to the A chord is in keeping with cadences associ-ated with E phrygian.

The choruses of the song become increasingly more complex from both textual and musical perspectives. Chorus 1 states the main thought of the song about the protagonist reading his lover's note. It changes tonal focus from E phrygian to C major through a key-defining Dm7–G7–C chordal pro-gression (ii7–V7–I). The chorus returns to verse 2 by means of a transitional C–Bm–Am chord succession.

Chorus 2 is more expansive textually as it focuses on how the mayor of Bal-timore will never get the protagonist's support or a quotation from his lover's note. To match the text, the music grows in intensity. McCartney expands the key areas of this chorus by modulating first to D minor, then to C major, before returning to the transitional chordal succession of chorus 1 that even-tually takes the music to verse 3. In this instance, it is repeated six times, fol-lowed by a guitar solo based on the chorus.

Chorus 3 repeats the thought of chorus 1, but in a more intense manner, reiterating it several times. Although it modulates to the same keys as chorus 2, chorus 3 does not have another verse to go to, thus it must somehow con-clude the song. It does so by ending with the transitional chordal succession (C–Bm–Am) that was used in the two previous choruses. This results in the song ending rather inconclusively in A minor, which might be a reflection of the fragmented text.

If there ever was a song that could serve as fodder for McCartney's detrac-tors, it is "She's My Baby," written by McCartney for Eastman. It is an inane pop song with trite lyrics and images, as witnessed by Eastman being com-pared to gravy, just begging to be mopped up by McCartney. Nonetheless, the song must have had some importance for him, because he rearranged it for Eastman's memorial services in 1998 and rerecorded it for his *Working Classical* album in 1999.[19]

As suggested by John Blaney, "She's My Baby" was influenced by the then-current vogue for bass-heavy dance music.[20] With that in mind, and ignoring the lyrics for the most part, the song is a pleasant, almost-disco dance number that displays McCartney inventiveness. The song is cast in a verse/refrain–bridge structure with outro. In each verse, the singer lauds the attributes of his "baby" to an eight-measure parallel period in C major, with the first phrase ending on a dominant G7sus4 and the second a tonic C chord. The refrain, "She's My Baby," closes each phrase of the verse. The melody con-tains short musical figures that sound in a sparse texture, although with a prominent, driving bass part. As expected, the bridge begins with the sub-dominant harmony F. It consists of two phrases, the last ending on a retransi-tional dominant chord, G7. But more interestingly, the beginning of each phrase is driven by a chromatic bass line, beginning on F and ending on D. The bass line includes two chromatic harmonies sounding above, one of which is an Fm chord borrowed from C minor: F–*Fm*–C–E♭*dim*–Dm7.

Finally, after the last verse and an instrumental break, the song proceeds to the outro and fades out.

In contrast to the danceable and superficial "She's My Baby," "Beware My Love," the next track, is a complex and substantial rocker, demonstrating that Wings had not given in to light disco music. The song's text focuses on the singer warning his love of the attentions paid to her by an unscrupulous rival. The song is in D minor and consists of a prelude, intro, and outro framing a series of alternating verses and bridges, which can be represented formally as ABCDED(inst.)EDEEC, with most of the song's verses represented by E, and the bridges by D.

"Beware My Love" begins with a harmonium prelude (A) in C major. The prelude's last sonority, an A5, is cross-faded with the song's intro (B), an acoustic guitar vamp in A that is repeated four times. This unsettling succession of keys is resolved by the time verse 1 (C) and its key of D minor enter. McCartney structures verse 1 harmonically by means of an ascending tetrachord, A–B♭–C–D, in the bass, sounding the line's respective chords, A–B♭–C–Dm (V–VI–VII–i), above. (Descending tetrachords in the bass drive the music of bridges 1–3 and verses 2–5.). After two iterations of the tetrachord come alternating Dm and G chords (i–IV). Verse 1 features multitracked vocals by Eastman, who, serving as the voice of the song's protagonist at the beginning, exhorts his love to beware.

After Eastman's vocal prelude, McCartney as protagonist sings in bridge 1 (D). He informs his love that although he may be wrong, he believes that his rival is not the one for her. McCartney structures his melody around a descending tetrachord in the bass consisting of the notes B♭–A–G–F, which results in the use of a B♭–Dm/A–A–A/G–Dm/F harmonic succession (VI–V_4^6–V_3^5–V_2^4–i6). He concludes bridge 1 by informing his love that while he must depart, he will leave her a truthful message in his song. To accentuate this lyric, McCartney embellishes the bridge's harmonic succession by changing the B♭ chord to B♭m (vi), using modal mixture yet again in his music for structural and expressive purposes. He follows the B♭m sonority with an F/A (III6), before the rest of the chords are sounded as is.

In verses 2–5 (E), McCartney as protagonist gets more intense as he goes through a litany of complaints about his rival. In like manner, the music of the verses becomes more intense, assuming the characteristics of a dynamic rock song. As with all of the bridges in the song, he organizes verses 2–5 by means of a descending tetrachord in the bass, this time involving the notes D–C–B♭–A. This tetrachord spans eight measures, with two measures allotted to each bass note. Above the pattern sound Dm, C, B♭, and A chords (i–VII–VI–V).

The bridges contrast with verses 2–5 by functioning as structural counterweights to their forward motion and drive. In other words, at each appearance, the bridges slow down the song's momentum through jerky musical gestures. For added contrast, bridge 2 has no vocal solo per se, whereas bridge 3 repeats bridge 1. Finally, the outro (C) repeats the music of verse 1, but in a much more animated vein, as Eastman's multi-tracked vocals return. The outro ends after "Beware my love" is sung frenetically seven times over a Dm–G chordal accompaniment, ending abruptly with the G chord.

"Wino Junko," "Cook of the House," and "Time to Hide," the fifth, seventh, and eighth tracks, respectively, of *Wings at the Speed of Sound* deserve little comment. In keeping with the democratic nature of the album, McCartney gave space on the album for Jimmy McCulloch and Colin Allen's "Wino Junko" and Denny Laine's "Time to Hide." McCulloch sang lead vocal on "Wino Junko," a dark song purportedly about his alcohol and drug use, and Laine, of course, sang lead on his song, "Time to Hide." McCartney wrote "Cook of the House" for Eastman, a silly, 1950s-style rock 'n' roll song. He even played double bass on the track using the same instrument played by Elvis Presley's bass player, Bill Black. Critics of *Wings at the Speed of Sound* have either ignored "Cook of the House," chalking it up to it only being natural that McCartney give the wife something to sing on the album, or panned it.

"Silly Love Songs," the sixth track of the album and the first to be released as a single, has McCartney answering criticisms of his music as cute, lightweight, and sentimental (in comparison with the more critically acclaimed music by ex-Beatle John Lennon) by mocking himself as well as celebrating his values. Inspired by the thought that what he was writing was not in style, as seen by the likes of Alice Cooper's "No More Mister Nice Guy" (1976), McCartney wanted to strike a blow for old-fashioned, sentimental love songs.[21] And boy did he strike that blow. In the summer of 1976, "Silly Love Songs" was a smash hit and Wings' best-selling single, going gold and reaching No. 1 in the US, even spending five weeks at the top of *Billboard* magazine's charts.[22]

"Silly Love Songs" is a pleasant disco tune in the key of C major and cast in a verse–chorus–bridge structure with an intro and interludes. In the song's four verses, three choruses, and bridge, McCartney makes the case for writing silly love songs, stating that people still crave them. He also celebrates the love he and Eastman share through exclamations of love and statements of their feelings for each other. In keeping with aspects of McCartney musical style, the melody of verses 1 and 4 consists of different gestures that begin with repeated notes and end with a descending figure. Conversely, the melody of verses 2 and 3 features ascending and/or descending scalar figures, while the melody of each chorus consists of slower-moving notes that leap up a fifth and then move either up or down a step (G–D–E, G–D–C). Three chords, C, Em7, and Fmaj7, dominate the harmonic language of the song's verses and choruses, although verses 1–3 include a cadential dominant chord on G to move the music forward. The bridge provides harmonic variety through Em7, Am, Dm7, C, and G11 chords, as well as textural variety through stop time, where the group suddenly stops supporting McCartney's vocal line every other measure.

In verses 2–3 and chorus 3, McCartney heightens the song's message of domestic love by incorporating a warm, musical dialogue between him and Eastman. In verse 2, as McCartney sings the words, "I can't explain, the feelings plain to me . . . ," Eastman sings the chorus's line, "I love you." In verse 3, they continue in the same vein as in verse 2, with McCartney asking how can he tell you about his loved one. In chorus 3, which is the climax of the song, McCartney combines all three lines in a display of contrapuntal skill. McCartney sings the words of the chorus, while Eastman sings the words of verse 2. Next, McCartney joins in with words from verse 3. Finally, "Silly Love Songs" is topped off musically by a superb bass line, excellent horn parts, and disco-esque strings that make it charming. It ends rather inconclusively on an Em7 chord, asking the question, why is it wrong for some people to write silly love songs.

McCartney composed "Must Do Something About It" and, after laying down the song's backing track, gave it to drummer Joe English to sing. Despite lyrics that center on loneliness, English's performance of the song conveys a surprisingly sunny disposition. "Must Do Something About It" is played in the key of D major on the guitar. However, the guitar is capoed on the first fret and tuned flat to sound closer to E♭ major. The song has a verse/refrain–bridge form with an intro, outro, and acoustic guitar tag. In each verse, the protagonist describes his lonely existence, such as playing cards by himself or watching a sunset alone. But in each refrain, he resolves to do "something about it," that is, change his life. The music reinforces the protagonist's situation. The instability generated by the asymmetrical five-measure lengths of the verses, along with the move away from the tonic harmony on D to an Em chord (preceded by its dominant, B7: V7/ii–ii), underscores the unsettling nature of the protagonist's existence. The stability produced by the symmetrical four-measure length of the refrain, along with a possible return to the tonic via A7sus4 and A7 chords, indicates, on the other hand, the possibility that the protagonist may transform his life.

The lyrics of the bridge continue to describe the protagonist's drab and lonely existence. The bridge consists of one eight-measure phrase, parsed into two-measure units. Its harmonic language, however, is not as drab as the descriptions contained in the text. The chords of the bridge move, for the most part, by descending fifths, arriving on the retransitional dominant A7: Am7–Dsus4–D–Gm7–C7sus4–C7–G7–Dm–A7sus4–A7. This series of chords reflects McCartney's penchant for modal mixture: all of the chords in the series, except for Dsus4, D, A7sus4, and A7, are borrowed from D minor.

"San Ferry Anne" is a short song about the lifestyle of a presumably rich and sophisticated woman. The singer comments on various aspects of her energetic existence, noting how she seems to have it all together. Although casting some doubt as to whether or not she is truly content ("And if things are what they seem''), the singer encourages the woman to be happy in a world that keeps turning happily ever after.

"San Ferry Anne" is in A minor and, in keeping with the urbane and sophisticated nature of the main character of the song, includes jazzy flute, trumpet, and saxophone obbligatos, as well as horn interludes and an outro in which the flute, trumpet, and saxophone take turns playing riffs. The song's form is simple, comprising three verses, with the first two followed by instrumental interludes, and the third followed by an outro. Verses 1–2 consist of two phrases that begin with the tonic harmony on Am and end with a half cadence on E. McCartney plays a descending bass line, A–G–F♯–F–E, that assists the motion to the E chord at the end of each phrase. Although the last verse is similar structurally to its two predecessors, it eventually modulates to D minor, setting up the harmonic scheme of the outro that sounds the primary chords of that key—Dm, G, A—over a D–C–B–A bass line as the music fades out.

"Warm and Beautiful" closes *Wings at the Speed of Sound*. McCartney wrote the song for Eastman and rearranged it for inclusion on his *Working Classical* album. It is a sentimental, idealistic, but compelling love ballad. It is in C major and consists of an intro, two verses, bridge, interlude, bridge, and verse. Textually, the verses view love as everlasting, and in conjunction with faith and hope, as helping one overcome a world touched by sadness. The bridge gets more personal as McCartney uses the images of a sunlit morning and moonlit water to describe his love for Eastman. Formally, each verse consists of a parallel period, while the bridge includes two phrases. This prosaic approach to form, however, does not spill over into the song's use of melody and harmony. Rather, melody and harmony are what make the track.

The melody of the verses has a wide arc. In the first phrase of each verse, the melody begins on C, moves up to an F, and then descends by way of leaps to D. The second phrase of each verse traces a similar melodic path but concludes with a highly expressive descending diminished seventh followed by an ascending minor second, A♭–B–C. The harmonic setting of the first two measures of each phrase consists of a C–C + –F–Fm chordal succession, with the Fm chord, borrowed from C minor, employed to support the word, "beautiful." While the last two measures of each first phrase conclude with the dominant harmony G, the last two measures of each second phrase conclude with a G7♭9–C harmonic succession (V♭9–I), supporting the poignant A♭–B–C in the melody.

The melody and the harmonic setting of the bridge are equally expressive. The melody contains leaps complemented by stepwise motion, usually in the opposite direction. Harmonically, the first phrase of the bridge begins on the subdominant harmony F and concludes with an authentic cadence, G–C (V–I). This sets the stage for a heightening of the music's expression in the second phrase. The ascending minor sixth, A–F, in the melody of the first phrase that was harmonized by an F chord, is transformed into a major sixth,

A♭–F, in the second, now harmonized by a modally altered Fm chord. The move to the second phrase's retransitional dominant G is enhanced by two secondary dominants, A7 (V7/ii) and D7 (V7/V).

When it was reissued on compact disc as part of *The Paul McCartney Collection*, *Wings at the Speed of Sound* included three singles as bonus tracks that were recorded or overdubbed in Nashville in 1974: (1) "Walking in the Park with Eloise," (2) "Bridge on the River Suite" (the flip side of "Walking in the Park with Eloise"), (3) and "Sally G" (the flip side of "Junior's Farm"). McCartney's father Jim originally composed the instrumental "Walking in the Park with Eloise" in the early 1950s, although neither he nor anyone else wrote it down.[23] At the urging of guitarist Chet Atkins, McCartney decided to record it. Country piano player Floyd Cramer joined McCartney, Atkins, and Geoff Britton, along with Atkins's pickup band, the Country Hams, to play on the track. McCartney improvised the melody of what was to become "Bridge on the River Suite" during the recording of "Country Dreamer," the flip side of "Helen Wheels," in 1973.[24] He recorded the song's basic tracks at EMI's studio in Paris in December 1973, adding overdubs in Nashville a year later. "Sally G" is a delightful country-music-style number, demonstrating McCartney's versatility as a songwriter, and I shall discuss it here.

McCartney wrote "Sally G" after being inspired by the country-music singer Diane Gaffney and a visit to a bar called the Skull's Rainbow Room in the Printer's Alley district of Nashville.[25] Besides the 1974 lineup of Wings playing and singing on the track, McCartney secured the services of various studio musicians, particularly Johnny Gimble, who played for Bob Willis and the Texas Playboys, on fiddle.

"Sally G" is in the key of G major and through a verse–chorus structure complemented by an intro, outro, and instrumental interludes, narrates the story of its female protagonist. The intro begins with an incomplete progression, A7–Am7–G/B–C, before settling down with the tonic harmony on G decorated by its subdominant C. In verse 1, the singer introduces Sally G and the song's locale of Nashville. The harmonic setting of verse 1, as well as that of verses 2–3, includes chordal sequences anticipated in the intro, G–A7–Am7–G and G–A7–Am7–C–G. The chorus that follows expresses the main message of the song, that Sally G is "no good" and has hurt the singer emotionally. The harmonic setting of the chorus develops the paradigms found in the intro and verses. Although the first and third lines alternate C and G chords, the second line introduces a series of fifth-related chords, A7, D7, and G7, whereas the fourth line essentially repeats the chordal sequence of the intro's opening.

Verse 2 advances the story line by placing the singer at a bar in Printer's Alley. The bridge has the singer reflecting upon his relationship with Sally G, noting how it was initially blossoming but deteriorated because of Sally's lies to him. He concludes that he must "move along." Harmonically, the bridge does not follow the standard model of beginning in the subdominant and ending with a retransitional dominant. Instead, the bridge's first phrase is supported by an Am–Em–G–D harmonic succession, and the second phrase by Am–G–Am–Em–C chords. Verse 3 serves as the song's epilogue. The singer has left Sally G. As he reflects on his relationship with her, he notes that the letter "G" does not stand for anything good. The song concludes with an outro that repeats the music of the intro.

LONDON TOWN (1978)

Preliminary work on *London Town* began in February 1977 at Abbey Road Studios.[26] In keeping with McCartney's zest for recording albums in exotic locations, as he did with *Band on the Run* (Lagos, Nigeria), various singles such as "Junior's Farm" (Nashville), and *Venus and Mars* (New Orleans), recording sessions for *London Town* (originally titled *Water Wings*) continued in April 1977 on a yacht called the *Fair Carol*, moored in Watermelon Bay off the island of Saint John, US Virgin Islands. (McCartney may have actually wanted to compose and record songs for *London Town* in international waters to avoid paying taxes to the US Virgin Islands.) The yacht was outfitted with a 24-track recording studio. McCartney brought in three other yachts for his family and the other band members to use for eating and sleeping. Wings recorded nine tracks on the *Fair Carol* during the month they spent in the Virgin Islands. Seven of the songs made it onto *London Town*. In late 1977 and continuing into early 1978, Wings worked at Abbey Road Studios to finish the album by recording overdubs and main vocals.

During the recording of *London Town*, Jimmy McCulloch and Joe English left Wings. Their absence from the group is seen on the cover artwork of the album where only McCartney, Eastman, and Laine are pictured. After *London Town* was released in March 1978, McCartney hired guitarist Laurence Juber and drummer Steve Holly to replace McCulloch and English. Although this was yet another turnover that aggravated McCartney, it indicated a deeper, artistic situation. For McCartney, "Wings was starting to become tense. Sometimes you sense when you've done what you set out to do."[27] Thus, *London Town* signaled the beginning of the end of Wings. In two short years, McCartney would move onto the next stage of his solo career.

London Town shipped platinum (1 million copies) and was the second best-selling album of 1978 next to *Saturday Night Fever*, and the best selling Wings album since *Band on the Run*. It contained five McCartney/Laine collaborations, the most of any Wings album. McCartney pulled "With a Little Luck" from *London Town* and released it as a single in March 1978. It hit No. 1 in the US and made the Top 10 in the UK.

McCartney and Laine wrote the album's title track, "London Town." McCartney began the song in November 1975 while Wings was in Perth, Australia and completed the number with Laine in Scotland between tours.[28]

Through the song, McCartney and Laine provide a quixotic picture of the people of London, reminiscent of what McCartney had done with the people of Liverpool in "Penny Lane." However, loneliness as a theme permeates the song, as expressed by the protagonist's alienation from the city's populace.

This soft rock ballad begins in the key of E major and includes a sophisticated use of harmony. Although obscuring the tonic key of E by beginning with D/F♯, Dmaj7/F♯, G, F♯7/A♯, and B chords, the harmonic structure of the intro establishes E major near the end of the intro's first phrase through a plagal progression, A–E. For its harmonic support, the intro's second phrase employs a varied form of the first phrase's chordal succession, with the concluding harmony on E functioning as the first chord of the ensuing verse.

"London Town" contains four verses interspersed with two bridges, instrumental interludes (including a guitar solo), and an outro. Structurally, verses 1 and 4, and 2 and 3, are related. Verses 1 and 4 contain the same E-centered chord progressions and close with the song's refrain that ends with the tag, "London Town." Textually, both verses describe the protagonist's adventures on the streets of London where he is stopped in each instance by a colorful character, only to have silver rain falling down on the city's dirty streets. Verses 2 and 3 contrast both musically and textually with verses 1 and 4. They begin and end with A chords, suggesting a focus on the subdominant instead of the tonic. Rather than describing colorful characters he meets on the street, the protagonist expresses his frustration about how it is impossible to meet ordinary people (verse 2) and comments on the emotional emptiness experienced by an unemployed actor (verse 3). Instead of including the refrain of verses 1 and 4, verses 2 and 3 have their own as the protagonist exclaims, "Well, I don't know," which indicates that these verses, in the final analysis, center on commentary, whereas verses 1 and 4 center on idealized observation.

Bridges 1–2, which follow verses 2–3, respectively, continue the latter sections' musical and textual thrust. The bridges emphasize A major through chromatic chordal successions that end with A as a point of arrival (F♯m7–Gdim7–E7/G♯–A). They pose the question about knowing where to go to in the town. Bridge 1 concludes with the textual phrase, "I don't know," supported by D/F♯, G, and E7/G♯ chords. Since A major is emphasized in bridge 1, the E7 chord at the end sounds like a half cadence, making the phrase "I don't know" sound open-ended, suggesting that the protagonist is wandering the streets of London with no purpose.

After a second interlude and a guitar solo, the song concludes with an outro in A major. The outro derives textually and musically from the bridge and refrain of verses 1 and 4. The protagonist reiterates that someone out there has to know what to see in London as F♯m7–Gdim7–E7/G♯–A chords provide harmonic support. The song concludes with the refrain from verses 1 and 4, but instead of suggesting E major through plagal motions, the harmonic setting features a double plagal progression involving G (G7–G6–

Gsus4–G), D, and A chords in A major (♭VII–IV–I). The conflict between the keys of E and A major heard throughout the song reinforces the uncertainty felt by the protagonist, who is unsure about where to go in London.

McCartney composed "Café on the Left Bank" remembering his trips to Paris, especially one with John Lennon in 1961.[29] The song has the distinction of being the first track recorded by Wings on the yacht *Fair Carol* in the Virgin Islands in 1977. Like "London Town" and even "Penny Lane," "Café on the Left Bank" deals with observation, this time involving people in Paris. This rocker is in the key of D minor and employs a simple verse–bridge design with an intro, outro, and two guitar solos. Each verse and bridge, moreover, contains only one phrase.

In verse 1, the singer describes a café on the Left Bank of the Seine River in which he observes people drinking ordinary wine and men watching women. The phrase's harmonic structure, which is used in all verses, is routine, employing basic chords from D minor that end with an authentic cadence featuring a major tonic triad: Dm–Gm–C–Gm–Dm–A7–D (i–iv–VII–iv–i–V7–I). In verse 2, the singer turns his attention to a group of Frenchmen watching Charles de Gaulle on television. Bridge 1 shifts the scene to people dancing after midnight and drunks sprawled over automobiles. Fortunately, continental breakfast awaits everyone the next day in the bar. Harmonically, the bridge begins with the subdominant Gm alternating with the tonic Dm, before the music cadences on the retransitional dominant A7. In verse 3, the singer describes a loud, boisterous group of English people drinking beer.

The rest of the song proceeds in a predictable manner with the repetition of verses (4 and 5 repeat 1 and 3, respectively), the insertion of guitar solos, and the appearance of bridge 2, which varies the text of bridge 1: while people are still dancing after midnight, they are crawling to their cars as a cocktail waitress remains inside. The outro has the singer repeating the line, "Café on the Left Bank," accompanied by a guitar obbligato, as the song fades out.

Composed by McCartney and recorded on 5 May 1977 on the yacht *Fair Carol* in the Virgin Islands, the love song "I'm Carrying" was supposedly inspired, curiously enough, by one of McCartney's former girlfriends instead of Eastman.[30] The song's instrumentation includes McCartney's double-tracked acoustic guitar, overdubbed strings, and an instrument called the Gizmo, invented by former members of 10cc, Kevin Godley and Lol Creme. It is a small handheld gadget for guitar that vibrates the strings.

"I'm Carrying" has a plain but melancholy text that conveys three ideas. In the ever-present chorus, the singer informs his lover that he is carrying something for her. Verse 1 describes how the singer will be at his lover's room at dawn with a carnation hidden by his gifts of love for her, whereas verse 2 draws attention to the singer's long absence and lack of style when he comes back. "I'm Carrying" is simple musically, alternating verse with chorus and based on a harmonic vocabulary of four chords in the key of E major, E, Edim, F♯m7, and Bsus4.

McCartney, Eastman, and Laine recorded "Backwards Traveller/Cuff Link," a two-song medley, without Jimmy McCulloch and Joe English in October 1977 and completed it in January 1978.[31] Both songs are throwaways. "Backwards Traveller" is in an A–B–B[1] form (verse–chorus 1–chorus 2) in the key of C major (because a C chord initiates each section). Its lyrics describe the song's protagonist as a traveler going back in time, "sailing songs" and "wailing on the moon." "Backwards Traveller" is a mid-tempo rocker, with McCartney's repeated-chord accompaniment on the organ giving the song a retrospective, 1960s-style sound. "Cuff Link" is an unimaginative instrumental number in D minor.

Written by McCartney and Laine, "Children Children" was inspired by a waterfall in McCartney's garden.[32] It is a folk-like song with a Caribbean flavor, centering on children playing hide-and-go-seek in a forest by a waterfall. The trio of McCartney, Eastman, and Laine recorded the song at Abbey Road Studios. Besides bass, guitar, and keyboards, McCartney plays violin and autoharp on the track. "Children Children" is in G major and cast in an alternating verse–chorus design with an intro and instrumental interludes. Laine sings lead vocal and delivers it in a George Harrison-esque style. The harmonic vocabulary of the song is straightforward, consisting of G major's basic chords—G, C, D, along with other diatonic triads, such as Em and Am.

McCartney wrote "Girlfriend," the album's next track, with Michael Jackson in mind.[33] At the suggestion of his producer Quincy Jones, Jackson recorded the song and included it on his critically acclaimed album *Off the Wall* (1979). This association blossomed into actual collaborations between McCartney and Jackson in the early 1980s. The two wrote and recorded "Say, Say, Say" and "The Man" for McCartney's *Pipes of Peace* album (1983). McCartney sang a duet with Jackson on the latter's "The Girl Is Mine" for Jackson's monumental *Thriller* album (1982). After Jackson bought the rights to the Beatles song catalogue in 1985 via his purchase of ATV music, which McCartney contested, McCartney and Jackson's professional association ended.

"Girlfriend" demonstrates McCartney's versatility as a songwriter. It truly sounds like an R & B ballad that either Jackson or the Jackson Five would sing. Assisting in the song's musical likeness are the number's vocals, which include McCartney's falsetto and Eastman and Laine's high-pitched backing vocals. The text of the song tells the story of a love triangle. The protagonist is going to inform the rival for his girlfriend's attentions that he and his girlfriend are in love, and that nothing will stand in the way of their relationship.

The song is in the key of G major and set in an AABA form (verse 1–verse 2–bridge–verse 3) with intro, interludes, and outro. In the song's first two sections, the protagonist informs his rival that he and his girlfriend are in love, especially by showing the rival letters his girlfriend has written to him. Each of these sections contains a G6–Am7–D13 harmonic succession (I–ii7–V13) that accompanies the first two lines. Thereafter, McCartney varies this scheme by using a G–Em7–Am7–F7–F6–F–G6 succession (I–vi7–ii7–♭VII–I) to accompany the rest of the lines. Besides being a substitute for dominant harmony on D, the subtonic chords on F are a part of a prolongation of ♭VII via a descending line, E♭–D–C, a compositional technique similar to what McCartney used to prolong the dominant in the bridge of "Maybe I'm Amazed."

After a wordless vocal interlude, the protagonist characterizes the magnitude of his love in the bridge in terms of rivers, wind, and flowers doing the impossible by ceasing to flow, gust, or grow, respectively. At this point, McCartney abandons his falsetto and sings with his natural voice, accompanied by a series of chords based on an interlude that separates verse 1 from 2. Next comes a guitar solo in A major, then minor, after which follows a repetition of the last two lines of verse 2. Finally, verse 3 has the protagonist urging his girlfriend that the two of them must inform his rival of the strength of their love. The song's outro combines the previously heard wordless vocal interlude and melody from the bridge to close the song.

Wings recorded McCartney's "I've Had Enough" on the *Fair Carol* in the Virgin Islands. It is a guitar-dominated rocker in D major, and in keeping with that genre, is simple musically, with an intro and alternating verses and choruses. The harmonic vocabulary is likewise simple, involving only four chords, D, A, Asus4, and E. The lyrics do not say much either, expressing frustration at various situations one encounters in life. But there could be a deeper meaning to the song's text. As John Blaney has noted, McCartney may be signaling that Wings was getting old, that the group had accomplished all that they could have possibly done.[34] The personnel changes were irritating, furthermore, for McCartney and did not help matters. Looming over the horizon was a need to move on to new musical associations and projects.

McCartney wrote "With a Little Luck" in Scotland and, like the previous track, recorded it with Wings in the Virgin Islands.[35] He finished mixing the song at Abbey Road Studios, London later that same year. He released "With a Little Luck" on both sides of the Atlantic in March 1978 where it hit the No. 1 position in the US.

Serving as a stylistic foil to the harder-edged "I've Had Enough," "With a Little Luck" is another formulaic soft-rock song that characterized Wings' sound during the 1970s. It is in the key of E major and has a verse–bridge structure with an intro and outro. It is thoroughly optimistic in tone, especially in the lyrics of the bridge where the singer maintains that there are no limits to what he and his love can do together. In the verses, the melody is wide-ranging, encompassing ascending and descending leaps, whereas in the bridge, it features more stepwise motion. Harmonically, the three verses are set to the same changes, as is the bridge. The verse features a key-defining progression in E major, with the first two lines supported by E, E/G♯, A, A/B or B11, and E chords (I–I6–IV–V11–I). The next two lines contain the same chords except for the last one on E, which is replaced by a C#m7 (vi7), resulting in a deceptive cadence (V–vi).

The bridge begins in F# minor, the song's supertonic key (ii). The harmonic structure alternates F#m and C#7 chords (the dominant of F#m) before concluding on the retransitional dominant, B11. The outro contains vocal sections framing an instrumental one, generating an A–B–A form. The vocal sections are based on the song's verses. The instrumental section is supported initially by a new harmonic scheme that includes E, B7sus4, A/D, and C#m7 chords. But it eventually repeats the harmonic designs of both verse and bridge as synthesizer leads sound above.

McCartney wrote "Famous Groupies" while in Scotland.[36] Wings recorded the comedic, tongue-in-cheek number on the *Fair Carol* in the Virgin Islands. Indeed, Howard Elson characterizes the song as "[v]audeville re-visited à la Don Partridge, a British busker who enjoyed chart success in England in the 1960s."[37] The lyrics describe a humorous fantasy tale about musicians and the real stars of rock music, groupies. The form of "Famous Groupies" is simple. Following a count-off, there are three choruses and four verses, as well as one instrumental solo. The song begins with the chorus, which features the refrain, "Take a snap [photo] of the famous groupies for me," accompanied by a C–Em–Am–G chordal succession that suggests C major. Following chorus 1, verses 1–4 relate the tale of two famous groupies and their adventures with a bongo player, a lead guitarist, and Rory the roadie who practices voodoo on the side. The verses are cast in the key of D minor in their first half and G major in their second (ending with half cadences on D in verses 2 and 4). The last section of the song, chorus 3, is the most expansive of all choruses as the singer speaks at length about the physical attributes of these groupies.

Composed by McCartney and Laine, "Deliver Your Children" is a folk rock song in the style of Bob Dylan or Paul Simon, with Laine singing lead vocal accompanied by acoustic guitars. Despite the title of the song, which suggests a coherent message of hope, the lyrics of the song are not completely lucid. The verses ramble from topic to topic, from people fleeing torrential rains, to the singer seeking God's assistance, to the singer's unfaithful lover, to an unscrupulous dealer who cannot fix the singer's broken-down truck, to the singer robbing the dealer in order to get even with him, to an invitation of singing the song again. The text of the chorus, on the other hand, is a plea for responsibility in the face of the pessimism of the verses. Although the song sounds in A minor, it is played in D minor, capoed on the seventh fret.

Having established the textual roles of verse and chorus in the song, McCartney and Laine highlight their differences through dissimilar harmonic settings. They accentuate the stark imagery of the verses by setting them in the Dorian mode (D–dorian for verses 1–2, and G–dorian for 3–4) through i–VII–i–IV–i–VII–v(7)–i–v(7)–i harmonic progressions. Conversely, they reinforce the chorus's message of hope through deliverance by highlighting the key of C major. After moving to G dorian for verses 3 and 4, the music returns to D dorian for the song's acoustic guitar solo and outro.

McCartney's "Name and Address" is a tribute to his teenage musical idol, Elvis Presley. That the song pays homage to Presley can be confirmed easily from McCartney's Elvis-style lead vocal, complete with imitation Sun Records reverb. He, Eastman, and Laine recorded the song at Abbey Road Studios, because by this time, English and McCulloch had left Wings. McCartney played lead guitar, bass, and drums on the track. In keeping with its rockabilly style, the song's form and harmonic vocabulary are basic. The song takes an AABA design as its frame of reference, but enhances that format predictably with an intro, guitar solo, repetition of a verse, and outro. Moreover, each verse, as well as the bridge, concludes with the refrain, "If you want my love, leave your name and address." The song's harmonic vocabulary is limited to the three basic chords of its tonic key, E major: E, E5, E/B, A7, and B5. Each verse begins with the subdominant harmony A7 moving to the tonic E, before eventually progressing to a B5, then E5, to conclude the section. Since it is a truncated and harmonically varied form of the verse, ending with the refrain, the bridge adds nothing substantially new to the song's form.

McCartney and Laine collaborated on *London Town*'s next track, "Don't Let It Bring You Down." McCartney began the song in a hotel room while on tour with Wings in Aberdeen, Scotland, in 1975.[38] He and Laine finished the song at a later point in time. Wings then recorded the track on the *Fair Carol* in the Virgin Islands. "Don't Let It Bring You Down" is a musical contrast to the previous up-tempo rockabilly number, "Name and Address." It is reminiscent of not only Irish reel music but also the type of material done by the Chieftains, enhanced by flageolets (Irish tin whistles) played by McCartney and Laine.[39] The song is in the key of D minor and begins with a lengthy instrumental intro that includes the song's opening melody and its accompanying harmonic changes: Dm–C–G/B–G–A7–A7sus4–A7, F–G–A7–Dm (i–VII–IV6–IV–V7, III–IV–V7–i).

McCartney's optimism shines forth in "Don't Let It Bring You Down," although in a more subdued manner. The song's three verses all open with textual images of problems in life that are at times hard to bear, followed by the resolute refrain, "Don't let it bring you down." McCartney and Laine distinguish these ideas musically with a parallel period, with the first phrase associated with something negative and the second with something positive, that is, encouragement. Textually, bridges 1 and 2 offer more encouragement in the form of advising one not to run away from problems. Harmonically, an Am chord (v) initiates each phrase of the bridge before culminating on the retransitional dominant A7, elaborated by an A7sus4 (A7–A7sus4–A7). Finally, the song includes an instrumental solo and an outro with vocals that are based on the harmonic structure of the verse. The music ends by repeating the tonic chord on Dm, over which sounds Jimmy McCulloch's fuzz-tone guitar solo, dissipating the energy of the song in the process.

McCartney wrote "Morse Moose and the Grey Goose" in collaboration with Denny Laine. It emerged from a Wings jam session while on the *Fair Carol* in the Virgin Islands. At the time, McCartney and Laine experimented with an electric piano, whereby McCartney would play a series of notes suggesting Morse code, while Laine would give the instrument an occasional thump.[40] Using this as a foundation, McCartney added a bass lick while the other members of Wings supplied other parts. The band finished the track at Abbey Road studios by adding vocals, lyrics, a countermelody, and parts for Mellotron and acoustic guitars.

A sea chanty in the key of D minor, "Morse Moose and the Grey Goose" tells the story of the ship the *Grey Goose*, which went down to the bottom of the sea, presumably during a storm. Morse Moose is a character in the song who is sending a frantic signal to the ship, wondering if it has received his communication. "Morse Moose and the Grey Goose" is cast in a free-flowing A(intro)A(chorus)A(inst.)B(verse 1)B(verse 2)B(verse 3)B(inst.)A(inst.)B(verse 4)A(outro) form. The song begins with an instrumental intro, complete with imitation-Morse code played on the piano through a fuzz box, along with radio dialogue, all over a Dm–G6–Dm7–Dm vamp (i–IV–i7–i). Through the chorus, Morse Moose enters the scene, singing the frantic communiqué to the *Grey Goose* over the intro's vamp.

The verses narrate the story of the ship. Verse 1 declares the *Grey Goose* a steady ship, although not inspiring confidence on the part of the public. But one night, when the moon was high, it sank. Verses 2–4 tell the story of the ship's sinking, from the ship sailing around rocks, dealing with bad winds, facing imminent disaster—which had its crew preparing to face eternity—and, finally, reaching tranquility as it sinks into the stormy sea. Each verse ends with the refrain, "The *Grey Goose* flew away," indicating the ship's demise. Harmonically, and still keeping the music in the key of D minor, McCartney supports the vocal lines of verses 1–3 with Dm, F, A7, Dm, Am7, and Dm chords.

After instrumental interludes based on B and A, along with a statement of verse 4, the chorus returns in the form of an outro, bringing the song to a feverish climax. Compared to its earlier appearance in the song, this chorus as outro is more developed, with parts added to make it more dynamic and intense. In the final analysis, the outro heightens the tragedy of what just occurred in the song's story.

Reissued in 1993 as a part of the *Paul McCartney Collection*, *London Town* included "Mull of Kintyre" and its flip side, "Girls School," as bonus tracks. Because "Mull of Kintyre" was one of the biggest-selling singles in the UK (outstripping the Beatles' "She Loves You" in 1963, and eclipsed only by Band Aid's "Do They Know It's Christmas" in 1984) and, more importantly, the biggest hit of McCartney's career, I shall discuss it below.

Begun in 1974 and finished with the help of Denny Laine and Tony Wilson, pipe major of the Campbeltown Pipe Band, "Mull of Kintyre," a Scottish waltz, should not have been the huge hit that it was, given the fact that, at the time, punk rock was dominating the British musical scene. "Mull of Kintyre" celebrates the Scottish countryside near McCartney's farm. He elaborates:

> It occurred to me that no great Scottish songs had been written for quite a while. I looked into it: all the bagpipe stuff was from the previous century and some of the popular folk songs were really old—and, I noticed, written by Englishmen. I wondered if I could write one, too—I certainly loved Scotland enough. So I came up with a song about where we were living, an area called Mull of Kintyre. It was a love song, really, about how I enjoy being there, and imagining I was travelling away and wanting to get back to it.[41]

After making a demo at Rude Studio, McCartney developed a plan as to how the bagpipes would fit in the song.[42] He invited Wilson to come to his Scottish farm and help him work out the technical details. McCartney observed that much of what Wilson was playing was in the key of D major, so he decided to use the keys of A and D major in the song. On the recording, the pipe band plays on all choruses and verses after a solo in which it plays the chorus's melody in D major. However, for a chorus and verse in A major, McCartney made adjustments to the bagpipe parts, due to the different key. Subsequent to this meeting, Wilson brought the Campbeltown Pipe Band to McCartney's farm to record the song in the mobile studio installed in the barn. The band came fully dressed in their kilts and sporrans.

"Mull of Kintyre" begins in the key of A major and ends in D major. It is in a conventional chorus–verse arrangement augmented by an intro, bagpipe solos, and outro. The melody of the opening chorus is varied and expansive, moving from E up to C♯ before settling on A. In the opening verse, the melody is equally expressive, although more expansive, hitting a high D before descending then ascending to its final A. (Of course, these gestures are simply transposed to D major for later verses and choruses.) The harmonic vocabulary is limited to each key's primary chords, A, D, and E for A major, and D, G, and A for D major.

After a chorus–verse–chorus sequence in A major, the music modulates to D major via a bagpipe drone on A (a common tone between the two keys) that crescendos, which creates a dramatic and hair-raising effect. After the bagpipe band plays the melody of the chorus in D, verse 2 and chorus 3 follow in the same key, with the bagpipe band playing an accompanying part in verse 2 and doubling the melody in chorus 3. Following another bagpipe solo based on a motive from the chorus's melody, verse 3 sounds in A major, as does the ensuing chorus 4. In verse 3, the bagpipe band provides a drone on A, and in chorus 4, doubles some notes of the melody. The music then modulates back to D major for chorus 5 in which bagpipes double the melody. These two musical devices greatly enhance this expressive pinnacle of the song. "Mull of Kintyre" ends with a vocal outro based on the second bagpipe solo.

BACK TO THE EGG (1979)

Back to the Egg, by its very title, was intended to be a fresh start for Wings, a "back-to-basics, garage band kind of feel," as guitarist Laurence Juber recalled.[43] However, despite Juber and drummer Steve Holly coming on board (replacing Jimmy McCulloch and Joe English, respectively) for the album, adding energy to the group by making it a five-piece band again, *Back to the Egg* turned out to be Wings' epitaph. Despite the new band's attempt to broaden its style by experimenting with a "progressive concept rock album played out punk-style in as few takes as possible,"[44] things were not working musically, as evident by the poor reviews *Back to the Egg* garnered. Although an intercontinental tour loomed on the horizon, McCartney's drug bust in Japan on 16 January 1980 put an end not only to that tour after its British leg but also to the group itself.

The songs on *Back to the Egg* are uneven in quality. Unlike recent efforts by Wings, it featured no standout singles. Besides concessions to the punk/new-wave style and an attempt to strive for a harder sound, *Back to the Egg* still contained fare typical of McCartney and Wings: ballads, dance music, rockers, and 1940s-style numbers. Most interesting are two tracks, "Rockestra Theme" and "So Glad to See You Here," for which McCartney assembled an all-star lineup to form the Rockrestra, the first rock supergroup. This was a blatant attempt on his part to seek new musical horizons, something that he would do a year later with his solo album, *McCartney II*. Finally, Wings recorded *Back to the Egg* in 1978–79 at the Spirit of Ranachan Studio, Scotland; Lympne Castle (dating from the twelfth century) in Kent, England; Replica (a recreation of Abbey Road Studio Two in the basement of McCartney's MPL offices in Soho); and EMI Studios, London. McCartney enlisted the aid of Chris Thomas to coproduce the album. Thomas assisted George Martin with the Beatles' *White Album* (1968) and had been recently involved in the punk/new-wave style through his associations with the Pretenders and the Sex Pistols.

"Reception," a short instrumental, opens *Back to the Egg*. Ian Peel characterizes it as the "sound of a listener turning the dial of a radio, in search of something new."[45] Recorded at Lympne Castle, this track features a funky, two-measure bass ostinato played by McCartney within an E7 harmonic framework, suggesting the key of E major. Above the ostinato sounds an equally funky guitar riff in thirds, derived from the bass part, played by Juber on a guitar synth and an ARP avatar (a guitar-controlled synthesizer).[46] The number is overlaid with musique concrète effects, such as a random radio broadcast and a text from Vivian Ellis's "The Poodle and the Pug," a song from her 1946 opera *Big Ben*, recited by one of the castle's owners, Mrs. Dierdre Margary.

McCartney composed "Getting Closer" in 1974 and made a demo of the song later that year.[47] In 1978, Wings took up the song, sped it up, and made it into a driving rocker. Laine and McCartney shared vocals on the number, with McCartney later adding guitar and keyboard overdubs to generate a thick, dense sound. "Getting Closer" was the last British single by Wings, although it hardly registered in the UK pop music charts. It fared better, however, in the US.

"Getting Closer" is in the key of A major and proceeds verse–chorus–bridge–verse–chorus–bridge–verse–chorus–outro. The text of the song focuses on a love triangle. In verse 1, the singer exhorts his lover to turn away from his rival, whereas in verse 2, he asks to see her, and in verse 3, he informs her that he is getting closer to her. McCartney sets each verse as a parallel period, supported by A, E, D, F♯, Bm, and E chords (I–V–IV–V/ii–ii–V) in the first phrase, and the same series of chords concluded by the tonic harmony A in the second. In the chorus, the singer exclaims optimistically that he is getting closer to winning his lover's heart. The melody ascends from an E to a D followed by an F♯, highlighting the word, "closer," before descending stepwise to a C♯. A mixture chord, Dm/A, heightens this expressive point, signifying the importance of modal mixture in McCartney's compositional techniques.

The text of the bridge does nothing to substantially advance the song's narrative. It suggests that the singer is in his car driving to his lover's residence, listening to the radio as the rain pours down, even rolling a joint in the process. At this point, both melody and harmony are rather prosaic, with unimaginative two-measure melodic gestures supported by tonic and dominant harmonies on A and E, respectively. The outro is based harmonically on the last four measures of the chorus and its Dm and A chords, where it is repeated until it fades out.

McCartney wrote "We're Open Tonight" while in Scotland.[48] It was supposed to have served as the title track of the album but Eastman suggested "Back to the Egg" instead. "We're Open Tonight" is a short song about a place open for fun where everyone is encouraged to bring their friends. The song features a wide-ranging melody characterized by rising arpeggiated figures followed by predominantly stepwise motion in the opposite direction. But the track's tempo and harmonic language contradict its upbeat message. "We're Open Tonight" not only is played at a slow tempo but also includes a static harmonic vocabulary composed of alternating G6 and Gm6 chords played by acoustic 6- and 12-string guitars over a G pedal point (implied in the first verse, occasional bass notes in the second verse, and outro). Enhancing the sound of the accompaniment is the natural echo produced by Juber when he recorded his 12-string guitar part on a spiral staircase at Lympne Castle.[49]

"Spin It On" is a primitivistic rocker that acknowledges the new, emerging punk/new-wave style. Simplistic in structure and content, it is a frenetic, hard-edged, two-chord song in the key of A minor featuring electric guitars with added distortion, keyboards, bass, and drums, with a repeated-note vocal sounding above. Formally, "Spin It On" includes an intro and choruses alternating with either loud guitar solos or verses. The intro presents the two-chord riff that permeates the song, an A5 chord alternating with the note G, followed by an E5 chord alternating with the same note. In the song's four choruses, the singer declares to his lover that they should "spin it on" (that is, engage in sex) because he has a "whole lotta love" for her. In the verses, the singer rattles off a series of nonsensical lyrics, such as how his lover goes to the movies with her underwear wet with urine or to the fair with curlers on, or about cousins who did not go to the pleasure dome or spend the night in an aircraft hangar. All in all, "Spin It On" is McCartney-esque whimsy on punk steroids.

(Denny Laine composed "Again and Again and Again," the only song on *Back to the Egg* not written by McCartney and, of course, sang lead vocal. Wings recorded the song's basic track live at the Spirit of Ranachan Studio. Since McCartney did not share any cowriting credits on the song, I shall not discuss it here but will move on to the album's next track, "Old Siam, Sir.")

The next track on *Back to the Egg*, "Old Siam, Sir," has been characterized as "Jimi Hendrix signs up for the cast of *The King and I*."[50] Like "Spin It On," it acknowledges the punk/new-wave revolution dominating Britain at the time. The text of "Old Siam, Sir" tells the story of a woman from a village in Siam who comes to the UK because she wants to find a husband. After going to Walthamstow and Scarborough, she finds a man in the East End of London whom she almost marries. Instead, on the advice of a relative, she returns to her village in Siam, living without a purpose in life.

"Old Siam, Sir" is in the key of E minor and combines five verses recounting the story of the woman from Siam with guitar solos and instrumental interludes that convey a primitive punk feel. According to John Blaney, Eastman developed the song's E-minor-based, four-measure riff during rehearsals, with McCartney and Laine finishing it later.[51] The riff is Wings' attempt to add a picturesque, exotic atmosphere to the song. In keeping with punk's primitivistic aesthetic, the intro, all of the song's verses, three instrumental interludes, and the outro are based on a repeated E5 chord followed by the notes D and E. The two guitar solos sound over an A-minor framework: first, a series of Am chords driven by a descending then ascending bass line—Am/A–Am/G–Am/F#–Am/G–Am/G#; next, a D/A–Am7 harmonic succession.

McCartney recorded "Arrow Through Me" at the Spirit of Ranachan Studio, adding overdubs at Replica Studio, London. Due to the absence of guitars and the use of synthesizers, brass, Fender Rhodes electric piano, and drums (two drum tracks, one regular, one double speed), the song is reminiscent of the techno-pop style of Stevie Wonder. Although a McCartney love song, which suggests that it should sport an optimistic orientation, "Arrow Through Me" has uncharacteristically pessimistic words in which the composer casts himself as a rejected lover.

"Arrow Through Me" is in the key of E major with a formal structure that shapes its text. In verses 1–2, the singer expresses the pain of his rejection, while in bridge 1, he reflects on what could have been had his lover chosen otherwise. Verses 3–4, which are separated by an interlude, and bridge 2 repeat the pattern of lament followed by rumination. McCartney distinguishes verse from bridge by making the bridge more chromatic harmonically. With the exception of verses 3 and 5 that have different concluding chords, the song's verses accompany their single phrases with a harmonic progression that begins on the tonic harmony E and ends with the dominant harmony B11. Within its confines, the progression includes chromatic chords, such as an E7 (V7/IV) and a C#7 (V7/ii). While the bridge ends with an expected retransitional dominant (B/D#), it gets there through a circuitous chromatic route. It begins by alternating Cmaj7 and B♭maj7 chords, which can be analyzed, respectively, as a chord borrowed from E minor and a dominant harmony whose root and quality have been altered. The bridge sets up its culminating retransitional dominant by preceding it with an Em7–Cmaj7–A6–D chordal succession, which again involves mixture chords ($i7$–♭$VI7$–IV–♭VII).

The brass-dominated outro uses F#m7, G9, F#m7, Fmaj9, and E chords, which are an expansion of an F#m7–G9 chordal succession heard in the last line of the song's final verse. The chromaticism represented by these harmonies (F#–G–F#–F–E) serves as an emotional—albeit somewhat dynamic—release for the singer's pain at the thought of his rejection.

For "Rockestra Theme" and "So Glad to See You Here," the eighth and thirteenth tracks of *Back to the Egg*, McCartney formed the Rockrestra, rock's first supergroup, to record the songs. On 3 October 1978, he invited some of Britain's most noted rock musicians to join Wings and its brass section at Abbey Road Studios to record two tracks. The lineup included (1) Denny Laine, Laurence Juber, Dave Gilmour (Pink Floyd), Hank Marvin (Shadows), and Pete Townshend (the Who) on guitar; (2) Paul McCartney, John Paul Jones (Led Zeppelin), Ronnie Lane (formerly a member of the Small Faces), and Bruce Thomas (Elvis Costello's Attractions) on bass; (3) Paul McCartney, Gary Brooker (Procol Harum), John Paul Jones (Led Zeppelin), Linda Eastman McCartney, and Tony Ashton (Ashton, Gardner, and Dyke) on keyboards; (4) Steve Holly, John Bonham (Led Zeppelin), and Kenney Jones (Small Faces) on drums; (5) Speedy Acquaye, Tony Carr, Ray Cooper, and Morris Pert on percussion; and (6) Howie Casey, Tony Dorsey, Steve Howard, and Thaddeus Richard on brass. In 1979, "Rockestra Theme" won a Grammy Award for Best Rock Instrumental Performance.

"Rockestra Theme" is in C major and is simple in both structure and content. The instrumental proceeds intro–verse–bridge–verse–bridge–verse–

outro. A descending bass line, C–B♭–A♭–A♮, drives the structure of the verse, a compositional strategy seen in "Dear Friend" and "Beware My Love." Above these bass notes sound C, B♭, A♭, and F/A chords, respectively. The melody begins on A and winds its way down to C (A–G–A–G–G–F–G–F–F–E–C–C). The bridge features a series of pentatonically driven power chords, B♭5–F5–E♭5–C5, over a C pedal point, lending a static air to a dynamic music. These chords culminate on a G5, followed by F5 and C5 chords, to conclude the bridge. The outro features a chromatic riff that winds its way up from G to C, concluding on a C7 chord.

Unlike "Rockestra Theme," "So Glad to See You Here" is more complicated in both structure and content. It is in a large-scale, three-part form, with the first two parts composed of a verse–verse–chorus sequence, and the third part, a verse–link(inst.)–outro. In each verse, the singer invites a friend to come over, presumably, to a place where exciting things are happening. In the chorus, the singer welcomes the friend upon his or her arrival. Finally, the reggae-influenced outro affirms the song's idea of escaping to a better place by repeating the line from "We're Open Tonight."

"So Glad to See You Here" is complex harmonically, employing mode mixture to color its chordal progressions and key relationships. The verse is in A major and consists of two phrases. Anticipated in the intro, the harmonic language of the first phrase alternates the tonic harmony on A with a C6 chord borrowed from A minor (I–♭III). The second phrase, however, involves not only more mixture chords but other chromatic harmonies as well. It begins with two mixture chords, Dm and C6 (iv–♭III), followed by a secondary dominant and its intended tonic, B7 and E7 (V7/V–V7), before closing with a mixture tag found in Beatle songs such as "Lady Madonna": F–G9–A (♭VI–♭VII9–I).

The chorus is in C major, the key of A major's chromatic mediant (♭III). The harmonic language of the chorus is basic, involving C major's primary harmonies Ĉ/G, F, and G. A chromatic bass line from G to A, in conjunction with a G–G/G♯–Am–A chordal sequence, takes the chorus to the next verse. After the song's last verse and an instrumental link, the outro enters, with words drawn from "We're Open Tonight," supported by the mixture tag, F–G–(F/G)–A.

A moderate rocker, "To You" centers on questions put forward by the singer to his lover regarding whether or not she would appreciate people treating her badly, especially if she received the same treatment that she put the singer through. Later in the song, the singer states that he wants no part of any bad situation, and muses that if it occurs, it will not be as severe as it used to be—in other words, he can handle it.

The song has an alternating verse–chorus structure that is framed by an intro and outro and varied by an electronically manipulated guitar solo inserted between choruses 3 and 4. Juber played the solo through an Avonside harmonizer while McCartney, who could hear Juber's playback in the control room, altered the guitar's pitches by manipulating the harmonizer's settings as Juber played.[52] Juber could hear what he was doing on the guitar and what McCartney was doing in the headphones he was wearing. They could not anticipate, however, what the other was doing during the solo, thereby creating random (but ultimately imaginative) effects. Juber's guitar effects are also heard as an obbligato during the song and at the beginning of the outro.

"To You" is not cast in a single key, which may highlight the ambiguity of the emotional situation experienced by the singer. Although the melody does not strongly define key areas because of its nondescript stepwise gestures and repeated notes, the chords do through their harmonic implications. The verses suggest D major through their D, A, Am, and Em chords (I–V–v–ii). The choruses, conversely, suggest E major through an initiating tonic harmony on E alternating with its chromatic submediant on C, borrowed from E minor (I–♭VI). Things get more expansive in choruses 2 and 4 as the music departs from E major to suggest D major. After alternating E and C chords, the music sounds D and C chords before concluding on a G harmony, which is a signal for the ensuing verse to occur.

McCartney believed that the gospel-influenced songs "After the Ball" and "Million Miles" were not strong enough to stand on their own as individual numbers, so he combined them into a medley.[53] The lyrics of "After the Ball" convey an apprehensive and tentative tone in which the protagonist is looking for security and hoping for deliverance from his downbeat existence. "Million Miles" attempts to provide answers to those questions about security and deliverance, but ultimately fails.

The form of the medley is simple, with "After the Ball" comprising the medley's opening chorus–verse–chorus, and "Million Miles" its outro, with a guitar solo connecting the two songs. In the choruses of "After the Ball," the lyrics describe how the protagonist searches for his lover, who will provide the security he craves. In the verse, after arriving at a party, he looks for her, but only after going to sleep and then awakening after the party is over does he find her, waiting to bring him out of his sleep. In keeping with its dance connotations, "After the Ball" is in 3/4 time, and its phrase structure is regular: the choruses consist of two eight-measure phrases, whereas the verse contains a sixteen-measure parallel period.

After the guitar solo, "Million Miles" enters as the outro of the medley. The protagonist is wondering if he will ever find security and gain deliverance from his downtrodden condition by constantly asking the question, "How many million miles, Deo?" Ultimately, the query is not answered. Structurally, "Million Miles" is in G major and, with one exception, proceeds as a series of four-measure phrases that are punctuated by authentic cadences (V–I). The song has an unusual sound, featuring McCartney singing a solo and accompanying himself on a concertina, an accordion-like instrument.

Like the previous track, "Winter Rose/Love Awake" is a medley. McCartney made a solo demo of "Winter Rose" at Rude Studios in 1977 and recorded the song with Wings at the Spirit of the Ranachan Studio in July 1978.[54] He played piano and harpsichord on the track, and Laine and Juber acoustic guitars. Wings recorded "Love Awake" at Lympne Castle, with the Black Dyke Mills Band overdubbing horn parts later at Abbey Road Studios. Because of their positive metaphors and symbolism, McCartney probably wrote both "Winter Rose" and "Love Awake," as with most of his love songs at the time, for Eastman.

"Winter Rose/Love Awake" is longer and more complicated musically than the album's previous track. The medley is cast as a series of verses and choruses enclosed by an intro and outro. "Winter Rose" takes up the first verse and chorus, along with an instrumental solo, while "Love Awake" takes up choruses 2–3, verse 2, and the outro. "Winter Rose" is a plaintive song in B Aeolian. In the verse, the singer has followed his lover throughout the summer and will bring her a rose for the winter that is coming. In the chorus, the singer extols the rose, which symbolizes the love that he and his lover share. The Aeolian-derived chords in both verse and chorus accentuate the tenderness of the song, particularly the cadential gestures in the chorus involving the minor dominant F♯m progressing to the tonic Bm.

"Love Awake" is brighter than "Winter Rose" in both lyrics and musical style. With all of its references to love awakening, one could even consider the winter rose of the previous song as blossoming into a summer one in "Love Awake." In choruses 2–3, the singer exclaims that love is alive and vibrant. In verse 2, the singer reflects on the nature of love, especially its tenuousness. The outro has the singer invoking seasonal metaphors, noting how summer—love—always comes again. McCartney brightens the sound of "Love Awake" by casting it in the key of D major, the relative major of the previous song's key of B minor. Choruses 2–3, verse 2, and the outro feature diatonic chords from D major, with phrases often ending with half cadences on A or authentic cadences on D.

"The Broadcast" is the most experimental track in Wings' entire output. It sounds as if radio stations are weaving in and out of the track. Laurence Juber explains the genesis of the number:

> It's a bit hazy but the guy [Mr. Harold Margary] that owns the castle where we were recording, both he and his wife had these very plummy kind of voices . . . . I think it was like, "Oh, wouldn't it be fun to have them read some classic English literature material and use the orchestral background to be just this kind of weird interlude." And they were kind of game for it.[55]

After having selected books randomly from the castle's library, McCartney had the Margarys recite sections on the recording. Mr. Margary read from *The Sport of Kings* by Ian Hays and *The Little Man* by John Galsworthy.

Mrs. Margary's reading of Vivian Ellis's "The Poodle and Pug" did not make it onto the track; instead, McCartney inserted a few lines into "Reception." The piano-dominated instrumental accompaniment of "Broadcast" is in the key of F♯ major and consists of a three-chord pattern, F♯–G♯7sus4–C♯11 (I–V7/V–V11), repeated until the number fades out.

McCartney originally wrote "Baby's Request" for the Mills Brothers to record.[56] He met the group backstage after one of their performances while vacationing in France. He cut a demo of the song and offered it to them, but eventually had Wings record the tune after hearing that they insisted he pay them for recording it. "Baby's Request" is a 1940s-style song that matches the type of music the Mills Brothers performed. McCartney's lead vocal and Juber's jazz guitar playing enhance the song's period feel. Typical of the formal structure of popular songs from the 1940s, "Baby's Request" consists of an outro, two verses, bridge, solo based on the verse, bridge, and last verse, all in the key of G major. In verses 1–2, the singer conjures up colorful images of the moon resting on a pillow, stars settling down, and birds flying away, as he requests that a song associated with his lover be played, presumably by a band in a nightclub. In keeping with its jazzy feel, the melody of the verse has a wide arc, moving up and down from a low D to a high E. The harmonic setting is characterized by a plethora of seventh chords, although traditional progressions are still emphasized (for example, Am7–D7–G [ii7–V7–I]), and the expressive use of a mixture chord, Cm7, at the end of the first phrase.

The bridge of the song has the singer informing the band that although his lover knows the tune in question, they know it better. Thus, after the band plays it, the singer and his lover will retire for the evening. The melody of the bridge features syncopated gestures followed by notes in dotted, shuffle-like rhythms. The harmonic vocabulary continues to be distinguished by seventh chords, with Bdim and D+ chords thrown in to enhance the bridge's sound. Finally, there is a video associated with the song in which the members of Wings are depicted as a 1940s period band, dressed in World War II military uniforms entertaining the troops in the African desert.[57]

In 1993, McCartney reissued *Back to the Egg* as part of *The Paul McCartney Collection* with three bonus tracks: (1) "Daytime Nighttime Suffering" (the flip side of "Goodnight Tonight"), (2) "Wonderful Christmastime" (a solo effort by McCartney dating from 1979), and (3) "Rudolph The Red-Nosed Reggae" (another solo effort, the flip side of "Wonderful Christmastime"). In 2007, this version of *Back to the Egg* was reissued on iTunes, with the addition of a disco remix of "Goodnight Tonight." To conclude my discussion of *Back to the Egg*, I shall examine "Daytime Nighttime Suffering."

During the mixing of *Back to the Egg*, McCartney supposedly challenged the other members of Wings to write a song over a weekend, with the best one to be recorded and included on the album.[58] When the time came to assess everyone's efforts, and after each band member played his or her song,

McCartney offered his, "Daytime Nighttime Suffering," which easily won the competition through its outstanding melody.

"Daytime Nighttime Suffering" is in the key of C major and begins with a free-flowing intro that exposes the song's thematic elements found in both chorus and verse. Thereafter, the song progresses chorus–chorus–verse–chorus–bridge–verse–outro. McCartney wrote "Daytime Nighttime Suffering" to focus on the plight of women. In choruses 1–2, the persona as observer wonders what a woman gets out of a relationship with a man. He concludes nothing but day and night suffering. The melody of the chorus consists of a 2 + 2 + 4 structure, with the first two units composed of gestures that flow downward from a high G, whereas the last melodic unit is cut up with rests. The harmonic setting of the chorus is unremarkable with chords drawn primarily from C major. The chorus ends, moreover, with a half cadence on a G7 sonority. The bridge that follows chorus 3 reaffirms the reality of the woman's suffering, stating that her relationship is not the fairy tale she envisioned.

In the song's verses, the persona offers a more encouraging picture for women by likening a woman's capacity to love with a mighty river that is capable of eradicating her suffering. By overflowing people, neighbors, and the persona himself—who compares himself to a stream that might represent men—with love, this mighty river becomes a force for positive change. McCartney distinguishes verse from chorus by setting the former in the key of C minor, the parallel minor of the song's tonic key. Like the chorus, the harmonic setting of the verse is unremarkable, mainly sticking to C minor's primary triads, Cm, Fm, Gm, and G, except for a D♭ chord, a Neapolitan harmony that supports a climactic A♭/F in the vocal line.

By 1979, McCartney felt that Wings had lost its artistic luster. He sought new directions, desiring to purge himself of the 1970s rock that his band represented. He felt that he had essentially accomplished all he could do with Wings, and it was now time for a change. Not surprisingly, McCartney retreated to his Scottish farm in July 1979 to start work on a solo project that not only would be a departure from his previous work but, more importantly, suggest some of the future artistic directions that he would pursue in the 1980s, the subject of the next chapter.

With the disappointing bookends of *Wings Wild Life* and *Back to the Egg*, Wings opened and closed their recording career with their least acclaimed albums. Things were a bit more tense in 1979, as seen by yet another lineup change, this time involving Juber and Holly; continuing squabbles regarding the payment of royalties and salary; and the artistic and commercial disappointment of *Back to the Egg*, despite the best of intentions to get back to the basics. McCartney's drug bust in Japan on 16 January 1980 exacerbated the strife already in the group. MPL productions canceled the projected tour of Japan as well as follow-up tours of other countries, which meant huge financial losses for everyone. As a result, Laine, Juber, and Holly resented

McCartney for the losses, especially since it resulted from a cavalier attitude toward marijuana. After the fiasco in Japan, all members of Wings worked on solo projects. In November 1980, they actually began to rehearse for a projected follow-up album to *Back to the Egg*, but things fell apart. McCartney's reluctance to tour because of John Lennon's murder on 8 December 1980, an event that occasioned death threats against him and his family, was the final blow. The group broke up in April 1981.

Comparisons with the Beatles always bothered McCartney when he was with Wings. Critics assailed his music as superficial and saccharine compared to that by the Beatles. McCartney would counter that both the Beatles and Wings were bands that only wanted to be true to themselves, and that such comparisons were meaningless and unfair. But as Garry McGee comments,

> Out of the ashes of the most successful band of the 1960s arose one of the most successful bands of the 1970s. It was a group that accomplished almost as much as the Beatles had, from gold records and Grammy Awards to sold-out concerts and successes on the music charts.
>
> Wings won a legion of new fans, including some who never knew its leader had been in another group.[59]

4

Collaborating with Others, 1980–89

McCartney II (1980)

Paul McCartney came full circle with his aptly titled solo album, *McCartney II*, released in May 1980. Like *McCartney*, his debut solo album of 10 years earlier, he made *McCartney II* a homespun affair, recording it, presumably, on his farm in Scotland, and singing all vocal parts (except for wife Linda Eastman's harmony vocals on two tracks) and playing all instruments himself.[1] As with its counterpart issued after the Beatles broke up, *McCartney II* was a way to reinvigorate its author artistically as Wings was beginning to disintegrate. McCartney originally conceived of the album as an experiment for private consumption only, and did not initially intend it as a means to relaunch a solo career. To record the songs, he rented a 16-track tape recorder from EMI and two microphones that he could plug straight into the recorder. He used no mixing board and employed variable tape speeds in which he would combine one track at a regular speed with either a sped-up or slowed-down backing track. McCartney also played drums in the bathroom or kitchen for echo effects. He mixed the tracks and produced the album himself.

As noted by Ian Peel, *McCartney II* is a "full-blown investigation into synthesisers, with much of the album based on the kind of heavily sequenced loops that were coming from the likes of Sparks . . . , whom McCartney referenced in the video for the album's hit single 'Coming Up'."[2] Accordingly, the album is full of musical experimentation and features a sparser musical sound than his previous LPs. McCartney originally recorded over 20 tracks for a planned double album, but he eventually pared it down in order to release a more commercially viable single album. In any event, although receiving mixed critical reviews, *McCartney II* was a commercial success.

McCartney II opens with the studio version of "Coming Up." The song was released as a single in both studio and live versions in April 1980. McCartney recorded the studio version in July 1979 and recorded the live version with Wings on 17 December 1979 during their last British tour at the Glasgow Apollo, Glasgow, Scotland.[3] "Coming Up" was a hit on both sides of the Atlantic, with the live version outperforming the studio version in the US as it not only sold more copies but also topped the charts.

"Coming Up" is disco funk with sped-up backing vocals, showing off McCartney's ability to assimilate different musical styles. Cast in the key of E♭ major, with a Mixolydian flavor due to a constantly recurring D♭, "Coming Up" is in an alternating verse–chorus structure with an intro that sounds the song's omnipresent riff and synthesizer horn interludes. In the song's four verses, the persona poses a series of questions to his lover having to do with her insecurities about love. In the number's five choruses, the persona offers his lover security by stating that his love is "coming up like a flower," hinting that their love will blossom. Harmonically, the verses are static, as they are situated on E♭6 and E♭9 chords. The choruses show more movement through A♭maj7–B♭m7–Cm7–D♭, and E♭–Fm7–F♯dim–E♭/G harmonic successions. Finally, McCartney created a delightful video of the song, featuring a rock group called "The Plastic Macs," a pun on John Lennon's Plastic Ono Band. Aside from Linda Eastman's contribution in the form of portraying backup vocalists, McCartney played all the members of the band himself, which included, among others, Hank Marvin of the Shadows on guitar, Ron Mael of Sparks on keyboards, "Beatle Paul" playing his Hofner bass, and John Bonham of Led Zeppelin on drums.

"Temporary Secretary" recalls McCartney's Beatle song, "Paperback Writer," as the lyrics are associated with writing a letter to a "Mister Marks" of the Alfred Marks Agency about securing the services of a "temp."[4] The song has a space-age riff generated electronically by a synthesizer sequencer, suggesting a futuristic, highly automated typewriting pool. Along with synthesized sounds, McCartney employs guitar and drum parts as a part of his synthpop sonic landscape.

Although it has a traditional verse–chorus–bridge structure in the key of D♭ major, "Temporary Secretary" includes chromatic harmonies in all of its sections, giving the song a dynamic edge. The verses utilize modal mixture in the form of a minor subdominant harmony on G♭ alternating with the tonic on D♭ (iv–I). The choruses have McCartney shouting out "Temporary secretary" to an F♯–D–F–F motive, accompanied by D and D♭ chords. The bridge involves a chromatic harmonic sequence beginning on a D chord and ending with an F, heightening the tension of the song as the bridge culminates with a return of the chorus. During these harmonic changes, McCartney sings a series of repeated notes based on the root of each chord.

Having previously laid down its backing track, McCartney wrote the lyrics of "On the Way" after being inspired by a television program on the blues hosted by British bluesman Alexis Korner.[5] The song is in the key of E♭ minor and contains an intro, verses interspersed with instrumental interludes, and an outro that ends with an E♭ major chord. In keeping with its blues orientation, the lyrics of the song deal with love and all of its painful trials. Musically, the song features bluesy gestures in the vocal and guitar solos, echo effects, and a three-chord vocabulary composed of E♭m, A♭7, and B♭7 chords, all situated within a sparse textural framework.

"Waterfalls" is the best song on *McCartney II*. Taking its name from McCartney's cottage near Rye, Sussex, "Waterfalls" sports a simple message of caution, probably addressed to McCartney's children: do not engage in risky behavior because you are needed and loved by others. McCartney probably wrote "Waterfalls" before he began his solo project in July 1979. The song features a hauntingly beautiful melody, accompanied by an electronic piano and synthesizer string sounds.

McCartney conveys the textual message of "Waterfalls" through a verse–chorus structure in which verses advance the storyline and choruses reflect upon it. Verse 1 has the singer cautioning his loved one against jumping off waterfalls, verse 2, against chasing polar bears, and verse 3, against running after automobiles, because all of these risky activities could lead to harm. The choruses express the singer's need for love and possible emotional loss if something injurious happened to his loved one. "Waterfalls" is in a mixolydian-flavored B major. The phrases of each verse include an A placed at the beginning of their second measures. The harmonic setting of the verses likewise suggests B mixolydian through a B–Add9–F♯m–C♯m–Aadd9–B chordal succession. The choruses, on the other hand, suggest B major via its three closing chords: E11, F♯11, and F♯7 (IV11–V11–V7).

"Nobody Knows" is another bluesy number inspired by the same television program on the blues hosted by Alexis Korner.[6] Textually, the words are non-sensical and do not tell a coherent story; in a word, they are employed for their effects rather than for any meanings they might have. Musically, the song is in the key of A major and governed by a 12-bar blues progression involving I–IV–V7 chords.[7] Enclosed by an intro and outro, "Nobody Knows" includes three verses and two choruses that are similar from melodic and harmonic standpoints; however, choruses differ from verses by featuring less singing and varied repetitions of the verses' last two lines.

"Front Parlour" and "Frozen Jap," the sixth and eighth tracks of *McCartney II*, are experimental synthpop instrumentals. McCartney recorded "Front Parlour" in an actual front parlor, complete with old wallpaper and a little fireplace.[8] The song's ad hoc generation in terms of both its composing and recording summarized McCartney's approach to his new solo album. Recent technological advances in synthesizers and recording devices allowed him the freedom not to be, in his words, "that Paul McCartney fellow."

Accordingly, "Front Parlour" is not characteristic of McCartney at all, as it includes timbres never heard before in any of his songs: a flute-like synthesizer melody sounding above an accompaniment driven by a quasi-banjo part; a pulsing, heavily compressed, slap bass line; and percussion provided by a drum machine. "Front Parlour" begins in the key of E major and ends in D minor, and is cast in an ABCADABCDADAE form, with the A section serving as a refrain.

McCartney wrote "Frozen Jap" before his drug bust in Japan. The song is in F major and is characterized by an exotic, oriental-style melody in perfect fourths. Unlike "Front Parlour," "Frozen Jap" has a stronger rhythmic drive, and its harmonic setting is more static, with relatively longer stretches of one of only three chords used in the song: F, Dm, or C. In order not to offend the Japanese market, McCartney changed the title of the song to "Frozen Japanese" for LPs sold in Japan. However, "Frozen Jap" is inappropriate and offensive no matter how you see it, whatever market outside Japan for which the album was intended. In any event, "Front Parlour" and "Frozen Jap" were "completely avant-garde compared to almost anything McCartney's rock and roll contemporaries were recording at the time."[9]

Inspired by an unnamed classical-sounding piece, McCartney composed "Summer Day's Song" initially as an instrumental, only later changing it into a song after he decided to include it on the original double-album version of *McCartney II*.[10] "Summer Day's Song" is a ballad in F major and has a simple text supported by an equally simple musical structure and harmonic language. The text has a positive message of hope for anyone struggling with life's problems: the singer observes that although someone is having a bad dream, it will end, because the world will be awakening to a summer's day. The song reiterates this text in two verses, with an instrumental intro, interlude, and outro serving to enhance the optimism of the song's words. "Summer Day's Song" begins with a slow, synthesizer intro that sets the emotional tone for the track. The intro's harmonic language is elemental, sounding an F–C–Bb–F chordal succession. Verse 1 consists of an eight-measure phrase ending with an authentic cadence. Its beautifully constructed melody begins on an A, reaches up to a G before descending to an F an octave lower. With the exception of one secondary dominant (V7/vi), its harmonic language is diatonic, emphasizing tonic, subdominant, and dominant harmonies. The ensuing flute/string dominated synthesizer interlude develops previously heard musical materials, while the outro that follows verse 2 restates the melody of the verse.

McCartney wrote "Bogey Music" after reading the popular British children's book, *Fungus the Bogeyman*, by Raymond Briggs.[11] With his wife Mildew and son Mould, Fungus lives in Bogeyland, a place located in subterranean tunnels where filth and slime abound. Noting how the young people in Bogeyland rebel against the old people who hate music in Briggs's book, and seeing parallels between that situation and the generational conflict associated with rock 'n' roll music, McCartney improvised a rock 'n' roll track.

However, he should have taken more care to develop the lyrics and music. The song moves haphazardly from one idea to another with no direction, making "Bogey Music" one of the weaker tracks found on *McCartney II*.

McCartney sings the vocal of "Bogey Music" Elvis-style, complete with irritating echo effects generated by a reverb unit. "Bogey Music" is in the key of A major and based on the twelve-bar blues pattern, with an intro, four verses, two instrumental interludes, two bridges, and an outro. The instrumental interlude introduces a theme that is used near the end of verse 2 and during bridges 1–2 and the outro. The harmonic language of the song is simple, consisting of A major's three basic harmonies, A, D, and E, along with a Dm mixture chord to liven things up. Unfortunately, nothing can save the song.

For "Darkroom," McCartney revisited a recording practice used on the *White Album* and *McCartney* of layering parts onto the multitrack tape of a tape recorder, beginning with drums, proceeding to other instruments, and then adding vocals. The resulting song involved a one-line lyric built on a funky groove replete with variable-speed vocal effects and different synthesizer sounds. The lyrics of "Darkroom" are sexually suggestive as the singer invites a woman to a place that could be a photographic darkroom, or a room that is just dark. Although the vocal is varied, containing several different melodic figures, the harmonic setting is not. In keeping with its funky groove, the song's harmonic support is static, composed of an Fm7 chord. Thus, melody and rhythm are the forces that propel the music forward.

McCartney composed "One of These Days," the last track on *McCartney II*, after being inspired by the serene demeanor of a follower of Hare Krishna who visited him while he was recording the album.[12] This ethereal, reflective song contrasts greatly with the mechanical sounds found on most of *McCartney II*. The text of the song centers on stripping away all of the obstacles that hinder happiness and seeking self-fulfillment. On the guitar, McCartney plays "One of These Days" in G major, although it sounds in A♭ major because he capos up one fret.

The song is in a verse–chorus–bridge structure supported chiefly by diatonic chords that enhance its gentle melody. Verses 1–4 have the singer reflecting on the uneasiness of life and the need to please oneself. The choruses that follow each verse emphasize the need for self-fulfillment, expressed symbolically by breathing fresh air. The harmonic structure of the song reinforces this textual dichotomy through half cadences that end each verse (C–D, IV–V), which reinforce the open-ended nature of the verses, and plagal cadences that end each chorus (C–G, IV–I), which highlight the resolve of the singer to do what is right for his life. In the bridge of the song, the singer states that happiness is there to be found. The bridge's harmonic setting intensifies this thought through chromatic chords, especially Dm7 mixture chords accompanying the significant words, "there" and "found."

As a part of *The Paul McCartney Collection* issued in 1993, *McCartney II* contained three bonus tracks. They are: "Check My Machine" (the B–side of "Waterfalls") and "Secret Friend" (the B–side of "Temporary Secretary"), which were included as bonus tracks on the original CD issue of *McCartney II*; and "Goodnight Tonight," a 1979 hit for Wings recorded during the making of *London Town*. To conclude my commentary on *McCartney II*, I shall discuss "Secret Friend" and "Goodnight Tonight."

"Secret Friend" is a long, Latin-flavored dance piece dominated by a fast synthesizer sequence. The track proceeds through a series of spacious choruses and verse/refrains that describe the singer's uncertainty as to where life will take him and his muse. But the singer concludes rather optimistically that things will work out if she agrees to be his secret friend. The song begins with the aforementioned synthesizer sequence sounding B♭–, B–, and, when the voice enters, E♭–based pentatonic riffs over different octaves. These three riffs then form the harmonic basis of the song's ensuing vocal sections and instrumental interludes. Accordingly, they envelop the long, drawn-out notes of the electronically altered vocal line with a static harmonic framework that accentuates the track's hypnotic atmosphere. The song still exhibits, however, strong dynamic qualities through the speed of the sequence, artificially generated muted trumpet obbligatos and solos, and lively salsa-like percussion parts. Overall, for the *McCartney II* sessions, "Secret Friend" is one of the most avant-garde numbers its composer wrote and recorded.

"Goodnight Tonight" is McCartney's homage to the disco craze of the late 1970s. It is a great pop song, pure and simple, containing well-constructed lyrics and music. Having recorded "Goodnight Tonight" after Wings' *London Town* sessions in 1978, McCartney was reluctant to release it as a single, but eventually did after some reflection. The song became the first single by Wings to be released on the Columbia Records label, with which McCartney was associated at the time, becoming a Top 10 hit on both sides of the Atlantic. Columbia wanted him to include "Goodnight Tonight" on *Back to the Egg*, but McCartney refused, stating that the song did not fit the album's punk/new wave sound.[13]

"Goodnight Tonight" is in the key of E major and has a straightforward verse–chorus structure with intro and instrumental interludes.[14] The intro begins in the key of E minor, the parallel minor of E major, as the guitar plays Em and C chords, which give way to Em7 and A7 chords. Near the end of the intro, the harmonic progression that dominates both the verses and choruses is introduced: Emaj7–C#m9–F#m7–B7♭9 (I7–vi9–ii7–V♭9). Except for their slightly altered last lines, verses 1–2 feature the same lyrics. All the choruses contain the catchy hook, "Don't say it," as the persona encourages his love not to go by saying "goodnight tonight." Interspersed throughout the song are three instrumental interludes, the last two recalling the intro's harmonic scheme involving E minor.

TUG OF WAR (1982)

Tug of War is the best album McCartney released since *Band on the Run* in 1973. For this LP, he was reunited with his former Beatles producer, George Martin. He collaborated with Stevie Wonder on two of the album's songs, "Ebony and Ivory" and "What's That You're Doing." He also invited noted musicians Stanley Clarke, Steve Gadd, Denny Laine, Andy Mackay, Carl Perkins, Ringo Starr, and Eric Stewart to play and sing on the album. McCartney recorded part of the album in George Martin's AIR Studios on the island of Montserrat.

As a producer, Martin reined in McCartney's initial plan of recording a huge backlog of songs for his new album by insisting that he revise some of the songs he wanted to record and discard others because they were second-rate and not salvageable.[15] This is exactly the type of advice that McCartney needed in order to create the quality album *Tug of War* became. In other words, Martin brought some needed discipline and polish to the album, enabling McCartney to shine as an artist.

The title track, "Tug of War," opens the album. Its lyrics center on the struggles and vicissitudes of life with the idea that if there were less struggle between people, things might be better for everyone. McCartney skillfully combines both metaphor and music in "Tug of War" to evoke aspects of gloom that are uncharacteristic of him. He arranges a simple but powerful text in a series of choruses and verses. The three choruses acknowledge life's struggles by beginning with the words, "It's a tug of war." Flowing from that statement are thoughts about the difficulties of life where one expects more but is ultimately disappointed, or where one must cling to a loved one or everything will fall apart. In the song's two verses (which essentially involve the same lyrics), McCartney conveys a sense of hope that one will triumph over life's tug of war through the symbolic images of being in a different world, standing on a mountaintop, flag planted, or of being in a future time where life will dance to a presumably more optimistic drum. The bridge expresses the need to empathize with people and their hardships before it is too late.

The song's brooding lyrics are set to a melody composed of sweeping, usually stepwise, descending and ascending gestures in C major. The track's chord changes involve C major's basic harmonies, C, F, and G, played on an acoustic guitar, each harmony usually sounding over long stretches of time. The bridge distinguishes itself timbrally from chorus and verse by introducing electric guitars. "Tug of War" concludes with an eloquent string outro that ends with an Fmaj7–G–A chordal succession ($\flat$VI7–$\flat$VII–I) in the key of A major, McCartney's cadential signature incorporating mixture chords, although here sounding with a sense of touching poignancy.

Although McCartney wrote "Take It Away" originally for Ringo Starr, he decided that the song fit his voice better and decided to record it himself.

Joining McCartney, who sang lead vocal and played bass, guitar, and piano, were Starr and Steve Gadd on drums, Linda Eastman and Eric Stewart on backing vocals, and George Martin on electric piano.

"Take It Away" is in the key of A major and cast in a chorus–verse structure with intro, bridge, and outro. The intro lays out the chord changes that underlie the song's five choruses, which consist of the tonic harmony A alternating with dominant and subdominant harmonies on E and D, respectively. The lyrics of the chorus consist of a plea to an imaginary band to keep playing, even if the lights are turned off and the place is empty. The lyrics of the verses switch scenes by telling the story of a band manager who, after arriving by car, gives a message to the band and then goes off to a bar after hours. To accentuate this change of scene, the music modulates to D major in the verses. The harmonic language here is jazzier than that found in the choruses, with dazzling vocal harmonies enhancing its sound. The words of the bridge advise the band to play well, for they may never know who might be listening to them. The harmonic language of the bridge returns to the simplicity of the verses as it alternates F#m7 and Bm chords (vi7–ii). Finally, the outro repeats the music of the verses with wordless, jazzy harmonies as the song fades out.

McCartney wrote "Somebody Who Cares" with bassist Stanley Clarke and drummer Steve Gadd in mind. This jazzy song features an interesting blend of instruments, with McCartney playing acoustic and Spanish guitars; Denny Laine, guitar and synthesizer; Clarke, bass; Gadd, drums and percussion; and Adrian Brett, pan pipes. While the verses of "Somebody Who Cares" recite a litany of life's frustrations, the choruses remind everyone that there is somebody out there who still cares. The song is in the key of A minor, with the opposing ideas of verse and chorus differentiated by modal mixture: verses are in A minor, ending with a half cadence on an E7 chord; choruses are in a brighter A major, ending with a plagal cadence, D–A. The bridge emphasizes E minor before moving on to an E7 chord, indicating a return to the key of A minor. "Somebody Who Cares" ends with a restatement of the bridge and its half cadence in A minor, suggesting that the song's message is unresolved.

During a studio jam session at George Martin's AIR Studios, McCartney cowrote "What's That You're Doing" with Stevie Wonder. On the finished version of the song, McCartney and Wonder shared lead vocals, with McCartney, Eastman, and Stewart providing backing harmonies. Instrumentally, Wonder played synthesizer; McCartney, bass, drums, and guitar; and Andy Mackay, Lyricon, a wind-instrument synthesizer. "What's That You're Doing" is a jazz-funk number in E♭ major with its choruses situated on the tonic harmony E♭ and its verses on the subdominant harmony A♭ and dominant B♭ (at the end). Bluesy riffs in both the vocal and instrumental parts drive the song, with jazzy vocal harmonies enhancing the song's bridge and its move to the mixture chord, C♭ (♭VI). Finally, the bridge serves as the outro of the song, with Wonder adding a creative twist by quoting the chorus of the Beatles, "She Loves You," as the song fades out.

McCartney composed the touching ballad "Here Today" as a tribute to John Lennon. It was a way for McCartney to vent his feelings for his former collaborator and friend, something he wished he could have done while Lennon was alive. The song is essentially a letter to Lennon telling him that despite their differences, McCartney cared for him deeply. McCartney included the song as a part of his "Back to the USA" tour, which moved audiences immensely, something that I can attest to having heard the song at McCartney's concert at Gund Arena in Cleveland, Ohio, on 4 October 2002. In order to match the emotion of the song, McCartney and Martin decided to include a string quartet as a backing ensemble with McCartney's vocal and acoustic guitar part, despite the obvious similarities with "Yesterday."

"Here Today" is in the key of G major and consists of a series of verses varied by a bridge and extended middle section. Verses 1–2 have McCartney asking Lennon that if he were here today, how would he respond to McCartney saying that he knew him well. Lennon would probably remark that they were worlds apart. To highlight the poignancy of this image, McCartney uses the minor subdominant on C moving to the tonic harmony on G at the beginning and end of the verse. The sound brightens at the bridge with its emphasis on the major subdominant on C embellished by moves to its own subdominant, F6. Here, McCartney recalls the good times he had with Lennon, and with great emotion, professes his love for his dear friend. The lyrics of the middle section recall other poignant times with Lennon. McCartney distinguishes this section from others by moving to an aeolian-flavored E minor through its D7–Em cadences. In verse 3, which closes the song, McCartney expresses his love for his friend one last time as the music ends with the minor plagal cadence Cm–G.

"Ballroom Dancing" is McCartney's homage to his teenage years in Liverpool when he would go out to the city's ballrooms and dance halls to have a good time. The song also refers to *Come Dancing*, the British television show that broadcast ballroom-dancing contests, as its announcer, Peter Marshall, can be heard on the track providing commentary.[16] Although the song has elements of both big band and rock 'n' roll styles, "Ballroom Dancing" sounds like "Walk of Life," a Cajun-style number recorded by Dire Straits three years later (1985). The song is in the key of B major and features verses alternating with choruses. While recalling the carefree days of his youth in the song's verses, the singer gleefully states in the choruses that ballroom dancing made a man out of him. The song is dominated by the sound of B5 and E5 guitar riffs (B/F♯–B/G♯ and E/B–E/C♯), enhanced by guitar and horn licks. To sum up, it is a delightful number.

"The Pound Is Sinking" consists of two unfinished songs, one carrying the track's title that centers on the vicissitudes of the stock market, and the other entitled "Hear Me Lover." The two songs, unfortunately, do not blend into a coherent whole. In the first part of the song (verse 1, chorus 1), the persona rattles off the names of different currencies and how they are doing in the stock market. At the end of the chorus, he states that the market has tanked. In verse 2, the persona suddenly changes the song's message by singing about the limited perspectives of his lover, only to rattle off more names of different currencies and their performances in the stock market in the following chorus (2). The ensuing bridge takes us back to the persona addressing his lover again, this time arguing with her. The song then closes with verse 3, which repeats the words and music of verse 1. Exacerbating this fragmented text are the tempo changes associated with the song's different sections. Lastly, "The Pound Is Sinking" is in F–aeolian, with the more upbeat choruses suggesting A♭ major.[17] It ends inconclusively on a B♭m chord, with the sound of a coin spinning on a hard surface in the background.

McCartney composed "Wanderlust" after almost being busted for marijuana by US customs officials aboard a yacht moored off the Virgin Islands while recording *London Town* in 1978.[18] After arguing with the ship's captain about the incident, McCartney took his family to the *Wanderlust*, another yacht in the harbor, where he could be free to do as he pleased. Given his views on soft drugs, McCartney viewed the *Wanderlust* as a symbol of freedom, a means of escape, to engage in an innocuous, harmless pastime.

The song "Wanderlust" is a pop music hymn cast in a verse–chorus form with intro, outro, and instrumental interlude, all in the key of D major. Verses refer, however ambiguously, to McCartney's views about smoking pot, while choruses speak to the *Wanderlust* as a vessel that lights out to sea in order to escape the darkness of conventional social norms. The song's verses are structured primarily as parallel periods supported by conventional chord progressions. The choruses become more intense harmonically, with minor subdominant harmonies on G used in the last two lines to highlight the symbolic significance of the *Wanderlust* as a vessel of liberation. The record's final touch is perhaps the most extreme: brass parts played by the Philip Jones Brass ensemble that intensify the fervent religiosity of the song's message.

In "Get It," McCartney was able to sing and play with one of his boyhood idols, rock 'n' roll legend Carl Perkins. On 21 February 1982, Perkins arrived at George Martin's AIR Studios in Montserrat to record McCartney's song.[19] Before they commenced recording, they performed several songs together to warm-up, such as Perkins's "Boppin' the Blues," "Honey Don't," and "Lend Me Your Comb." At the end of "Get It," Perkins can be heard laughing in response to McCartney's use of an expression of his regarding how good the take was. Earlier in the week, Perkins attended a party with McCartney on a lavish yacht. Remarking on the posh setting, Perkins said that it reminded him of "shitting in high cotton." Thus, when McCartney said the same thing at the end of "Get It" (which was deleted), Perkins burst out laughing.

"Get It" is a laid-back rockabilly number in the key of E major. McCartney and Perkins take turns singing parts of the song as well as sing together. The four choruses include the song's title as both McCartney and Perkins urge everyone to go out and "get it." The verses set forth several images, ranging from bent Spanish guitars, loving people, telephones ringing about songs sung, and Cadillacs. Throughout the song, Perkins plays great rockabilly guitar licks that enhance the song's cozy atmosphere. The harmonic vocabulary centers on E major's primary sonorities, E, A, and B, with F♯m and D chords included in the verses in order to highlight the drive to each verse's cadence, A–B9–E–E6 (IV–V9–I).

"Dress Me Up as a Robber" follows the link "Be What You See." McCartney began the song in 1977, and at producer George Martin's insistence, polished the song in order for it to be included on *Tug of War*. On the cut, McCartney sings lead vocal, backing vocals (Eastman also provides backing vocals), and plays guitar and bass; Denny Laine plays synthesizer and electric guitar; Martin, electric piano; and Dave Mattacks, drums and percussion. The song's text proposes that no matter how many different outfits the protagonist's lover may dress him up in (that is, try to change him), he will always be true to himself and love her. "Dress Me Up as a Robber" is in the key of E minor by way of the tonic harmony serving as a point of initiation or arrival within musical phrases. Verses are distinguished harmonically by a descent and ascent from an Em chord—Em–Dm–Cm–B♭m–Dm–Em, whereas choruses by an ascent from an Am to E/Em chord—Am–Bm–C–D–E–Em. The song has a jazz/funk sound through an E–minor-based riff that occurs at the beginning, middle, and end of the song; McCartney's falsetto singing in the verses; a funky accompanimental guitar groove; and acoustic guitar solos.

In the song "Ebony and Ivory," McCartney conceived of the black and white keys of the piano and how they produce harmony when played together, as a metaphor for harmonious race relations between blacks and whites. He got the idea from Spike Milligan, a British comedian and former member of the comedy troupe the Goons.[20] As McCartney developed the song, he wanted to get a black singer to perform the song with him, and secured the services of Stevie Wonder after the number was completed. Wonder arrived in Montserrat on 25 February 1981 to record the song with McCartney the following day, with McCartney adding more parts to the song when he returned to the UK. McCartney released "Ebony and Ivory" as a single in March 1982, one month before the release of the album *Tug of War*. It reached the top of the charts on both sides of the Atlantic.

Critics panned "Ebony and Ivory" for being lightweight in relation to the message it was trying to convey. The song, in other words, was too sentimental and sugary to be taken seriously. But McCartney believed that less seriousness would take some tension out of the topic of race relations.[21] After a synthesizer chordal intro, "Ebony and Ivory" opens with its familiar chorus. McCartney sings a melody in E major that constantly soars up to a high G♯, with Wonder providing a harmony part a third lower. The melody is supported by a series of key-defining chordal successions (E–F♯m7–B11 [I–ii7–V11]). The song's two verses include the same text in which the singers describe people as being the same everywhere, with good and bad in everyone. The verse's melody is more sedate compared to that of the chorus, as it is more restricted in range. The harmonic language, however, is more varied, with D6, Ddim, and C♯7 chords enhancing the verse's drive to its half cadence on B11 (♭VII–♭vii°–V7/ii–ii–V11). The bridge and its repetition of the first line of the chorus provide needed variety to the alternating chorus–verse scheme through its synthesizer riff and F♯maj7–G♯m7–C♯11 harmonic successions that culminate with the retransitional dominant harmony, B11.[22] The song closes with an outro in which the first line of the chorus, sung in thirds over E–F♯m7–B11 chordal changes (I–ii7–V11), is repeated continuously. As the song fades out, Wonder and McCartney exchange bluesy vocal riffs.

PIPES OF PEACE (1983)

Released in 1983, *Pipes of Peace* was the sequel to the popular and acclaimed album *Tug of War*. As Ian Peel puts it, they are bookend efforts, both produced by George Martin, with *Tug of War* dealing with pain and *Pipes of Peace* with absolution.[23] (In fact, McCartney was going to call *Pipes of Peace Tug of War II*, but decided against it for fear of associations with trivial movie sequels, such as *Rocky I*, *Rocky II*, and *Rocky III*.[24]) When recording *Tug of War* in 1981, McCartney amassed a backlog of songs that did not make it onto that album, hence he included some of these songs on *Pipes of Peace*. Like *Tug of War*, *Pipes of Peace* featured collaborations with other artists, such as Stanley Clarke, Steve Gadd, Michael Jackson (on "Say, Say, Say"), Denny Laine, Dave Mattacks, Ringo Starr, and Eric Stewart. However, unlike *Tug of War*, critics gave *Pipes of Peace* generally unfavorable reviews, especially in the British press, where it was dismissed in *The New Musical Express* as a "dull, tired and empty collection of quasi[-]funk and gooey rock arrangements."[25] Commercially, *Pipes of Peace* did not do as well as *Tug of War*, reaching the No. 4 spot on the UK charts and a disappointing No. 15 on the US charts. In the eyes of some critics, *Pipes of Peace* marked an artistic decline for McCartney that lasted until the end of the 1980s.

McCartney initially wrote "Pipes of Peace," the title track of the album, at the behest of jazz musician George Melly, who informed McCartney that a children's organization wanted him to write a song for children about a hopeful future.[26] McCartney agreed, but then the song developed into something for him rather than the organization, a hymn of peace in which all people could come together in a spirit of love and reconciliation. He wanted "Pipes of Peace" to serve as a positive counterweight to the more depressing thoughts found in "Tug of War" in which life's struggles tended to weigh people down.

"Pipes of Peace" evinces a simple verse–chorus structure but a more complicated tonal/harmonic setting. The song opens and closes with the same section of music, with its interior consisting of alternating verses and choruses, all varied by the inclusion of an instrumental interlude. In the intro, the singer extols love as the answer to the world's problems, quoting the Indian poet Rabindranath Tagore's idea that in love all problems disappear.[27] Musically, the intro consists of two phrases in E major, the first ending with a half cadence on B, and the second with a deceptive cadence on C, which prepares the chromatic mediant key of the song's verses and choruses, C major. The verses raise questions about problems faced in the world, whereas the choruses respond by exhorting people to pursue joy and peace by playing the symbolic pipes of peace. The harmonies of the verse pursue a diatonic path from the tonic on C to the dominant on G. The harmonic setting of the chorus is more adventurous, beginning with a Dm chord (instead of a more stable tonic harmony on C) that sounds over a chromatic bass line descending from D to C. With the exception of one secondary dominant, E/G♯ (V6/vi), the harmonic setting continues on a diatonic path, culminating, like each verse, on the dominant harmony G. These half cadences may suggest that the world's problems will have to await another day to be solved. Finally, the intro returns as the song's outro, reiterating the thought that in love all problems disappear.

McCartney wrote the duet "Say, Say, Say" with Michael Jackson. After he recorded McCartney's song "Girlfriend" upon the advice of his producer Quincy Jones for his *Off the Wall* album in 1979, Jackson composed a duet, "The Girl Is Mine," for his upcoming *Thriller* album with McCartney in mind. McCartney agreed to record the song, and cut it with Jackson in Los Angeles in between sessions for *Tug of War* in April 1982. The song, let alone the album *Thriller*, was a success in 1982 and beyond, with McCartney receiving a songwriting co-credit on "The Girl Is Mine" for some last-minute assistance. Thus, it should come as no surprise, given this up-and-coming relationship that dated from the 1970s, that Jackson would call McCartney on Christmas Day 1980 and ask him if he wanted to record some songs with him. McCartney agreed, thus the stage was set for two tracks on *Pipes of Peace*, "Say, Say, Say" and "The Man."

McCartney and Jackson wrote "Say, Say, Say" quickly in London in early 1981. Recording the song, however, took longer, with final overdubbing taking place in February 1983 in London while Jackson was staying with McCartney and Eastman. McCartney released "Say, Say, Say" as a single in October 1983, and with the help of a video featuring McCartney and Jackson as con men in the old West selling "Mac and Jac's Wonder Potion" to anyone who was gullible (they actually donate their proceeds to an orphanage), the song reached the top of charts.

"Say, Say, Say" continues to show McCartney's creativity as a songwriter in terms of musical structuring, the backing track having been done by

Jackson.[28] The song is in B♭ minor and after an instrumental intro, opens with the chorus sung by McCartney, who as one of the personas in the song, tells the story of a troubled relationship. McCartney sings a syncopated, ascending arpeggio (B♭–D♭–F–A♭), followed by stepwise figures in the opposite direction. The chorus's harmonic support, given the R & B nature of the song, is limited, sounding B♭m7, E♭7, E♭m7, and B♭m7 chords.

In the verses, Jackson picks up on the theme of the troubled relationship articulated by McCartney. Jackson sings short, ascending, stepwise vocal gestures that contrast with McCartney's more sweeping melody. Jackson's vocal line includes a more varied harmonic support centered on E♭, moving to a B♭m7 at the end of the first phrase and a jazzy Faug9 at the end of the second. Given that their chord changes are based on the chorus and that they occur after statements of the verse, the song's two instrumental interludes (the second performed by brass) and outro (with prominent brass parts) function as varied forms of the chorus, providing the song with textural and timbral variety. Finally, the bridge has McCartney and Jackson singing about the troubled relationship once again as a subtonic harmony A♭ alternates with the tonic harmony B♭m7 before concluding with a jazzy retransitional dominant, the Faug9 from the verse.

McCartney and Jackson likewise collaborated on "The Man," the sixth track of *Pipes of Peace*, with McCartney composing the music and he and Jackson both writing the lyrics. The style of the song is reminiscent of the later softer-edged soul music of the Isley Brothers, a group that influenced both McCartney and Jackson in their earlier years. Although the lyrics held no special significance for McCartney,[29] the references to the "man" strongly suggest that Jackson was acknowledging the importance of God in his life, as the lyrics talk about a man who is alive and here forever, and who can do anything.

"The Man" opens with a striking dissonant sonority, a B♭m/A harmony that resolves to an A chord. The song vacillates between the keys of D major/D minor and B♭ major. After an intro in D minor, verse 1 moves to the key of B♭ major as McCartney and Jackson sing about a man who plays the game of life extremely well. In the ensuing chorus, McCartney and Jackson sing about the virtues of this man over B♭maj7–Am harmonic successions. In the climactic phrase, "This is the man," the music moves to the key of D major via Dmaj7–A/D chordal successions. After a repetition of the chorus with some minor harmonic changes, the formal pattern of verse–chorus–chorus is repeated again. After this point, the opening dissonant sonority and its resolution, B♭m/A–A, returns, followed by a guitar solo based on the chord changes of the intro. The rest of the song consists of one more statement of the verse–chorus–chorus scheme and an outro.

If the album *Pipes of Peace* does not match its predecessor *Tug of War* in terms of musical quality, it is because of songs like "The Other Me." This is not one of McCartney's better efforts. In the song, he explores a kinder and gentler side to his personality that he prefers come out but at times does not.[30] Despite the interesting premise, the song does not go anywhere from both textual and musical perspectives. In the verses of "The Other Me," the singer apologizes to his lover for his mistreatment of her, while in the choruses, he promises her that the kinder and gentler version of himself ("the other me") will surface and not let her down. Unfortunately, both of these sections involve lyrics that can be best described as pedestrian. Musically, the song is in D major and cast in a verse–chorus–bridge format with outro, with no instrumental solos in its interior. For the most part, the harmonic language is diatonic, given that "The Other Me" is a gentle rocker, although there are some chromatic chords present in the song, such as secondary dominants D7 and B7 in the verses, (V7/IV and V7/ii, respectively) that move, respectively, to their intended chords of resolution, G and Em7.

In August 1980, McCartney recorded "Keep under Cover," the fourth track of *Pipes of Peace*, as a demo at Park Gate Studios in Sussex.[31] Later on 7 and 8 December, he recorded the song during sessions at AIR London, and in early 1981 on the island of Montserrat at George Martin's AIR Studios, Stanley Clarke added bass overdubs. "Keep under Cover" begins with a slow vocal introduction in C minor before the song proper begins in the key of E minor with a series of verses and choruses. In each verse, the singer poses a series of metaphorical questions exploring whether or not something is beneficial if it is separated from its usual context, such as butter without bread. This sets up the main point of the chorus in which the singer realizes how empty he is without his lover by his side.

Musically, McCartney precedes verse 1 with an Em–B7–Em chordal succession played by strings, a sound reminiscent of one used by Procol Harum on their song "Conquistador" in 1968. This string chordal riff serves to demarcate various parts of the song. McCartney structures the beginning of the verses by employing a descending stepwise bass line, E–D♯–D♮–C–B, a device he used in songs like "Beware My Love" from *Venus and Mars*, with the line's respective chords, Em–Em/D♯–Em/D♮–C–Cm–G/B, sounding above. Next, D and Am chords alternate before the music moves to the string chordal riff. The chorus is still situated in E minor as it opens and closes with Em–A chordal successions. A guitar interlude and the string chordal riff separate chorus 1 from verse 3. The song closes with an outro that follows chorus 2 where the words "Keep under cover" are repeated, accompanied by a dynamic guitar part.

"So Bad" is a gentle, Motown-sounding ballad inspired by McCartney's wife and children, particularly his young son, James.[32] The song is in G major and cast in a simple verse/refrain–bridge form with intro. In verses 1–2, McCartney sings about how love may be so strong to the point of being painful, ending with the refrain, "Girl, I love you so bad." In verse 3, McCartney informs his loved ones that since they are with him, he has no fear. To include his son into the mix, he expands the refrain by singing, "And she said boy, I love you . . . so bad." In the bridge, McCartney comments, in somewhat curious language, on his domestic bliss.

The melody of the verses has a descending arc, beginning on a high B that gradually sweeps down to a B an octave lower. This vocal line is harmonized diatonically in G major, closing with a plagal cadence, Cadd9 moving to G. The bridge features jazzy harmonies that first ascend then descend, culminating on the retransitional dominant D. Throughout the song, McCartney sings in falsetto.

The "Sweetest Little Show," the album's seventh track, materialized slowly. McCartney elaborates:

That ["Sweetest Little Show"] just came out of a jam, just a little chord sequence that was lying around for a while . . . . It nearly got into a medley with two other pieces, and we suddenly didn't like the two other pieces, but we liked the "Sweetest Little Show" bit. So[,] then I added the guitar show—I fancied playing a bit of guitar—so I played a little bit of acoustic in the middle of it. And that got a little bit of applause, and that became the Little Show.[33]

The "Sweetest Little Show" mixes the sound of the early Temptations and country music. Its text is not complicated, relaying the need to be valued and to stand steadfast in the face of criticism. The song's form is straightforward, proceeding intro–verse–chorus–bridge–verse–chorus–solo–outro. The intro introduces the harmonic sequence about which McCartney speaks that will form the basis of the chorus ("You've got the sweetest little show"): Am–Bm–C–G (ii–iii–IV–I). The chord changes in the verses and bridge are likewise diatonic, with the verses closing with the chorus's chord sequence. After chorus 2, McCartney plays an acoustic guitar solo over a G chord, the solo that is the "Little Show," inserted from an apparently live take, as applause can be heard after it. The outro is based on the chorus, but is altered to conclude on a D7sus4 chord, which sounds like a half cadence at first, but because it is sustained into the next track, "Average Person," is transformed into a subdominant harmony that resolves to a tonic chord on A.

After rehearsing and recording different versions of "Average Person" from 1980 to 1981, McCartney felt that he finally got it right with a version of the song he recorded with Ringo Starr, including it subsequently on *Pipes of Peace*. Deriving from the British music-hall tradition, the song tells an unfortunately unimaginative story about ordinary people and their ambitions. The track begins with the chorus where the singer encourages everyone to consider the average person one would meet on the street and imagine what makes him or her tick. The verses have the singer telling a story about three people and their desires. Verse 1 describes how a former engine driver's greatest ambition was to work with lions in a zoo; verse 2, a waitress who did not win her Hollywood audition, which forced her to grow up; and verse 3, a boxer who wished he were taller. The song is an upbeat rocker in the key of

A major with its musical interest deriving from the use of mixture chords. After a series of diatonic chords, the chorus ends on a C chord (♭III), followed by C–A chordal successions. The verses include a Dm chord (iv) used often with the tonic harmony on A.

"Hey Hey" is a dynamic instrumental that emerged from a jam session involving McCartney and Stanley Clarke, two of the music industry's premier bass players, the day after Clarke arrived in Montserrat.[34] The co-composers recorded the song on 9 February 1981 at George Martin's AIR studios. "Hey Hey" is in a ternary form, with the opening section returning after a contrasting middle. The song's guitar riff evokes the one that opens McCartney's "Birthday" from the Beatles' *White Album*. Both songs are in the key of A major and feature riffs based on an A7 chord—A–C♯–E–G—that are then sounded on other scale degrees.

"Tug of Peace" is an upbeat version of "Tug of War," with extended instrumental sections. By including this song on *Pipes of Peace*, McCartney wanted to link this album with the message of its predecessor, *Tug of War*, effecting a sense of coherence in the process. Like its earlier counterpart, "Tug of Peace" is in C major, with McCartney singing forceful melodic counterpoints that include the phrase, "Learn to play the pipes of peace" (alluding to the album's title track), against the words and melody of "It's a tug of war." From a rhythmic point of view, the song has a strong Caribbean flavor through its percussion parts and incessant drum beat. As a part of the song's ethnic sound, McCartney and Martin bang garden canes on the floor.[35]

The last track on *Pipes of Peace*, "Through Our Love," is a gooey love ballad dedicated to McCartney's wife, Linda Eastman, with the message that love makes all things possible. The song begins in the key of E major, and during its middle, modulates up a half step to F major as the song becomes more intense. The form of "Through Our Love" is simple, consisting of a vocal intro followed by a series of verse–chorus pairs. In verses 1–2, McCartney sings about spending all of his time with Eastman, because she has the power of love. In choruses 1–2, he comments on how their love will allow them to better their existence in unimaginable ways. Harmonically, the verses begin with the tonic harmony E/F and end on the dominant B/C. Choruses, on the other hand, begin with the tonic E/F and feature a more varied harmonic language, ending with the tonic harmony E/Emaj7/G♯–F/Fmaj7/A alternating with its subdominant A/B♭.

When it was reissued on CD as part of *The Paul McCartney Collection* in 1993, *Pipes of Peace* included three bonus tracks: (1) "Twice in a Lifetime" (the title song for a 1985 film), (2) "We All Stand Together" (from the 1984 *Rupert the Bear* project), and (3) "Simple as That" (from a 1986 anti-heroin charity LP). Since McCartney conceived of *Pipes of Peace* as a companion album to *Tug of War*, and because these three songs were composed and recorded after *Pipes of Peace*, I shall not examine them in this book.

GIVE MY REGARDS TO BROAD STREET (1984)
AND SPIES LIKE US (1985)

Released in 1984, the album version of the soundtrack of *Give My Regards to Broad Street* included 12 songs, six of which were written by McCartney during his Beatle days: "Yesterday" from the album *Help!*; four cuts from *Revolver*; and "The Long and Winding Road" from *Let It Be*. The album also included "Silly Love Songs" from *Wings at the Speed of Sound*, "Ballroom Dancing" and "Wanderlust" from *Tug of War*, and three new songs written for the film, "No More Lonely Nights," "Not Such a Bad Boy," and "No Values" (a number supposedly arising from a dream involving the Rolling Stones). In the remastered version of the album included in *The Paul McCartney Collection* in 1993, *Give My Regards to Broad Street* contained additional versions of "No More Lonely Nights," an extended version and a special dance mix, along with "Goodnight Princess." "No More Lonely Nights" is played throughout the movie and is essentially the film's theme song. For that reason, I shall discuss it here.

After conferring with the film's director, McCartney composed "No More Lonely Nights" for a scene in *Give My Regards to Broad Street* that they both felt needed music. While jamming at AIR studios, he fashioned the song out of a bass riff played through a repeating echo device,[36] which can be heard before the song begins on the album. McCartney developed the number into a gentle ballad to match the scene's mood, not to further the movie's plot. Although there are different versions of "No More Lonely Nights," including a "Playout Version," that is, exit music for the audience at the movie theater, produced at the request of Twentieth Century Fox, all arise from two different recordings of the song.[37]

The ballad version of "No More Lonely Nights," which I shall discuss here, addresses the anxieties of love. Cast in a verse–chorus–bridge structure in the key of F major, the song exhibits a superbly constructed melody and harmonic setting. In verses 1–3, the persona sings about the pain of separation, only to express his resolve in choruses 1–3 of being reunited with his love. The melody of the verses consists of four wide-ranging gestures involving leaps, stepwise motion, and a 2/4 measure interpolated into a 4/4 metric framework. The harmonic language of the verses includes a strategically placed A7 chord (V7/vi) that enhances the ideas of the persona's heart being on a string, and that the separation of the two lovers can be blamed on both. The melody of the chorus features gestures that are stepwise and in a high vocal range, emphasizing the persona's resolve that there will be "no more lonely nights," that is, being separated from his love. Harmonically, strong chordal progressions emphasizing F major, B♭–F/A–B♭–C–F (IV–I6–IV–V–I), underscore the text, "no more lonely nights," before eventually cadencing on the dominant harmony C.

"No More Lonely Nights" also includes two bridges, the second longer than the first, a guitar solo based on the chord changes of the verse, and another solo functioning as an outro. In both bridges, the persona informs his lover that he will not go away until his lover promises him that he will not be alone at night. His emphatic tone is matched by an equally emphatic melody and harmonic accompaniment: the melody consists of a single, unbroken gesture harmonized by subdominant and dominant chords on B♭ and C, respectively, over a C pedal point (B♭/C–C [IV–V]). The outro's guitar solo is improvised over an A♭m7 chord as the music fades out.

At the request of director John Landis, McCartney composed and recorded the title song for the comedy film *Spies Like Us* (1985), starring Dan Aykroyd and Chevy Chase, in September 1985 during the *Press to Play* sessions.[38] Except for a synthesizer played by Eddie Rayner of Split Enz, McCartney performed all the instruments on the track. Joining him on backup vocals were Linda Eastman, Ruby James, Kate Robbins (McCartney's cousin), and Eric Stewart. "Spies Like Us" became a Top 10 hit for McCartney in the US, the first to be released under McCartney's new contract with Capitol Records. Its popularity was assisted by a video featuring McCartney, Aykroyd, and Chase in a spoof of the cover of *Abbey Road* interspersed with scenes from the movie. Finally, "Spies Like Us" can be found as a bonus track on the 1993 reissue of *Press To Play* as a part of *The Paul McCartney Collection* (the other bonus track is "Once Upon A Long Ago").

Set in the key of G major, "Spies Like Us" is characterized by a catchy refrain, powerful drum beat, and hard-driving bass riff. Of course, the song's text is replete with comedic images related to the movie. The number is in a straightforward verse/refrain-bridge form with instrumental interludes and an outro. Most verses are four measures long, using G major's primary chords as harmonic support. A dominant Daug9 that resolves to the tonic G at the end of each verse not only intensifies the hard edge of the song but more importantly accentuates the refrain, "spies like us." The bridge begins with the subdominant harmony on C, progresses to B♭ and F chords (♭VII–IV in C major), and then culminates with the retransitional dominant on D. After the last verse and an instrumental link that connects verses in the song's interior, the music moves to a frenetic outro that repeats the song's refrain incessantly.

PRESS TO PLAY (1986)

After the commercial failure of *Give My Regards to Broad Street* in 1984, McCartney felt that he needed to rehabilitate his image and music. In order to project a new, harder-hitting pop sound for his next project *Press to Play*, his fifteenth album since leaving the Beatles, McCartney enlisted the aid of Hugh Padgham, who worked with the likes of Peter Gabriel, Genesis, Phil

Collins, The Police, and XTC, to co-produce the album. After eight largely lackluster years with Columbia Records in the US, McCartney was reunited with his old label, Capitol Records, and looked forward to the future.

Having composed many new songs since *Pipes of Peace*, especially with collaborator Eric Stewart, McCartney began recording *Press To Play* in March 1985.[39] To play on the album, he enlisted the aid of his rock-star pals Phil Collins and Pete Townshend, guitarists Carlos Alomar and Stewart, drummer Jerry Marotta, and keyboardist Eddie Rayner. Yet, despite the new direction, producer, and more contemporary sound, *Press To Play* was a commercial flop. Part of the reason may have been Padgham's tendency to pile on the digitized sound effects, making the album sound lifeless and mechanical. Although it garnered surprisingly positive reviews, *Press To Play* failed to make any impact on the album charts in either the UK or US.

The album's first track, "Stranglehold," was the first song on which McCartney and Stewart collaborated.[40] This E-major-based rocker began life as an up-tempo groove, with words added later. The song begins with an E5 vamp played by McCartney and Stewart on acoustic guitars, suggesting a bluesy number to come. However, depending on whether or not one likes the sound of 1980s pop, this song is either enhanced or ruined when the horns enter. At any rate, in three verses, the persona tries to gain the attention of a woman, eventually asking her if she will take a chance on him. The vamp introduced at the song's beginning forms the basis of each verse's harmonic support. The first three lines of each verse are set, respectively, to E5–A, E5–A–B, and E5–A chordal successions. The fourth line, however, departs from E major's primary harmonies (I, IV, V) by sounding a colorful harmonic succession progressing by half steps, G–F♯–F–Em, followed by an equally colorful cadential tag, G–F♯–A.

In the chorus, the persona resolves to wait for the woman in any venue, hoping that she will come and see him. He then proclaims that she has a "stranglehold" on him, prompting him to desire her even more. The vocal line is accompanied by chord changes centered on E and then A, as well as horn licks that intensify the persona's expressions of emotion. The song includes another statement of the chorus near the end, bringing the music to a dramatic climax that is continued by the chorus-based outro and its acoustic-guitar vamp.

"Good Times Coming"/"Feel the Sun" consists of two songs, one a nostalgic but dark look at summers past, the other a yearning for a brighter future. According to McCartney, the three verses of "Good Times Coming" are linked with three summers.[41] Verse 1 deals with McCartney's days as a boy when he felt embarrassed to wear short trousers to Butlin's (British vacation camps launched by Billy Butlin). Verse 2 is linked with the Beatles, and it contains one of McCartney's favorite lines on the album: "That was a silly season, was it the best? We didn't need a reason, just a rest." Verse 3 focuses rather ominously on one memorable summer before the onset of a war. While the song's verses narrate a story about three summers, its three choruses present positive emotional reactions to them. Musically, "Good Times Coming" is a reggae-style number, with the verses suggesting E phrygian through their Em–Dm–C–D and Em–F chordal successions, and the choruses indicating C major through alternating B♭9 and C chords.

"Good Times Coming" segues into "Feel the Sun," a laid-back rocker in A major composed of a chorus, bridge, and outro. It begins with the chorus ("Feel the sun . . . "), a section that consists of four lines in which three close with half cadences on E, and the fourth a plagal cadence, D–A. The bridge's lyrics depart from the optimism of those found in the chorus by reflecting on a past troubled relationship, concluding that only love will restore it. The outro repeats the music of the chorus as the track fades out.

McCartney considered the next track on *Press to Play*, "Talk More Talk," as surrealistic. Indeed, the song's text is a stream-of-consciousness series of different images and word sounds that do not cohere. For some of the lyrics, McCartney took selected quotes from an interview with Tom Waits, such as "I don't like sitting down music."[42] "Talk More Talk" begins with Linda Eastman and their son, James McCartney, reciting a jumble of different texts ("A master can highlight the phrases") that are at times electronically manipulated and accompanied by synthesizers. After this intro and a synthesizer interlude, McCartney begins the actual song, a G-mixolydian number in a simple verse–chorus–bridge structure. The melody of the verse, replete with repeated notes, is accompanied by G–Em–A–G (I–vi–II–I) chords. The chorus features F–G iterations (VII–I) before it moves through Em–F–A–G (vi–VII–II–I) chords. The bridge contrasts with both verse and chorus through its static lyrics and harmonic content, "I'm happy to do it for you" repeated several times over a G chord. After additional statements of the verse and chorus, the spoken texts return to close the song before it fades out with digitized percussion.

McCartney first thought of the idea for "Footprints" in the winter of 1984–85 after observing a magpie scavenging for food in the snow.[43] Later, he and Stewart wrote a song around this theme, only they changed the bird to a lonely old man walking around in the snow looking for logs. Despite the obvious similarities with the character of "Eleanor Rigby," which McCartney has acknowledged, "Footprints" does not attain the emotional power of the earlier song, from the standpoint of either lyrics or music. This Latin-flavored track is tonally ambiguous, vacillating between A minor and E minor. It is in a verse–chorus–bridge format with an instrumental intro that returns as an interlude (in a modified form) and outro. As the verses proceed, the singer narrates the story of an old man looking for wood in the snow. In the chorus and bridge, we learn that the man's life is empty because his love has left him. In verse 4, we get an inkling of the original concept behind the song through the singer's mention of a magpie looking for food. Because the old man throws the bird a crumb, the singer wonders if he has found a friend in the bird.

McCartney recorded his ballad, "Only Love Remains," live at his 48–track studio, Hoghill, East Sussex.[44] The song is vintage McCartney, singer-songwriter at his best, augmented by Tony Visconti's orchestral arrangement. The lyrics focus on the prospect of the singer's lover not caring for him anymore and the potential angst caused by that situation. Cast in C major and a verse/refrain–bridge form, the song features a lush melody supported by complex chord changes that draw upon modal mixture. In verses 1–2, the singer describes his potential predicament and what he would do to chord progressions that include mixtures sonorities, particularly at the end, G–A♭maj7–C (V–♭VI7–I). The last two chords are repeated to support the refrain, "Only love remains." The bridge moves to C minor, the parallel minor of C major, sounding harmonies from that key before ending with a retransitional dominant on G. Finally, the refrain's harmonic support, A♭maj7–C, returns as a link in the middle of the song and an outro to accompany further statements of the lyrics, "Only love remains."

McCartney issued "Press" as a single in July 1986 before *Press to Play* was released two months later. The song was supposed to usher in the newer, more up-to-date sound he desired in order to remain a relevant force on the 1980s pop music scene. "Press" is characterized by a text driven by McCartney's penchant for words that magically flow from his subconscious and a digital technology that makes the song sound both glossy and mechanical. In the song's verses, the singer declares his love to a woman but believes that various things interfere with their relationship, such as people eavesdropping on their conversations. Consequently, he suggests that they devise a signal, such as a word or secret code in order to convey their feelings to each other.

The chorus does nothing, however, to develop this story line. The singer informs his lover that she should tell him to "press," which may mean that he push forward with his affection. Following these words is a possible sexual innuendo, "Right there, that's it, yes," unintentionally resembling a line from a song by the notorious Gary Glitter, "Do You Wanna Touch Me," from 1973.[45] Although the bridge's lyrics begin in a promising way, they ultimately fall flat with the line, "Oklahoma was never like this," which refers, according to McCartney, to a distant place, but how that place relates to the singer's state of mind is a mystery.[46]

"Press" is in C major and set in a verse–chorus–bridge form with an intro, guitar solo, instrumental interlude, and outro. The verses feature diatonic chords that end with half cadences on G. The choruses likewise include diatonic chords but end on the tonic harmony C. It is the bridge and the instrumental interlude based on its chord changes, however, that provide the song with musical contrast through modal mixture. The bridge begins with the subdominant as expected, but that chord alternates with a mixture chord on E♭ (♭III). At the end of the bridge, mixture chords on E♭ and A♭ support the climactic line involving "Oklahoma."

McCartney composed "Pretty Little Head" in collaboration with Eric Stewart. The song began life as an instrumental number with McCartney adding the song's quasi-psychedelic lyrics later. The track's personnel included McCartney on lead vocal, bass, guitar, and drums; Eric Stewart, backing vocals, guitar, and keyboards; Jerry Marotta, vibraphone; and Linda Eastman, Ruby James, and Kate Robbins, backing vocals.[47] Although McCartney selected "Pretty Little Head" as his thirty-eighth single in order to reverse the sluggish sales of *Press to Play*, the song did not materialize into the commercial hit he desired.

"Pretty Little Head" is dreamily abstract and includes a wash of electronically dense sounds. In the song's verses, the persona speaks of tribesmen coming down from the hills in order to sell their precious wares, and a presumably female ruler who is told not to worry her "pretty little head." In the chorus, the vocal ensemble chants "Ursa Major, Ursa Minor." McCartney casts the song in C minor and uses different riffs as ostinatos to heighten the song's primitivistic message. In the verses, he uses a repeated vibraphone riff combined with a series of chords that descend from Cm, Cm–B♭–A♭–G–Fm–E♭–B♭–Cm, to set the song's hypnotic, trancelike tone. The chorus continues this tone by including a repetitive vocal riff (C–C–E♭–D, C–C–C–B♭) accompanied by equally repetitive A♭–B♭–Cm chords. Verse and chorus alternate throughout the song, introduced by an intro featuring digitized drums, a sustained C, and the aforementioned vibraphone riff, and varied by an instrumental interlude and outro based on the chorus. After the persona speaks about how the tribesmen live in the upper reaches, one hears what appears to be a motorcycle driving off, and then the song ends abruptly.

In the cheeky, honky-tonk rocker, "Move Over Busker," McCartney developed an absurd storyline chock full of different characters that include the old Hollywood actors Mae West and Errol Flynn, improbable situations, and double entendres. The song begins in A major and modulates to D major, and is set in a verse–chorus–bridge form. In the verses, the singer advances the story line that includes the protagonist encountering a Nell Gwynne, presumably someone from McCartney's past, and Mae West and Errol Flynn. In the choruses ("Move over busker"), Gwynne and West rebuff the protagonist's amorous advances, while just before the last chorus, Flynn excuses himself in order to engage in a tryst. No matter the key, rock chordal changes dominate the song, with verses set to I–vi–♭VII–I harmonic successions (for example, A–F♯m–G–A chords in A major), while choruses feature IV–V–IV–V–IV–V–I chords. Finally, McCartney included the phrase, "Mae West's sweaty vest," in the song, an old Beatles inside joke that is hard to fathom, as is the rest of the song.[48]

McCartney and Stewart wrote the punkish song "Angry" in response to the day-to-day frustrations of life. In an interview with Kurt Loder, McCartney elaborates upon the motivations behind the song:

> I was thinking... about... British trade unions withdrawing coal when there's old ladies dying, and we kind of just go, "Yeah, well, the union's got a right." And Britain's attitude toward apartheid at the moment, which is just so crazy. I mean, *still*, after all those years of Martin Luther King and everything, they're *still* buggerin' around with black and white. It's so *insane*. Couldn't they just *wise* up? But there's Maggie [former Prime Minister Margaret Thatcher] saying, "We don't need to do sanctions," while everybody else—all the civil-rights groups—are saying, "But you *do*."[49]

On the song, McCartney is joined by Pete Townsend on guitar and Phil Collins on drums. They recorded the song live in the studio in a little over two hours.

In keeping with its hard-driving sound, "Angry" is simple from a variety of musical vantage points. It is in a standard chorus–verse structure with intro, guitar solo, and outro. It is in the "guitar key" of E major. McCartney screams the melody of the song to a limited set of chord changes, with long stretches of E-based chords in the chorus and verse, the only variety coming in the form of an A chord in the guitar solo. All of these musical factors combine to enhance the singer's lyric, which focuses on his anger against a corrupt society that should not be dictating morals and social behavior.

As Kurt Loder notes, "However Absurd" is "a stream-of-conscious stew of non sequiturs lifted from the works of such poets as W. H. Auden,"[50] suggesting comparisons with some of John Lennon's psychedelic songs from the later 1960s. Although McCartney has tried to avoid sounding like the Beatles in his solo music, he emulates their sound in "However Absurd," as the track sounds like Lennon's "I Am the Walrus" from both textual and musical perspectives. In the song, McCartney tries to break down language barriers in order to make meaningless words seem meaningful. The song's melody is disjointed, cast in a contextually established C major by means of C chords placed strategically at the beginnings and endings of phrases. In keeping with the song's subject matter, the chord changes are unorthodox, progressing primarily by step (e.g., C–D–Dm–C), with F–Bb–C progressions providing variety in the song's choruses. Although there is an attempt in this number to capture the grandeur of a late Beatles song, it does not reach those heights.

"Write Away" is another McCartney and Stewart composition. As with "P. S. I Love You," "Paperback Writer," and "Temporary Secretary," McCartney and his collaborator constructed the lyrics of the song around the penning of a letter. Indeed, the song even begins with a percussion intro that suggests the beating of a typewriter. "Write Away" is a soulful, funky song in C major with McCartney employing the homonyms "write" and "right" in the chorus. After an intro that sets the stage for the track's groove and chorus's harmonic changes, the song begins with the chorus. Above Fm and C chords, the singer encourages his lover, who is in need of love, to "write" him a letter, telling her because she needs love, "write" away, or is it "right" away? In the second line of the chorus, the singer informs his lover that completing the letter will lift her spirits, so she should send the letter "right" away, or should she "write" away? All of this recalls John Lennon's lyrical contributions to McCartney's Beatle song, "She Leaving Home," from *Sgt. Pepper's Lonely Hearts Club Band*. Singing the role of the distraught parents whose daughter has left them, Lennon plays with the homonyms buy, by, and bye. Lastly, in the verses of "Write Away," the singer encourages his lover that he can deliver the love that she needs. From a musical standpoint, the verses develop the modal mixture used in the chorus (i.e., Fm chord, iv) by employing Cm and Eb chords in the harmonic accompaniment (Cm–F–Eb–F–C).

In the ballad "It's Not True," McCartney goes after his critics who not only took him to task for his use of meaningless and obscure lyrics but also questioned Linda Eastman's role as a song collaborator.[51] Yet, in spite of it all, he uses the ballad as a vehicle to express his feelings for his wife. "It's Not True" is in a verse/refrain–chorus structure with intro and outro set in the key of D major. In the intro, McCartney and his backing vocalists (Stewart, Eastman, James, and Robbins) sing the track's title in exuberant outbursts accompanied by a strong digitized drumbeat, a sound suggestive of Queen's "We Will Rock You" (1977). When the verse enters, the ballad begins. In each verse, McCartney rails against both critics and people who disapproved of Eastman both musically and personally, punctuating his discourse with the refrain, "It's not true." In the song's chorus, McCartney gets more specific with his diatribe by mentioning that if Eastman helps him write a melody, he lets the words take care of themselves, a swipe at those who questioned Eastman's musical abilities and his approach to writing lyrics. Musically, McCartney supports the song's melody with diatonic chord changes, the only exceptions being a secondary dominant on E (V/V) and subtonic harmony on C (bVII) that precede a dominant harmony on A in the verse and chorus, respectively.

"Tough on a Tightrope" is the last track on *Press to Play*, and, unfortunately, a disappointing way to close an unfairly maligned album. In the song, the persona addresses his anxieties and worries about a relationship in which he is involved. The verses and choruses are bland from both textual and musical perspectives, with underdeveloped lyrics and simplistic chord progressions in D major—even the chromatic movement engendered by a Gm6 mixture chord progressing to a Bm chord (Bb–B♮) in the chorus cannot save the harmonic setting. The bridge, however, shows more creativity compared to the verse and chorus, evincing more convincing lyrics (the singer exclaims, "It's tough on a tightrope") and chord changes involving secondary dominants and mixture chords (Am7–D7–G–E7–Am7–F–D [v7–V7/IV–IV–V7/V–v7–♭III–I]).

Press to Play included two bonus tracks when it was reissued on CD as part of *The Paul McCartney Collection* in 1993, "Spies Like Us," and an alternative mix of the ballad, "Once Upon a Long Ago." Released as a single in the UK (and not in the US) on 16 November 1987, "Once Upon a Long Ago" reached No. 10 in the British charts. The song was also included on the British version of the *All the Best* hits package that was released on 2 November 1987. Produced by Phil Ramone, "Once Upon a Long Ago" includes a violin solo by classical musician Nigel Kennedy.

In the lyrics of "Once Upon a Long Ago," McCartney attempts to evoke the fairy-tale atmosphere implied in the song's title through a series of different, at times surrealistic, images. Included in the text are several musical references, such as learning and performing scales and broken chords, making up tunes in a minor key, and playing guitars on a bare stage. Formally, "Once Upon a Long Ago" consists of an intro and outro, and a series of alternating verse/refrains ("Tell me darling, ... ") and choruses ("Once upon a long ago") in the song's interior, interspersed with two instrumental solos—the first on tenor saxophone, the second involving electric guitar and violin—and a vocal interlude based on the chorus. The song is in the key of C major, although it is a C major established by a C chord used as a point of arrival at the ends of phrases rather than by tonic-dominant-tonic progressions. While the verses feature only two chords, F/B♭ and C, the choruses exhibit a more sophisticated harmonic palette, with a hint of the key of C minor through mixture chords A♭maj7, Cm, Cm/B♭, Fm, and Gm.

FLOWERS IN THE DIRT (1989)

Released in 1989, *Flowers in the Dirt* represents a renaissance for McCartney's career as a musical artist. After his acclaimed album *Tug of War* reached the Top 10 in 1982, McCartney suffered a series of setbacks during the 1980s with the disappointing commercial and critical reception of *Pipes of Peace*, *Give My Regards to Broad Street*, and *Press to Play* (although this writer considers these albums more satisfying than critics have maintained). Although it did not reach the Top 10, *Flowers in the Dirt* compares favorably not only with *Tug of War* but also *Band on the Run* in terms of consistent musical quality.

McCartney did two things to turn his career around in the late 1980s. First, he assembled a new, top-flight band in order to embark on a 1989–90 world tour. In addition to McCartney and Eastman, the group included: Robbie McIntosh, formerly of the Pretenders, on lead guitar; Hamish Stuart, formerly of the Average White Band, on guitar and bass; Paul "Wix" Wickens, a noted London session player, on keyboards; and Chris Whitten, who played with such stars as Edie Brickell, on drums. More importantly, in 1987, on his own initiative, McCartney began writing songs with Elvis Costello. After they helped each other with one another's songs in progress, McCartney and Costello wrote nine songs together, four of which were included on *Flowers in the Dirt*. This was a fruitful association for McCartney from several vantage points, as Costello challenged him in ways no one had since the days of John Lennon.

Although McCartney and Costello produced four songs they wrote together on *Flowers in the Dirt*, McCartney became dissatisfied with their raw sound and consequently brought in producers Mitchell Froom and Neil Dorfsman to help him record more conventional-sounding pop songs. He also enlisted the aid of Trevor Horn, famous for his work with Art of Noise, Frankie Goes to Hollywood, and Yes, to produce "Rough Ride" and "Figure of Eight," and David Foster and the team of Chris Hughes and Ross Cullum to work on other songs on the album. Perhaps spurred on by George Harrison's contemporaneous successes with his albums *Cloud Nine* and the *Traveling Wilburys, Volume 1*, McCartney was determined to make a great album, as reflected by his remarks in an interview with James Henke in 1989: "I really wanted an album I could go out on tour with, an album people could relate to. I just didn't want some crummy album dogging the tour."[52]

As opined by Walter Everett, "My Brave Face" is the "closest an ex-Beatle has ever come to " 'She Loves You'."[53] Composed by McCartney and Costello (real name Declan MacManus), the song centers on a man whose woman has left him.[54] At first, he is happy, but soon realizes how empty he is without her. The song's Beatle-esque qualities, surprisingly, come from Costello, not McCartney.[55] The song's harmonies, bridge, and melodic bass line played by McCartney on his iconic Hoffner bass were all Costello's ideas.

"My Brave Face" opens with a scintillating vocal intro in the key of E major. Next come two verses in which the singer advances the song's story line of a recently independent, seemingly happy man. But in the bridge, the man begins to express regret regarding the loss of the woman in his life. In the chorus, the man's pain is intensified to the point of him wanting to put on a brave face to mask the hurt he feels inside. Musically, the verses' first phrase opens with a melodic gesture that slopes down and then up, followed by vocal harmonies that include nonchordal tones resolving down by step, all over an E–F♯m–E (I–ii–I) chordal succession. The verses' second phrase develops the initial melodic idea of the first through sequence before returning to the tonic note E. The harmonic language expands during this second phrase to include more chords, E–A–G♯m–F♯m–B–E, which establish E as tonic.

In keeping with its contrasting lyrics, the bridge differs from the verses by featuring a melody that consists of a series of descending scalewise gestures harmonized by C♯m, C♯m(maj7), C♯m7, E7, A, Am, and E chords. This chord series reveals descending stepwise lines in its inner voices (C♯–C♮–B, corresponding to the first three chords, and D–C♯–C♮–B to the last four), a device encountered in McCartney's compositions. Yet, the device may actually stem from Costello, who not only was responsible for the bridge but also may have been emulating his songwriting partner's compositional techniques when devising that section.

The rest of the song includes an interlude and another verse, bridge, and chorus. Besides the harmonies, bridge, and melodic bass line, the song's Beatle-esque qualities stem from the sound of an electric 12-string guitar part reminiscent of George Harrison's guitar playing on the Beatles' album "A Hard Day's Night."

The next track on the album, "Rough Ride," is a blues-influenced song first recorded in October 1984.[56] McCartney decided to write the song after watching a television program on the blues, "trying to be Big Bill Broonzy" as he composed it. McCartney presented "Rough Ride," along with other song fragments, to producer Trevor Horn during a recording session for *Flowers in the Dirt*.[57] Horn decided he liked the unfinished "Rough Ride." Accordingly, he helped McCartney develop the song into a more horn-dominated, soulful funky composition, with him playing keyboards and his associate Steve Lipson playing guitar and programming a drum machine.

Because of the lack of a D♯ in the melody and any B-based chord in the accompaniment, "Rough Ride" is in a dorian-flavored E minor. It opens with a chordal riff composed of an Em chord alternating with a D chord. A 12-bar blues pattern limited to Em(7) and A7add6 chords govern the ensuing verse and chorus, with McCartney singing about the travails of love through a series of horn-like vocal riffs. After the second chorus, horns play some bluesy licks in an instrumental interlude that enhances the song's emotional atmosphere. Next, the bridge comes in as the song's harmonic vocabulary is expanded to three chords as a G chord alternates with Em before culminating on an A7. The rest of the song includes additional statements of verse, chorus, and horn interlude (with and without vocals) to close this fresh-sounding number.

Cowritten by McCartney and Costello, "You Want Her Too" suggests the interaction between Lennon and McCartney as singers and songwriters. In their collaborations, Costello instigated this working relationship. McCartney elaborates:

> I really resisted it at first. I said, "We can't do this, man. This is me and John." But Elvis said, "It's your style. There's nothing wrong with it." He really drew me a bit toward the Beatles thing. He made me think, "Why am I being resistant to it? What is the resistance?" You know, you don't want to be seen to be trying to be a Beatle again. It is not seemly.[58]

"You Want Her Too" centers on the emotional struggles a man goes through as he desires a woman. McCartney likened the man's conflicted state to a *Tom and Jerry* cartoon: "We imagined a Tom and Jerry cartoon, where there's an angel and a devil above, and one says, 'Go ahead, do it,' and the other says, 'No, don't do it.'"[59]

"You Want Her Too" is a waltz in C major that alternates verses and choruses, with a bridge inserted after the second chorus for musical and textual variety, all framed by an instrumental intro and outro. McCartney and Costello alternate singing the lines of each verse, with McCartney singing the sweet lines that Beatle Paul would, and Costello the caustic ones that Beatle John would. The harmonic support for each verse is basic, with C–Dm–G (I–ii–V) chordal progressions enhanced by Dm's secondary dominant (I–V+/ii–V7/ii–ii–V). The chorus has McCartney developing his melodic gesture from the verse, soaring to a high A and G in the process, supported by F and C chords (IV–I). The bridge introduces the prospect that the song's protagonist may have a rival for his woman's affections. It accentuates this idea harmonically by going further afield than verse or chorus, suggesting the key of E minor then major, particularly with a climactic F#m–B7 chord progression (ii–V7). The intro returns as an outro, only to be joined by a big band passage as the song fades out.

"Distractions" is a sentimental, Latin-flavored ballad McCartney wrote for his wife, Linda Eastman. Indeed, the song is similar in style to the light-orchestral music of Mantovani, whom the young McCartney despised, as seen by his response to producer George Martin when Martin suggested adding strings to "Yesterday" in 1965.[60] "Distractions" focuses on the inner turmoil faced by someone trying to balance a highly lucrative career with a stable home life. McCartney enlisted the aid of longtime friend Geoff Emerick to engineer the song, as well as arranger/conductor Clare Fisher to devise an orchestral arrangement, which was recorded at Mad Hatter Studios in Los Angeles.[61] "Distractions" is sophisticated from tonal/harmonic perspectives. Its instrumental intro features both melodic and harmonic chromaticism, with the passage ending on a D♭/C♭ chord (D♭$^4_2$), which proceeds to the verse's opening Gm7 chord. McCartney distinguishes the song's verse–verse–chorus structure by casting the verses in D minor and choruses in B♭ major. For the lengthy acoustic guitar solo based on the verse's melody, the music modulates to E minor. The music returns to D minor and then B♭ major for one last statement of verse and chorus.

"We Got Married" had a long gestation period, with the song written and finished in two creative bursts. With the help of American producer David Foster, McCartney recorded and produced an initial version of the song in late 1984.[62] It remained unfinished until the *Flowers in the Dirt* recording sessions. "We Got Married" benefited from this long path of maturation; while it sounds like a folk-rock song at the beginning, it develops into a full-blown symphonic pop song at the end. In the song's lyrics, McCartney celebrates the institution of marriage, but adds a slightly cynical tinge to it.

After an acoustic guitar intro on an Em chord establishing the key of E minor, McCartney sings about the ups and downs of marriage in the first two verses to the accompaniment of three chords, Em, Am7, and C. He then moves to the song's first bridge, continuing to sing about the realities of marriage to an expanded harmonic framework suggestive of C major at its beginning. An instrumental link returns the music to E minor via its reiterated Em7 chord, preparing the song's third verse. All the while, the song continues to grow in sound and excitement. Another instrumental interlude featuring a guitar riff (played by David Gilmour) heightens the entrance of verse 4 and bridge 2, as McCartney sings in an increasingly animated manner about what constitutes a strong marriage. It is at this point that the song completely leaves its folk-rock atmosphere through another instrumental interlude featuring a jazzy trumpet part. The song continues to build to symphonic proportions, closing with an outro that exhorts everyone to work at marriage if they want it to be successful.

On the surface, McCartney wrote "Put It There" in honor of his father Jim by incorporating one of his father's favorite sayings that referred to a hearty handshake, "Put it there if it weighs a ton." But in his late forties and cognizant of both past and future generations of his family, McCartney also wanted to honor his 12–year-old son James through the song, passing on the love he received from his father to him. Accordingly, "Put It There" is a warm, fuzzy number that celebrates father-son relationships. Indeed, in the video of the song, with its different images of fathers and sons, McCartney and his son James are pictured near the end.[63]

"Put It There" is in the key of D major and features McCartney singing to an accompaniment of acoustic guitar, acoustic bass, and percussion, joined later by strings. The song proceeds in a simple intro–verse–chorus–interlude (inst.)–verse–chorus format. With the exception of the intro and interlude that feature identical chordal progressions, the song's harmonic setting is diatonic, in keeping with its sweet, folk-like qualities. The verses feature plagal progressions where G and D chords (IV–I) alternate. As for the choruses, they are more varied, with Bm chords initiating lines 1 and 3 before a strong authentic cadence involving A and D chords (V–I) brings the music to a close.

According to John Blaney, in "Figure of Eight," McCartney wanted to coarsen the edges of producer Trevor Horn's perfectionist bent and techno-wizardry.[64] He recorded the vocals, bass, and drums live in the studio, and then allowed Horn to work his magic with technology, in order to generate a sound he preferred that was more rough than accurate. In a total of two days, the song was finished, a radical change from Horn's usually painstaking work as a producer.

"Figure of Eight" is a mid-tempo rocker in the key of E major. After a chordal guitar intro sounding E, F♯m7, E, F♯m7, G6, and F♯m7 chords, McCartney as persona sings about a troubled relationship in verses 1–2 where he seems not to be getting anywhere with his lover, dancing around in a figure of eight. In the chorus, the persona comments upon his situation by asking questions about the choices people make when they are in love. The song's melody features predominantly repeated-note gestures in keeping with the song's style. Not surprisingly, the harmonic language is blues-based, but with E major's primary triads joined by a C♯m7 chord in the verses, and G♯m11, C♯m11, and F♯m7sus4 chords in the choruses. After verses 1–2 and chorus 1, the rest of the song proceeds interlude (repetition of the intro), bridge, verse 3, and chorus 2 before the outro ends the song by repeating the chord progression of the intro until it fades out.

According to McCartney, his work as a songwriter falls under different categories, one of which is to construct a song around wordplay.[65] When he likes the sounds of words with which he is experimenting, he will create an entire song around them, "Biker Like an Icon," from the album *Off the Ground* (1993), being an example. For him, it is a surreal way to write. "This One" is a number that emerged from his compositional penchant for wordplay. In developing the lyrics, "This one" kept coming back to McCartney as "This swan." From there, he has the swan gliding over the ocean with a god upon its back, an image he derived from posters he picked up in India of the little blue god Krishna riding on the back of a swan. For McCartney, the image is surreal for Westerners, for the people of India, just a part of their folklore. Finally, according to McCartney, "This one" connotes an emphasis on the present ("this now"), not allowing it to slip away because of preoccupations with the past or future.

Cast in the key of A major, "This One" is in a conventional verse–chorus–bridge form supported by equally conventional chord changes. In the verses, the singer regrets those times he did not convey his most heartfelt feelings to his lover. He sings a melody that features ascending lines followed by repeated-note gestures, all set to a primarily diatonic chordal succession, A–F♯m7–C♯m–D–A–E–Em7–A (I–vi7–iii–IV–I–V–v7–I). In the first part of the chorus, the singer realizes that in his relationship, he was fixated on the future ("waiting for a better moment"), instead of the present ("this one"), when expressing his feelings. In the second part of the chorus, the text becomes surreal with the image of the swan and god on its back gliding over the ocean. The musical motion pick ups in the chorus through a more active bass line, which still supports, however, diatonic chordal progressions above. The song closes with an outro based on the second part of the chorus, fading out with vocal ad libs over a guitar vamp.

McCartney and Costello cowrote "Don't Be Careless Love." According to John Blaney, as with other McCartney/Costello efforts that were initially produced for *Flowers in the Dirt*, McCartney and producer Mitchell Froom reworked the song.[66] But this different, more pop-oriented version, with its gently flowing melody and soothing vocals, cannot hide the song's rather dark lyrics, which may be Costello's influence. The persona is worried about his love, keeping watch until she comes home. In a dream, he sees his love running but going nowhere, and falling through a spiral staircase. Although unclear whether in a dream or not, the persona reads in the newspaper about how his love was found dismembered, rolled up in a rug. Musically, the verses of "Don't Be Careless Love" are rather innocuous, with McCartney beginning the song by singing the melody accompanied only by backing vocals in D major. As the musical motion picks up in the chorus, things get more intense harmonically as the persona gets into his macabre story. A C#m–C–Bm–F#m chordal succession governs most of the chorus, moving through G–C–G chords before settling down on the dominant harmony A. The song's outro closes with some of the same chromaticism that characterized the chorus, only this time extended in order to end with a plagal cadence involving a mixture chord, Gm–D (iv–I).

"That Day Is Done" is another song by McCartney and Costello. It is a sad, gospel-like number, almost a funeral dirge, inspired by the death of Costello's grandmother. Costello started the song and McCartney helped him finish it, encouraging Costello that they should repeat the title in the song and develop it musically in order to give the song more power. Interestingly, the song includes the line, "flowers in the dirt," which McCartney took to name the album. "That Day Is Done" is in C major and triple time. Within its verse–chorus–bridge framework, the song conveys a powerful, almost majestic aura with broad sweeping vocal phrases delivered dramatically by McCartney. In keeping with its bluesy, gospel-like qualities, the harmonic language is basic, limited primarily to C major's three basic harmonies, C, F, and G, although in the chorus the harmonic palette is broadened to include chromatic chords.

"How Many People" is a reggae-influenced, politically motivated song by McCartney, written while he was vacationing in Jamaica. McCartney dedicated the song to the memory of the recently deceased Chico Mendes (1944–88), the ecological campaigner, as a sign of political support.[67] After an extended intro featuring synthesized strings and vocal ad-libbing, the ensuing verse has the singer remarking about the number of people who have been denied life's opportunities. In the ensuing chorus, while awaiting an answer to his comment, the singer posits another query as to how many people have died. He answers his own question in the bridge by saying, "one too many right now for me." In his view, he would like to see ordinary people living in peace. The song goes through another verse–chorus–bridge cycle, with similar lyrics in verse 2. Musically, "How Many People" is in G major. Its melodic language is simple, with a mixture of descending and ascending lines that frequently span the notes G and D. The harmonic language is equally straightforward, utilizing primarily diatonic chords to support the song's melody. Predictably, the bridge begins with the subdominant chord C before ending on the retransitional dominant D. Finally, as with "Ebony and Ivory," the light reggae sound of "How Many People" decreases the tension of the song's pointed political message.

In "Motor of Love," McCartney added elements of deep spirituality to an already highly emotional love ballad.[68] In "Let It Be," he referenced his late mother, Mary McCartney, who comes to him (presumably in a dream) in order to console him with soothing and wise words, telling him to "let it be." In "Motor of Love," he calls on his late father, Jim McCartney, in the line, "Heavenly Father, look down from above." "Motor of Love" is a gospel-inspired love song dedicated in all likelihood to his wife, Linda Eastman. It is in the key of D major, with a 9/8 meter enhancing an already powerful soulful feel. In the verses, McCartney gets highly personal with his lyrics, baring his soul as he expresses the depth of his love for his wife. In the choruses, he calls on his father to presumably bless the relationship. In both verse and chorus, McCartney created gentle, predominantly stepwise melodic lines that are supported by rich chordal changes. Overall, "Motor of Love" is yet another quintessential example of McCartney's ability to write powerful love ballads.

"Ou est le soleil," the last track on the album, was included only on the CD and cassette versions of *Flowers in the Dirt*. Arising from a jam session, this quirky song suggests the sound of Michael Jackson's album *Thriller*, coupled with a retro 1960s edge by means of its organ part. Cast in the key of E major, "Ou est le soleil" features McCartney's signature harmonic progression involving I–♭VI–♭VII–I chords, seen as early as his Beatle song, "P. S. I Love You" from 1962. This E–C–D–E harmonic progression begins the track and, after an Em7–F♯m7–G–A chordal succession and the song's bass vamp, is used during the singing of the verse's fragmented French lyric: "Ou est le soleil, . . . dans la tête, travaillez" ("Where is the sun, . . . in the head, work"). The Em7–F♯m7–G–A chordal succession also joins in to support the lyric before giving way to the song's bass vamp and repeated organ chords. After the verse's French lyric is repeated, the bass vamp is sounded again, this time with ad-lib vocals. The repeated organ chords return, now combined with distorted guitar licks. Bass vamp and repeated organ chords again continue, with the French lyric being both sung and spoken, then the song fades out, with vocals and synthesizer sounds in the background and repeated organ chords in the foreground.

As a part of the 1993 reissue associated with *The Paul McCartney Collection*, *Flowers in the Dirt* contained three bonus tracks: (1) "Back on My Feet," a song composed by McCartney and Costello, originally released as the flip side of the 1987 single "Once Upon a Long Ago"; (2) "Flying to My Home"; and (3) "Loveliest Thing." To close my discussion of *Flowers in the Dirt*, I shall discuss "Back on My Feet."

"Back on My Feet" is a song about social alienation that dates from McCartney's early collaborations with Costello in 1987. It was one of the unfinished songs that McCartney brought to his new songwriting partner as the two worked together to help each other fix one another's songs before they started writing from scratch. Costello helped McCartney with the song's lyrics, adding a cynical tone to the text, all to McCartney's benefit. "Back on My Feet" is in A major and proceeds through a verse–chorus–bridge structure. In the verses, the persona tells the story of a proud old homeless man living on a park bench. In the choruses, the old man declares that he does not need love, and with some help, will get back on his feet. He does not want to hear people telling him about his misery, nor does he want pity, because he has seen things others will never see. In both statements of the bridge, the persona observes that we are seeing life through the eyes of this old man. Finally, although the song is full of harmonic variety, it is the simpler A–C chord alternations (I–♭III) in the bridge that accentuate the pathos of the song's main character.

Flowers in the Dirt was more than just McCartney's comeback album of the 1980s. Rather, it reflected a new level of pop music mastery that he would continue in albums of the 1990s and beyond. With a new self-confidence brought about by the success of *Flowers in the Dirt*, motivating him not to avoid his musical past with the Beatles, McCartney would soon reach a new level of artistry that would surpass the work he accomplished with his former group. Although he would still write and record pop songs in the 1990s, new artistic challenges in the forms of writing classical music, along with reuniting with former Beatles George Harrison and Ringo Starr in order to complete two unfinished songs by the late John Lennon, loomed over the horizon.

Classical Music, Beatles Reunion, and Musical Roots, 1991–99

The Liverpool Oratorio (1991)

In June 1989, the Royal Liverpool Philharmonic Orchestra decided to commission a work in order to commemorate its sesquicentennial in 1991.[1] Through the orchestra's guest conductor, Carl Davis, the Royal Liverpool Philharmonic Society invited McCartney to write an oratorio on a Liverpool theme, an invitation he accepted. McCartney, who had no musical training, would work with Davis, who did. The finished composition would be performed as the culmination of the orchestra's 150th anniversary celebrations.

McCartney always had an appetite for new musical experiences, and the commission from the Philharmonic Society provided a perfect opportunity to expand his musical horizons, building upon his excursions into orchestral and choral music in order to compose a substantive classical work. As a member of the Beatles, McCartney was exposed to classical music not only when he lived in the home of the parents of his girlfriend Jane Asher, but also by attending concerts in London and, more significantly, through his interactions with the Beatles' producer George Martin. "Yesterday," "Eleanor Rigby," and "Penny Lane" come to mind as prime examples of Martin encouraging McCartney to incorporate musical sounds into his songs that were normally associated with classical music.

When he first got together with Davis, McCartney jokingly said to him that they should compose a three-minute string quartet, have it performed during the orchestra's celebrations, say "Happy Birthday," and then call it quits. But this would not be the case: what emerged was a full-scale, eight-movement oratorio lasting over 90 minutes. McCartney thought he had proverbially bitten off more than he could chew. In any event, McCartney and Davis worked together from 1989 to 1991, spending literally hundreds of hours composing, orchestrating, and reorchestrating the work.[2]

In the liner notes (p. 7) to the CD recording, McCartney commented on his collaboration with Davis:

> I prefer to think of my approach to music as primitive, . . . rather like the primitive cave artists, who drew without training. Hopefully, the combination of Carl's classical training and my primitivism will result in a beautiful piece of music. That was always my intention.

After long, arduous work on the composition, McCartney completed, with Davis's help, his first classical work, the *Liverpool Oratorio*. McCartney composed the music (which Davis shaped, notated, and scored) and wrote the text. Written in the tradition of an English oratorio, the *Liverpool Oratorio* recounts, in some measure, the story of McCartney's life in Liverpool: (1) his birth during World War II, (2) his days as a student at the Liverpool Institute, (3) his parents, (4) his aspirations as a boy, (5) and meeting his wife, Linda Eastman. The Royal Liverpool Philharmonic Orchestra premiered the *Liverpool Oratorio* on 28 June 1991 at Liverpool's Anglican Cathedral, with Kiri Te Kanawa (soprano), Sally Burgess (mezzo-soprano), Jerry Hadley (tenor), Willard White (bass), and Jeremy Budd (boy treble) as vocal soloists. Carl Davis conducted the Choristers of Liverpool Cathedral and the Royal Liverpool Philharmonic Choir and Orchestra. The *Liverpool Oratorio* received its US premiere at Carnegie Hall, New York City, on 18 November 1991. After its world premiere, the *Liverpool Oratorio* became a staple with classical music audiences, receiving performances around the world.

The *Liverpool Oratorio* is scored for three flutes (II and III, piccolos), three oboes (III, English horn), three clarinets in B♭ and A (II, E♭ clarinet; III, bass clarinet), three bassoons (III, contrabassoon), four horns in F, three trumpets in B♭, two tenor trombones, bass trombone, tuba, timpani, percussion (three players playing a variety of instruments), harp, organ, and strings. The soprano sings the role of Mary Dee; the mezzo-soprano, Miss Inkley, the Chief Mourner, and Nurse; the tenor, Shanty; and bass, the Headmaster, Preacher, and Mr. Dingle. Complementing the vocal soloists are a boy treble, boys' choir, and four-part (soprano/alto/tenor/bass) chorus.

The eight movements of the *Liverpool Oratorio* are entitled (I) "War," (II) "School," (III) "Crypt," (IV) "Father," (V) "Wedding," (VI) "Work," (VII) "Crises," and (VIII) "Peace." In the first movement, "War," set in 1942, the oratorio's fictional hero, Shanty (tenor), is born amidst the chaos and confusion of a nighttime air raid during World War II. The music depicts that hellish night through dissonant chromaticism, in the form of oscillating figures and ascending scales. Then enters the oratorio's motto sung by the boy soprano, derived from McCartney's school, the Liverpool Institute: "Non nobis solum / Sed toti mundo nati," which means, "But for the whole world were we born." The intensity of the music subsides to prepare for Shanty's solo in which he narrates the story of his birth. The movement closes with the chorus singing a chorale in four parts, reflecting on Shanty's birth as an allegory for hope and peace.

The second movement, "School," advances the story line to 1953. Shanty is now 11 years old and in school, celebrating his upbringing in the city. He skips school with some of his classmates and ends up sleeping on a gravestone in the cemetery of Liverpool Cathedral. There, he has dreams of ghosts from the past and future, one of which is Mary Dee (soprano), his future bride. Shanty wakes up and is back in school. He is in Spanish class, taught by a Miss Inkley (mezzo-soprano), who, according to the Headmaster (bass), was in the war fighting with the troops. He informs the classroom full of boys that they may address Miss Inkley as "Sir."

In keeping with its setting at a school, the boys' choir features prominently in this movement. Both Shanty and the boy's choir celebrate Liverpool by singing how they were all born in the city, which, according to them, carries certain responsibilities. During the scene at the cemetery, the music is more lyrical and sedate, with Shanty singing what I would call the "Ghosts of the Past" theme (E–F♯–E–D–E), taken up by Mary Dee as a ghost. When Shanty is back at school in class, Miss Inkley teaches him and his classmates Spanish via a Latin-flavored song full of changing meters. The movement closes with the choirs singing the Liverpool Institute's motto in English, followed by the celebration-of-Liverpool theme heard at the movement's beginning.

"Crypt," the third movement, is set in 1959 where Shanty is a confused 17-year-old. He goes to a church dance in a crypt, where he doubts both his existence and God's. Mary Dee materializes as a half-ghost and informs him that his father has died (in real life, it was McCartney's mother Mary who died while he was a teenager). At the beginning of "Crypt," which opens with brass and bells to evoke the inside of a church, Shanty sings an expressive melody telling the story of his life in 1959. It is interrupted and accompanied at times by boisterous, Renaissance-like dance music. The Preacher (bass) enters the scene, declaring how church must be made fun in order to get people to worship God there. Mary Dee then appears, singing the "Ghosts of the Past Theme," although Shanty cannot see her. She delivers the bad news. The music changes dramatically to support the sorrow of Shanty's loss, both slowing down and gradually getting softer.

The fourth movement, "Father," continues the narrative of the preceding movement. The year is still 1959. Mourners arrive for the funeral of Shanty's father. Shanty is confused and upset at the death of his father. He thinks about their relationship, and realizing that fathers are not perfect and fully human, asks for forgiveness. After an instrumental introduction, the chorus and Chief

Mourner sing lines in alternation that commemorate the life of Shanty's father. Shanty then enters, singing about his confusion, ultimately realizing that his father was only human. The music builds in intensity, with loud outbursts of "Father" from the choir. After a statement of the Liverpool Institute's motto sung in Latin by the chorus, Shanty not only declares that he will forgive his father but also asks his father to forgive him. Next, comes a trumpet solo in honor of McCartney's father, who played that instrument until his teeth gave out. The music closes with the Chief Mourner and choir singing a theme about Shanty's father heard earlier in the movement.

The oratorio's fifth movement, "Wedding," is set a few years later, presumably in the early 1960s. Shanty meets Mary Dee as he muses on top of a double-decker bus. She helps him learn how to cope with his anxieties and eagerness to succeed. They declare their love for each other and pledge to marry. Given the subject matter of this movement, the music begins in a highly lyrical vein, with Shanty and Mary Dee engaging in a dialogue about their budding relationship. The music builds in emotion and power, culminating in the choir pronouncing a blessing upon the couple, followed by their singing of words from the Gloria of the Mass ("Hosanna, . . . Gloria in excelsis Deo") that celebrate the couple's love. The music concludes with Shanty and Mary Dee vowing to live together, bathed in God's holy light.

"Work," the next movement, focuses on the life of the married couple. Mary Dee is a successful executive in charge of a company staffed solely by women. She issues orders but her workers lapse into romantic fantasies about love. Shanty works in an office, but is not as successful as Mary Dee. He is coaxed by his officemates to play around. Indeed, Mr. Dingle (bass) tries to get Shanty to go to the pub, while at home, Mary Dee realizes that she is pregnant. At the beginning of the movement, the music establishes the frenetic pace of office life through fast repeated-note gestures in the orchestra. At Mary's office, a women's chorus representing Mary Dee's staff and Mary Dee engage in a rapid-fire dialogue, with Mary Dee singing numerous repeated notes, evoking an office by imitating the sound of an old-fashioned typewriter. The scene then shifts to Shanty's office. The music begins in a similar manner to that associated with Mary Dee's office, but features oscillating vocal figures when the characters sing. In trying to get Shanty to the pub, Mr. Dingle sings a playful, Gershwin-esque vocal solo that is capped off by Mary Dee's realization that she is pregnant.

"Crises" is the oratorio's climactic movement. Mary Dee and Shanty are at home and have an argument. She sings to her unborn child, worrying about its future. Shanty comes home slightly drunk, demanding dinner. After their argument about money and Shanty's poor self-image, Mary Dee leaves, telling Shanty she is pregnant. In her anger, she runs into the street and is hit by a car. At the hospital, the nurse asks Mary Dee, "Do you know who you are?" (there are allusions here to the death of John Lennon's mother Julia through the accident and Lennon's death through the nurse's question). Mary Dee fights for the life of her baby while ghosts attempt to steal it. At her bedside is Shanty, who vows to reform if only both Mary Dee and the baby are allowed to live. To capture the drama of this movement, the music goes through several key, meter, tempo, and textural changes.

The eighth movement, "Peace," resolves the conflicts that reached a boiling point in the seventh, conveying the McCartney-esque theme that through it all, only love remains and will make all problems disappear. Shanty sings to the child, marveling at the wonder of being. Next, the boy soprano and boy's choir come in with one last statement in Latin of the Liverpool Institute's motto. After that, and throughout the movement, the chorus joyfully pronounces the security found in God's eternal love. The Preacher then comments on the fragile nature of family life. Finally, the oratorio ends peacefully as Shanty and Mary Dee celebrate their love for each other and future with their child.

OFF THE GROUND (1993)

Off the Ground was McCartney's follow-up to his acclaimed album *Flowers in the Dirt* and his eighteenth solo effort, coming off the heels of his new band's world tour of 1989–90.[3] The album began in 1991, after work was completed on the *Liverpool Oratorio*. McCartney made a number of rough demos of recently completed songs by recording them onto a cassette tape player, thereby leaving the arrangement of the song up to the band. In the past, he created demos that were essentially sophisticated arrangements of his songs. Band members usually played what was on the demo. In *Off the Ground*, McCartney's band mates actually provided more input into the songs than what had been done in the past. Perhaps as a response to the criticism leveled at him in the press, McCartney sought the aid of his friend, the poet Adrian Mitchell, to help him improve the lyrics of the album's songs.

In *Off the Ground*, McCartney was opting for a harder sound than his previous albums of the 1980s. Furthermore, this was the first time he had recorded with a band since *Back to the Egg* in 1979. But unlike the last lineup of Wings, McCartney was very pleased with the band of McIntosh, Stuart, Wickens, Eastman, and Blair Cunningham (drums) that he had assembled for his 1989–90 world tour. Since the songs of *Off the Ground* were to be developed in a cooperative effort in the studio, recording the album's tracks resembled the Beatles' recording practices. After being acquainted with the song through rehearsal, the band essentially did a live take of the song, which was McCartney's goal, spontaneity over perfection, with overdubs kept to a minimum. McCartney enlisted the aid of Julian Mendelssohn to produce *Off the Ground*. Released in February 1993, the album did reasonably well in the charts, reaching No. 5 in the UK and No. 17 in the US.

Off the Ground opens with its title track. Interestingly, unlike the "live band takes" of the album's other songs, "Off the Ground" is a more manufactured number. With the help of keyboardist "Wix" Wickens, McCartney developed the song from an unfinished fragment, adding electric guitar, bass, and percussion, with McIntosh adding vocal harmonies and a solo guitar part later.[4] "Off the Ground" is a laid-back rocker in G major, with a lilting melody accompanied by diatonic chords. In the song's verses, the persona attempts to console the object of his affections, concluding in the refrain that they both need loving, and it will take little to get their relationship "off the ground." The chorus is a lighthearted takeoff (no pun intended) on the song's title.

"Looking for Changes" reflects McCartney's involvement with green politics. Both he and his wife Linda Eastman had been vegetarians since 1975. Eastman authored a successful series of vegetarian cookbooks, beginning in 1989 with *Linda McCartney's Home Cooking*, coauthored with Peter Cox. In 1991, she launched a successful line of deep-frozen vegetarian meals under the company name *Linda McCartney Foods.* In December of that year, PETA presented her with a lifetime achievement award for her promotion of vegetarianism and animal rights.[5] In 1995, both she and McCartney lent their voices to an episode of the television cartoon show *The Simpsons*, entitled "Lisa the Vegetarian." Both McCartney and Eastman became involved with environmental issues and animal rights. They were incensed when they saw pictures of animals being experimented upon, especially one with a cat having its brain hooked up to a machine.

Accordingly, "Looking for Changes" is a protest song. Its two verses recount the horrors of a cat and rabbit, respectively, undergoing experimentation in a lab. The song's two choruses are a plea to stop the cruelty by "looking for changes" in the way human beings treat their fellow creatures on Earth. Musically, the song is a dynamic rocker in C major, perhaps a way for McCartney to vent his anger. Verses exhibit basic chord changes, as C5 and F5 chords alternate. In the choruses, the chord changes become more varied, as the band plays C5–A5–B♭5–F5 and C5–A5–B♭5–G5 chord successions.

"Hope of Deliverance" is the standout song on the album, a massive hit in Europe, particularly in Germany (although it did poorly in the US). Considering the generally rougher sound of *Off the Ground*, it is a surprise to find this lightweight-sounding song included on the album. But the seemingly easy-going, folk qualities of the song betray a set of lyrics that are religious in tone. "Hope of Deliverance" features textual metaphors of light and darkness to describe the human condition, with the phrase "hope of deliverance" serving as the light that will liberate people from their ignorance or the "darkness that surrounds" them. The song is in the key of C major and progresses in a verse–chorus structure. In keeping with its folk-like sound, the song's chord changes are limited, restricted to C, Am, F, Dm, and Dm7 chords. The melody exhibits, however, more variety, especially in the verses, with short stepwise gestures complemented by a line that traces the notes of a Dm7.

McCartney and Elvis Costello cowrote the album's next track, "Mistress and Maid," a song supposedly inspired by a picture painted by Vermeer.[6]

"Mistress and Maid" focuses on a dying relationship from a woman's perspective. The protagonist concludes that her husband or boyfriend is no longer in love with her and fears that he will focus his attentions on other women. But after realizing that all she has become is his "mistress and maid," she no longer is afraid and will not tolerate the situation any more. McCartney and Costello provide the song with a sophisticated musical setting. "Mistress and Maid" is a waltz in a mixolydian-flavored G with cadences that suggest D minor and D major, as well as secondary dominant (B7, V7/vi) and mixture chords (Cm6, iv) that enhance the song's harmonic coloring. The melody exhibits a wide arc, with some chromatic notes derived from its harmonic support.

"I Owe It All To You" is a ballad McCartney penned for his wife, Linda Eastman. The song's lyrics juxtapose verses that have McCartney recounting exotic images, such as the interior of Egyptian temples, the songs of seabirds, glass cathedrals, golden canyons, and glistening lakes of holy water shining like diamonds in the light, with choruses that have him recognizing how much he owes his happiness to Eastman. "I Owe It All To You" vacillates between the keys of A minor and C major. After a rubato-style intro on the Mellotron, McCartney plays an acoustic guitar accompaniment (Am–G11/B–C–G11/B) that establishes the A-minor framework for the verses to come. Choruses move to the key of C major, with a Dm–G–C (ii–V–I) chordal succession ultimately defining that key. The outro suggests that the song will end in A minor due to the return of the verses' chord changes; instead, it ends in C major via a Cmaj7.

"Biker Like an Icon" is a song arising from McCartney's penchant for wordplay. He just liked how those words rolled off the tongue. He then took his 12-string guitar and wrote a rough version of the song.[7] The track as heard on the album was its first take, with lead guitarist Robbie Mcintosh cutting a hot solo. In keeping with his back-to-basics recording aesthetic in which he preferred emotion to slick production, McCartney was pleased with the song, thinking that laboring over it until it was "perfect" would have ruined it.

"Biker Like an Icon" is a rocker in a dorian-flavored E minor that proceeds, after an intro, through a series of three verse–verse–chorus sequences, followed by an outro. The song's verses tell the dark story of a girl who is obsessed with a biker and follows him across America. She finally catches up with him in Hollywood. After meeting her, the biker does not let her go and possibly takes advantage of her, suggesting that she either attached herself to him in an obsequious way or met an untimely demise. Her concerned family tries to find her but to no avail. The dorian aspect of the song comes from the alternation of Em7 and A chords in the verses. The key of E minor emerges in the choruses through B7–Em (V7–i) harmonic successions. Despite the sometimes weak lyrics, the song succeeds because of its hard-driving rock sound.

song's bridge, which follows choruses 2 and 3. The Beatle-like vocals are intensified by the move to C major's parallel minor via Fm–Gm–Cm chordal successions.

McCartney wrote the last track of *Off the Ground*, "Cosmically Conscious," in 1968 while in Rishikesh, India. It is a short fragment lasting 1:49. Despite its dated mantra of how being "cosmically conscious" is "such a joy," the song encapsulated McCartney's environmental ideas of the 1990s. It progresses intro(inst.)–chorus–verse–chorus and is centered in E major via the strategic placement of an E chord at the beginnings and endings of phrases. In the choruses ("C'mon, be cosmically conscious … "), the chord changes involve E–F♯–A–E harmonic successions. The verse ("Such a joy, … ") features a chromatic chord succession, E–F–F♯–F, that helps to underscore the text's expression of joy, as its ascending and descending harmonic movement supplies a trancelike backdrop to the syncopated melody sounding above.

THE BEATLES ANTHOLOGY (1995–97)

In an interview with James Henke in 1989, McCartney mentioned a documentary movie about the Beatles entitled *The Long and Winding Road* that he, George Harrison, and Ringo Starr were planning to release in order to set the record straight about their history as a band.[10] What eventually became *The Beatles Anthology* began in 1970. Neal Aspinall, former Beatles road manager, personal assistant, and head of Apple Corps, wanted to produce a documentary about the group called *The Long and Winding Road*.[11] The project floundered for a number of primarily business reasons during the 1970s and 1980s. However, in 1989, with many business disputes behind them, the surviving ex-Beatles decided to revive the project, which would include performances by them. In his interview with Henke, McCartney even talked about writing music with Harrison, noting that he and Harrison had "*never* written [any songs] together, which [was] a staggering fact."[12]

Things began to fall into place for the documentary in the 1990s. Apple Corps named Geoff Wonfor as director in 1991. McCartney, Harrison, and Starr met in London in October 1993 to sort out what new songs they would record for the documentary, now referred to as *The Beatles Anthology* (probably at Harrison's insistence, because the original title was "too McCartney"), which was to include a six-CD set of outtakes and 10 hours of video. Through Apple Corps, the surviving ex-Beatles contacted Yoko Ono, Lennon's widow, in order to see if Lennon had left any rough homemade demos that they could transform into songs. Ono gave them cassette tapes of four unfinished songs by Lennon: (1) "Free as a Bird," (2) "Real Love," (3) "Grow Old With Me," and (4) "Now and Then." They chose to finish "Free as a Bird" and "Real Love."

In Los Angeles, producer Jeff Lynne, formerly of the Electric Light Orchestra and co-producer of George Harrison's *Cloud Nine* album (1987) and the two albums by the Traveling Wilburys (1988, 1990), instructed engineer Marc Mann to clean up the two songs electronically. Lynne and the three ex-Beatles then worked on adding overdubs to "Free as a Bird" (along with a "middle eight" or bridge) in 1994, and "Real Love" in 1995, at McCartney's Hog Hill Studio located on his East Sussex farm. As they worked on the tracks, McCartney, Harrison, and Starr pretended that Lennon had instructed them to finish the numbers while he was away on vacation. "Free as a Bird" was released as part of the *Anthology I* CD-set in 1995, whereas "Real Love" as part of the *Anthology II* CD-set a year later. In finishing Lennon's songs and singing and playing with him electronically, the three ex-Beatles imitated similarly conceived recordings done by Natalie Cole and Hank Williams, Jr. In her recording of "Unforgettable" (1991), Natalie Cole used her father Nat's original recording to sing a duet with him. In his arrangement of "There's a Tear in My Beer" (1989) by his father, Hank Williams, Sr., Williams, Jr. cleaned up his father's song electronically and added overdubs, singing and playing, consequently, with the father he never knew.

Of the two demos by Lennon, "Free as a Bird" was the more unfinished recording. "Real Love" had complete music and lyrics, and the "Threetles" (McCartney, Harrison, and Starr) performed as Lennon's session players on the track. As for "Free as a Bird," it contained an incomplete bridge by Lennon that commenced with the words, "Whatever happened to the life that we once knew." McCartney and Harrison completed the text of the bridge, as well as its music. According to Walter Everett, McCartney and Harrison alluded to the Beatles' past in the text that they wrote, with veiled references to their early days in the 1950s and 1960s and the rift caused by their financial disputes of the 1970s and 1980s.[13] Aside from vocal and instrumental overdubs, McCartney's only other contribution as composer/arranger to "Free as a Bird" seems to be the inclusion of his signature cadential ending, F–G–A, ♭VI–♭VII–I, to the song's added coda, a progression stemming from his days as both a Beatle and solo artist.

FLAMING PIE (1997)

Following his work on the commercially successful and widely acclaimed *The Beatles Anthology*, and inspired by the numerous hours of listening to tapes of the Beatles, McCartney decided to work on another album in 1995. He had released little music since *Off the Ground* hit the record stores in 1993 due to a hectic schedule working on different projects. Besides the *Anthology*, McCartney worked on another large-scale classical piece, *Standing Stone*, a follow-up to the *Liverpool Oratorio*; helped open the Liverpool Institute for the Performing Arts; and completed his *Oobu Joobu* radio series for

Westwood One Radio.[14] To produce most of the forthcoming album, McCartney secured the services of producer Jeff Lynne.

McCartney wanted to have fun making this album and to not take it too seriously. But he no longer had a band with which to play. The group that he formed for *Flowers in the Dirt*, his world tours in the 1990s, and *Off the Ground* was defunct. Accordingly, he got together with friends to make what would become *Flaming Pie*, which was released in 1997. In addition to Lynne, McCartney worked with the likes of George Martin, Geoff Emerick, Steve Miller, Ringo Starr, Linda Eastman, and even his own son, James McCartney, who made his professional debut playing lead guitar on "Heaven on a Sunday."

Critical and commercial reaction to *Flaming Pie* was positive. For the most part, critics praised the album, regarding it as McCartney's most successful musical outing since *Tug of War* in 1982. *Flaming Pie* received a 1997 Grammy nomination for Album of the Year, losing out to Bob Dylan's *Time Out of Mind*. Critics recognized, moreover, that it was McCartney's most Beatles-influenced solo work. In fact, the album's title and title track derive from an article John Lennon wrote for *Mersey Beat* in 1961 about the origin of the Beatles' name. In a vision, Lennon saw a man coming unto them in a flaming pie. The man bestowed the name Beatles on them with an "A." The album flourished commercially, reaching No. 1 in the UK charts and No. 2 in the US.

"The Song We Were Singing" is a nostalgic look back to the 1960s in an attempt to find meaning in life in the 1990s. McCartney comments: "I was remembering the sixties, sitting around late at night, dossing, smoking, drinking wine, hanging out. We were taking a sip, seeing the world through a glass, talking about the cosmic solution. It's that time in your life when you get a chance for all that."[15] Written in 1995 while McCartney was in Jamaica, "The Song We Were Singing" developed into a soaring folk ballad under McCartney and co-producer Lynne's work in the recording studio.

The song is in D major and alternates verse and chorus. In the verses, McCartney sings in a fast but understated way, talking about sitting down, smoking a pipe, sipping wine, and discussing a whole range of subjects in order to come up with the "cosmic solution." He accompanies his melodic line with a chord succession that ascends and descends stepwise, D–Em–F♯m–Em–D. The choruses are rousing in character, as McCartney sings in a more boisterous manner, recalling a song that was somehow meaningful, and provided answers to life's questions. Like the verses, the chord changes of the chorus involve three sonorities, Cadd9, G/B, and D, although here they provide a mixolydian flavor to the song.

McCartney wrote "The World Tonight" while vacationing in the US in 1995. Although the song was rather understated in its initial stages, it eventually developed into an aggressive rocker through Linda Eastman encouraging her husband to play "some real electric guitar" on the track.[16] The song also includes a line reminiscent of one found in McCartney's Beatle song, "Hey Jude": "The movement you need is on your shoulder." When asked for his opinion about the line by McCartney in 1968, Lennon insisted that he retain it in the song, which he considered as McCartney's masterpiece. Remembering that exchange, McCartney commented that if Lennon were alive and writing songs with him in the 1990s, he would have insisted that McCartney keep the line "I go back so far, I'm in front of me" in the chorus of "The World Tonight."[17]

In this song, the protagonist tells the story of a presumably famous person who is uncomfortable with his or her life. Through metaphors of discernment (seeing the world tonight and looking into the future), the choruses suggest that the protagonist not only is aware of the person's situation but also can predict what direction his or her life will take in the future. The song's unusual musical setting intensifies this message of alienation and angst through an energetic, guitar-oriented sound cast within an A-dorian framework. In its verses, "The World Tonight" features a melody composed primarily of chordal notes decorated by upper neighbors, supported by Am, C, and D chords that suggest the dorian mode. Both parts of the chorus continue the song's dorian framework, as melody and harmony avoid melodic G♯s or E-based chords that would signal the key of A minor.

McCartney originally composed "If You Wanna" in Minneapolis during his New World Tour in 1993, and supposedly was inspired by Prince to write the song.[18] However, "If You Wanna" does not sound like Prince at all; rather, it is closer to a country-rock song in the style of the Traveling Wilburys. Steve Miller joined McCartney to record the song. McCartney sang lead vocal and played drums, bass, electric guitar, and 12-string acoustic guitar, while Miller sang backup vocals and played electric piano and electric guitar.

"If You Wanna" centers on the rock topics of love and cars, with traveling on the road used as a metaphor for committing to a relationship. The verses describe the song's protagonist informing the woman he loves that if she cares for him, she will take a ride with him in his Cadillac. The choruses reflect the protagonist's determination to arrange the trip if she is ready. The bridge has the protagonist expressing his feelings of love, telling the woman that if she really cares for him, she will go on this trip.

The song vacillates between E aeolian in its verses and E dorian in its choruses, giving "If You Wanna" a hint of melancholy. Both verse and chorus share the track's prominent Em–D guitar strumming, used first in the intro and then throughout the track as an instrumental link, and finally in the outro. However, the verse includes C and Am chords, which cannot be derived from an E-dorian scale. Conversely, the chorus includes an A chord, which cannot be derived from an E-aeolian scale. Perhaps as a way to reinforce the protagonist's optimism about love, the bridge is brighter in sound, suggesting the key of G major through its D–G chordal successions. But the bridge returns to a darker harmonic quality with its B7–Em cadence, preparing for another cycle of modally based sections. Finally, excellent lead guitar playing enhances the country-rock sound of "If You Wanna," most notably by a solo over the verse's chordal changes and during the outro.

McCartney composed "Somedays" while accompanying his wife Linda Eastman to a photo session in Kent.[19] According to McCartney, while Eastman was busy for two hours, he decided to write a song in that time, an arbitrary deadline that both he and Lennon would impose on themselves when they wrote songs as Beatles. In any event, McCartney wrote this tender, personal ballad for Eastman, expressing the depth of his love for her. "Somedays" is another modally based song, this time in B–aeolian. Its instrumentation includes McCartney playing acoustic guitar, Spanish guitar, and bass, and an orchestra playing an accompaniment scored by George Martin.

The verses depict McCartney's love for Eastman through a series of poignant images, such as it being hard for him to believe that she loves him, or his fond memories of how young they once were through a picture on the wall. Since the song contains no chorus, its bridge serves as the only emotional foil to the atmosphere conveyed by the verses. The bridge projects McCartney's serene confidence that he and Eastman require no one to tell them what true love is. The modal setting of the song intensifies the touching emotions expressed by the verses. The bridge—and its optimistic message—are brightened by a move to the key of D major.

McCartney wrote "Young Boy" on 18 August 1994 while Eastman was cooking a lunch for a feature in the *New York Times*.[20] The song's theme explores the angst experienced by all young men and women who are looking for that special someone in their lives. McCartney recorded "Young Boy" at Steve Miller's studio in Sun Valley, Idaho. On the track, McCartney sang lead vocal and played guitar, bass, drums, and Hammond organ, while Miller sang backing vocals and played lead guitar. Set in the key of C major, "Young Boy" sounds remarkably like George Harrison through its use of melody, harmony, and texture. The verses are dominated by a series of short, repeated-note gestures, whereas the chorus includes more angular and expansive melodic ideas. The harmonic setting consists of diatonic chords, which is in keeping with the song's folk-rock style. The texture, especially the melody and the way in which McCartney strums the acoustic guitar accompaniment, is the decisive factor for Harrison's influence on the song.

"Calico Skies" (along with "Great Day") was not recorded during the *Flaming Pie* sessions of 1995–96 but in February 1992 at McCartney's 48-track Hog Hill Studio in East Sussex.[21] McCartney wrote the song in Long Island while housebound during Hurricane Bob's rampage. With "Calico Skies," he wanted to compose an acoustic-guitar song reminiscent of "Blackbird." And like "Blackbird," it has a social message. Although the lyrics initially point to a love song, that gives way in the third verse to an antiwar message. "Calico Skies" sounds in D♭ major, but McCartney most likely plays the song in D major with the guitar tuned down a half step. The song is simple in structure, with instrumental sections punctuating verse–chorus pairs: intro (guitar)–verse–chorus–link(guitar)–verse–chorus–link(guitar)–verse–chorus–link(guitar). McCartney sings and accompanies himself on the acoustic guitar. The harmonic vocabulary is limited to variations of four basic chords, D, G, A, and Bm. Overall, "Calico Skies" can hold its own and more with "Blackbird."

"Flaming Pie" is a rocker in A major, and given its origins in Lennon's article for *Mersey Beat* in 1961, is replete with witty, surrealistic, perhaps Lennon-esque images in its text. In the refrain to each verse, the persona identifies himself as the "man on the flaming pie." He narrates an improbable story redolent of the imagery found in the Beatle animated film *Yellow Submarine* (1968), although more sarcastic and edgier in tone. The "man on the flaming pie" mentions making love underneath a bed, sticking his tongue out to lick his nose, taking his brains out and stretching them on a rack, and cutting off his toes to spite his feet.

Both melody and harmonic setting accord with the driving rock style in "Flaming Pie." Indeed, the verses feature an A5–A6 guitar riff that shifts to G5, D5, and C5 chords before returning to the riff to conclude each verse. The bridge includes a secondary dominant of E (V/V), B,[22] moving to its intended chord, which in turn progresses to A, D, and E chords that accompany the conclusion of the vocal line. The melody drops out à la stop time so that instruments sound the retransitional dominant on E. Finally, McCartney plays a piano lick suggestive of the keyboard style of "Lady Madonna" during the song's instrumental link and outro, adding a further Beatles connection to the song.

McCartney composed "Heaven on a Sunday" while out sailing during a vacation in the US. For him, sailing was a relaxing experience, and during such times, he would write peaceful and tranquil songs.[23] Recorded on 16 September 1996, "Heaven on a Sunday" became a family affair, with wife Linda Eastman and son James contributing backup vocals and an electric guitar solo, respectively. In order to convey the intense peacefulness he felt while sailing, McCartney came up with the metaphor of "Heaven on a Sunday" for the song. The imagery of the title likens existence in heaven, which has traditionally been considered as the most blissful, peaceful place imaginable, to busy life on earth. If heaven, like earth, were busy Monday through Saturday, how much more peaceful could it be on a Sunday when, like life on earth, everything rested?

While the lyrics of "Heaven on a Sunday" allude to the intense peace felt by the song's protagonist, especially as he proclaims that given the choice of one love, he would choose that of his woman, something is awry. He observes that what the two of them call love may be a dream, and that their relationship ("learning a song") may not be a fulfilling experience ("a long and lonely blues"). "Heaven on a Sunday" is in the key of A minor. In keeping with the peaceful aura of the song, McCartney delivers a soft, laid-back vocal, accompanied by diatonic chords, although he distinguishes the chorus ("If I only had one love") from verse harmonically by using a chromatic Gm9 chord at its beginning.

McCartney and Steve Miller cowrote the Texas blues number "Used to Be Bad." Recorded on 5 May 1995 at Hog Hill Studios, the song developed from a jam session where Miller played numerous blues riffs on the guitar and McCartney played drums.[24] After they completed the lyrics, McCartney and Miller sang alternate lines of the vocal into one mike, completing the song in one take, in order to project a more personal and spontaneous feel to the song. "Used to Be Bad" is in the key of E major and uses a 12-bar blues progression involving I7–IV7–V7 chords, although McCartney and Miller insert a G7 chord before the concluding E7 (B7–A7–G7–E7 [V7–IV7–♭III7–I7]). This Texas blues number is outstanding, with terrific vocals and tasty guitar solos delivered by Miller.

McCartney composed and cut a demo of "Souvenir" while on vacation in Jamaica. When he decided to include it on *Flaming Pie*, he told co-producer Jeff Lynne that they should retain the flavor of the demo.[25] Recording commenced on 19 February 1996 with McCartney singing lead and backup vocals as well as playing a variety of instruments, including drums. He was assisted by Lynne and a horn section composed of Kevin Robinson, Chris Davis, and Dave Bishop that attempted to recreate the soul sound of the Memphis-based Stax Recording Studios of the 1960s. "Souvenir" sounds in the key of G♭ major but is probably played in G major on the guitar with the instrument tuned down a half step. It is in 3/4 time and cast in a verse–chorus–bridge structure. The song's lyrics cover familiar ground regarding the pain associated with broken relationships and how to overcome that pain through the promise of love. The melody has a wide range, spanning a low E♭ to high A♭. The chord changes are slow and deliberate, with one chord for every one or two bars.

Upon hearing the news of Maureen Starkey's death, McCartney turned to music for therapy by composing "Little Willow." Starkey, first wife of Ringo Starr, was a good friend of both McCartney and Eastman. McCartney felt the loss deeply and wrote "Little Willow" with Starkey's children in mind. He used the metaphor of a little willow tree to symbolize Starkey's children, their love for their mother, and their healing through the passage of time. As symbolized by a hard and cold wind blowing against a willow tree, McCartney alludes to life's difficulties that often come without warning. But just as a willow tree bends with the wind and does not break, love remains strong and unshakable. Later in the song, McCartney speaks about the little willow tree sleeping, attaining peace, healing, and growing to the heavens, words meant to console Starkey's children in their grief.

Cast in D major, "Little Willow" is a poignant and tender ballad, with McCartney singing a gentle and graceful melody, accompanying himself initially on the acoustic guitar. As the song develops, both McCartney and co-producer Lynne add more vocal and instrumental parts. The harmonic language involves D, D7, Em/D, Em/A, G, A, and A7sus4 chords, with the number's characteristic accompaniment alternating D and Em/D or Em/A chords. Finally, McCartney created a moving video of the song, a story about how a mother and her two children are still linked by love, despite the mother's death.[26]

After the "Threetles" finished recording "Free as a Bird" and "Real Love," McCartney invited Starr to drum on a few tracks for a new album that he was recording. Two of the tracks, "Really Love You" and "Beautiful Night," were included on *Flaming Pie*. Officially, McCartney and Starr cowrote "Really Love You," but Starr was surprised by the songwriting credit, because the song emerged from a jam session.[27] In any event, this three-chord rocker in E major comes off as a disjointed instrumental number with meaningless blues lyrics dealing with the pains of love added by McCartney on the spot. The melody lacks coherence, sounding over long stretches of an E7 chord that moves to A7 and B7 chords at each verse's end. In the final analysis, "Really Love You" cannot match "Used to Be Bad" in musical quality.

McCartney wrote "Beautiful Night" in the 1980s and recorded it in New York in 1986 with producer Phil Ramone.[28] Thinking it a good song but unhappy with the recording, McCartney shelved "Beautiful Night" for 10 years. When he and Ringo Starr decided to record again after their work on *The Beatles Anthology*, McCartney took the song off the proverbial shelf, revised the lyrics, and added a fast coda, in anticipation of recording it with Starr. When he and Starr got together in 1996, they recorded a basic track of the song, with McCartney singing lead vocal and playing piano and Starr playing drums. Nine months later, George Martin scored an orchestral accompaniment to the song that McCartney used. After the song was finished, it was not only included as a track on *Flaming Pie* but also released as the third single from the album. Both McCartney and critics agreed that the finished song sounded quite "Beatley." McCartney conceded that while he did not begin "Beautiful Night" with a Beatle sound in mind, he did not try to avoid it, an admission that he had finally come to terms with his musical past.

"Beautiful Night" is a song that is symphonic in scope. Set in A major, it begins as a lyrical ballad, with an expressive melody that soars over a colorful harmonic accompaniment. Its formal frame is simple, proceeding verse–verse–chorus–verse–bridge–chorus–coda. The first two verses describe the plight of the song's protagonist. For a variety of reasons, he is alone and asks why. The melody features some quick meter changes from 4/4 to 2/4 and back again near the end of each verse. In the harmonic setting, mixture chords, Fmaj7 and F6 (♭VI), accentuate the protagonist's question by sounding immediately before it is asked. The chorus has the protagonist pleading with the woman he loves to make the night beautiful for him, for it is a night for lovers. The melody consists of four gestures that descend by step, beginning with a high A and ending with an E. The harmonic support features mixture chords that accompany the first three gestures, Dm7, C, and Dm7 (iv7, ♭III, iv7), with the dominant harmony E accompanying the last gesture. At this point in the song, the orchestra joins the musical texture, becoming more prominent as the song develops.

As "Beautiful Night" progresses, the protagonist becomes more adamant in his pleas to his lover, asking her to join him this night. The musical setting matches the lyrics' growing intensity. In the song's bridge, the protagonist argues with his lover that no matter how things may turn out, he should be with her. At this point, both vocal line and musical accompaniment become bolder, with strings initially supporting the vocal line with vigorous repeated chords, followed by additional orchestral punctuations as the vocal line ends. The last chorus is the most intense of all, as McCartney sings the vocal line to a full-orchestral accompaniment. The music then segues into the song's added coda, a fast, upbeat, rocking affair in which Starr joins in on the vocals. At the end of the song, Starr acts the part of a doorman, throwing people out, which for McCartney was a "Beatley" thing to do.

"Great Day" dates from the early 1970s. McCartney resurrected the song because he wanted to include a short track on *Flaming Pie*. On the recording, he sings lead vocal and plays acoustic guitar and percussion, along with providing leg slaps, while Linda Eastman joins him on backing vocals. "Great Day" is a song of celebration in which the singer encourages everyone to embrace the day. It consists of one verse that is repeated at the song's end, interspersed with two statements of a chorus and an instrumental rendition of the verse. Although in the key of E major, McCartney shows off his harmonic ingenuity yet again by playing a mixture-driven Em7/D–Edim/D(a common-tone diminished seventh chord)–Am/D–E (i7–ct°7–iv–I) chordal succession, sounding over a pedal point on D, to accompany his vocal line in the verses.

Standing Stone (1997)

After completing the *Liverpool Oratorio*, and amidst his busy schedule of recording pop albums and working on *The Beatles Anthology*, McCartney found time to compose the first of a projected series of pieces for piano. Completed in 1994, "A Leaf" features seven linked movements that span a variety of moods. As with the *Liverpool Oratorio*, McCartney received help in realizing the piece, both from the standpoints of structure and notation, from John Fraser. Anya Alexeyev, a Russian pianist who was studying at the Royal College of Music at the time, premiered the piece on 23 March 1995 at Saint James Palace, London, in the presence of Prince Charles.

McCartney was happy with what he had accomplished with the *Liverpool Oratorio*, though he regarded it as a stretch for him as a composer.[29] As a result, he was looking for an opportunity to write another large-scale classical work. In 1993, Richard Lyttelton, EMI Classics president, presented such an opportunity by commissioning McCartney to write a symphonic piece to celebrate EMI's centenary year in 1997. McCartney accepted the commission. What he eventually composed, without the assistance of a full-time collaborator, was a four-movement symphonic poem entitled *Standing Stone* that dealt with the origins and meaning of life. The score required, moreover, a large orchestra with percussion and large chorus. In the final analysis, though he received assistance in notation and scoring, *Standing Stone* was truly McCartney's piece, not one compiled by others from several tunes he may have played on the piano or whistled to them.

The tragic death of McCartney's close friend Ivan Vaughan from Parkinson's Disease was the original inspiration behind *Standing Stone*. Vaughan had introduced McCartney to John Lennon at the village fête at Saint Peter's Church in Woolton on 6 July 1957. McCartney expressed his feelings about Vaughan's death through poetry, which was to become part of the epic poem he wrote to help him structure *Standing Stone*. McCartney used that poem as a framework for composing strongly contrasting themes as well as conveying a sense of coherence by their use. He did this because he did not know how to develop a theme properly throughout a symphonic movement. Derived from his research into the ancient world, especially that of Celtic legends, McCartney's poem focused on the origins of man and his development through time, along with perennial questions regarding the purpose of life. Since he had been painting for a few years, McCartney made pictures in order to help him visualize and further focus the work.

McCartney's approach to composing *Standing Stone* differed from that used in the *Liverpool Oratorio*. He did not spend hundreds of hours working with a collaborator writing the music for the piece. Instead, he composed and realized *Standing Stone* in different stages. First, he began composing source material for the work on the piano, recording these ideas on cassette tapes for jazz musician Steve Lodder to transcribe into musical notation. Second, McCartney used an Apple computer hooked up to a synthesizer keyboard to translate what he played onto musical staves. Next, he enlisted the aid of David Matthews to correct his computer-notated score in order to put the music into a more readable form. Finally, McCartney secured the services of composer and saxophonist John Harle as a "structural engineer" to give him further advice about how to shape the piece's architecture, and composer Richard Rodney Bennett to supervise the orchestration.

Standing Stone focuses on the history of life on earth as reflected by the ancient standing stones of the Celtic people. It tells the story of an ancient man who sails on a crystal ship to a distant land where the inhabitants welcome him. While there, he helps them fight off invaders and falls in love with a shepherd's daughter. Ultimately, the poem's message is about love, a central theme in McCartney's work as a musician. The London Symphony Orchestra and Chorus, under the baton of Lawrence Foster, premiered *Standing Stone*

Kahne playing or manipulating a sequence of string-like sounds on a synthesizer and Laboriel playing drums.

"Your Way" hearkens back to the sound of McCartney's first two albums of the 1970s. It is a country rock song reminiscent of "Heart of the Country" from *Ram*, and probably written for Linda Eastman. "Your Way" is in the key of D major and, for the most part, is limited to D, Em7, G, and A chords. It begins with an extended instrumental intro. The song's verses recount how Eastman gave McCartney love her way, which was what he wanted. Although the bridge switches to the present tense, the person referred to is most likely Eastman, because after almost 30 years of marriage the presence of a person in someone's mind cannot be erased overnight. Finally, the chords of the outro—D, Em7, G/D, and A/D are given a piquant touch through the addition of the mixture chord F/D following the D chord.

McCartney and his son James cowrote "Spinning on an Axis." The song originated in New Hampshire as father and son were watching the sunset.[5] They felt that the sun was not moving away from them but they away from it. McCartney and his son recorded a demo of the song, which McCartney later developed, expanding the lyrics to encompass notions of cyclical change as reflected by the sun's movements. "Spinning on an Axis" is in a contextually established F major and consists of an active, chattering-like melody accompanied by slowly moving chords. A rather ominous-sounding guitar riff, F–Ab, F–A, placed at the ends of verses and choruses, serves as a unifying musical element. Besides its recurrence, the riff's notes invade the vocal line, as part of the melody is derived from that figure. Although this was not the first song they wrote together, father and son's "Spinning on an Axis" is the first one to appear on a McCartney album.

McCartney composed "About You" for Heather Mills, thanking her for helping him get over his grief regarding the death of his first wife, Linda Eastman. This song of appreciation, however, is not a ballad, as one would expect given the topic, but a rocker with a loud guitar accompaniment. Moreover, it is not in a major key, which might better serve as a framework for a song of gratitude, but in minor, B to be specific. The song is cast in a verse/refrain–chorus–bridge form with intro and outro. In the verses, McCartney recounts the ways in which Mills has helped him move on with his life. The choruses reiterate the refrain, "about you."

McCartney composed the song, "Heather," with the new love of his life in mind.[6] One morning, Heather Mills heard McCartney improvising on the piano. Thinking his improvisation to be a Beatle song, Mills inquired as to the music's title. McCartney informed her that he was making up a song on the piano. Mills became excited and recorded McCartney working on the song, which later developed into "Heather." The song is in E major and opens with an instrumental that outlines the track's musical themes and harmonic accompaniment. The piano sounds an E-major arpeggio followed by chordal riffs, all derived from an E–Esus4–E–Esus4–E–C♯m–E/B–F♯/

A♯–A6–Bsus4–B harmonic accompaniment. Next, the music moves to a section composed primarily of E, A, and B chords before culminating with the same two chords that closed the first section, Bsus4, B. The music of the instrumental is then repeated twice, first with the addition of wordless vocal harmonies, and then with McCartney, using the themes already articulated in the song, singing carefree words about going to the moon and dancing with Heather, the queen of his heart.

"Back in the Sunshine Again" is another song by McCartney and his son James. McCartney composed the song in 1997 in Arizona while his wife Linda Eastman was battling cancer. James McCartney assisted with the song's riff and bridge.[7] "Back in the Sunshine Again" reflects, on the one hand, McCartney's anguish with Eastman's death and, on the other, his resolve to push ahead, however optimistically, with his life. It is a bluesy song set in A aeolian for its verses, choruses, and extended outro, giving the track a sense of despair that it never quite shakes off. These sections sound only three chords, Am7, Dm7, and Em7. Relief is found in the bridge, with relatively brighter harmonic sounds composed of B♭, Dm, and G chords coming to the forefront before the music cadences on the retransitional dominant Em7.

"Your Loving Flame" is another romantic ballad by McCartney inspired by the woman in his life, which in the past was Eastman, but by 2001, was Mills. McCartney performed a formative version of the song with him on piano and David Gilmour on guitar on 3 December 1999 on the *Michael Parkinson Show*.[8] He continued to refine the song, recording it for inclusion on *Driving Rain* on 19 June 2001. As John Blaney has noted, in this song, along with others on *Driving Rain*, McCartney was at an emotional crossroads in his life with respect to his relationship with Heather Mills.[9] Was she the right woman for him? (As we know from hindsight in 2010, no.) Blaney rightly compares "Your Loving Flame" with "Maybe I'm Amazed," as both come at pivotal emotional moments in McCartney's life.

"Your Loving Flame" sounds in the key of E♭ major but is probably played on the guitar in D major with a capo on the first fret. The verses describe how McCartney wants to become closer to Mills, whereas the bridge has him concluding that a life without her would be an unhappy one. The melody is yet another example of McCartney's inventiveness with highly varied, melodious gestures that seem to progress effortlessly and smoothly from one to another. Although the song's harmonic changes primarily involve chords diatonic to E♭ major, the bridge offers a more luminous harmonic quality each time it appears through a hint of the subdominant A♭ via a colorful E♭7–A♭7/E♭–E♭7–A♭7/E♭–D♭maj7–E♭6–A♭–A♭sus4–A♭ chordal succession.

Although "Riding into Jaipur" may recount a trip that McCartney and Mills may have taken to India in January 2001, and its melody may have originated while McCartney was vacationing with Eastman in the Maldives,[10] the song has to be a homage to George Harrison and the Indian music he composed while a Beatle, such as "Love You Too" (1966), "Within You, Without

You" (1967), and "The Inner Light" (1968). Set in D major, the song features Indian-like timbres, with numerous melodic figures sounding over a sustained tonic harmony on D. Later in the song, in a mantra-like fashion, McCartney sings about how he is riding to Jaipur with Mills, first individually then in thirds with himself via doubletracking.

"Rinse the Raindrops" began as poetry that was later put to music. With its minimalist haiku-like lyrics, and at 10:13 in length, it stands out as *Driving Rain*'s most avant-garde track. The song emerged from a 30-minute jam session. Producer David Kahne, who mixed and edited the resulting takes in order to put the album's 10-minute cut together, remarked that "Rinse the Raindrops" is:

> just one verse repeated over and over, but [McCartney] never sings it the same way twice, ... The song goes through different cuts back and forth between different takes. It's a very aggressive, pushy song where [McCartney] sings real low then real high—all over the place.[11]

"Rinse the Raindrops" is a multisectional track in D minor. It begins with an aggressive vamp that is followed by a strange instrumental passage, with chords sounding like they were borrowed from twentieth-century classical composers who did not use diatonic scales from which to construct their chords. After that point, the vocal comes in, followed by a series of different sections that assume assorted musical guises. The song's effect, in the final analysis, can be likened to that of a mind-altering trance.

McCartney wrote "Freedom" as a response to the terrorist attacks at the World Trade Center on 11 September 2001. The song speaks about the right to live in freedom against anyone who would want to take that right away. McCartney sang "Freedom" at the Concert for New York City on 20 October 2001. At Quad Studios, Eric Clapton enhanced the resulting live recording of McCartney's performance with guitar overdubs. McCartney then added "Freedom" as a bonus track to *Driving Rain*. With its impassioned plea to live in a world where people are free, catchy tune, and simple, repetitive chorus, "Freedom" would have made John Lennon smile.

CHAOS AND CREATION IN THE BACKYARD (2005)

Chaos and Creation in the Backyard is clearly McCartney's best album of the first decade of the twenty-first century. Coming off the heels of *Flaming Pie*, *Run Devil Run*, and *Driving Rain*, the album reflects his creative renaissance. *Chaos and Creation in the Backyard* could also be called *McCartney III*, for just like *McCartney* in 1970 and *McCartney II* in 1980, McCartney played almost all of the instruments on each track. The album is unusually personal and reflective, a welcome change from past albums and one that garnered it three Grammy nominations—one for Album of the Year. *Chaos and Creation in the Backyard* was the last album McCartney recorded for EMI, for in March 2007, he signed a deal with Starbucks' Hear Music.

After calling up George Martin for advice about whom to get to produce *Chaos and Creation in the Backyard*, McCartney went with Nigel Godrich, who had worked most notably with Radiohead, as well as Beck, R.E.M., Travis, and U2.[12] From the start, Godrich insisted that McCartney make an album that was "him." He challenged McCartney, refusing to let him record songs that he, Godrich, thought inferior, which led to McCartney ultimately respecting the young producer for his blunt appraisals of his work. Although there are some fine musicians who play on the album, McCartney played most of the instruments at Godrich's behest.

"Fine Line" opens *Chaos and Creation in the Backyard*, an upbeat, piano-dominated song in A major. McCartney plays nearly all the instruments on the track, with strings performed by the Millennia Ensemble. The lyrics are all about choices made in life, and whether if one is reckless or courageous, chooses chaos over creation, one should strive to be honest and true to oneself. "Fine Line" begins with an intro composed of a dynamic piano riff that has a long descending arc. The verses that follow feature a melody peppered with flatted thirds, a blues note, over a chordal accompaniment consisting of A, D, D7, Bm, and Esus4 chords. An instrumental passage based on A/F, A/F♯, and A/G chords connects the Esus4 chord of the verse with the A chord of the chorus via a near-chromatic bass line (E–F–F♯–G–A). This passage is used, more importantly, throughout the song as an instrumental refrain. Over the simple alternation of A and F♯m chords, the chorus exhorts one to reflect on the important aspects of life and pursue them with integrity. The instrumental refrain returns as an outro with McCartney singing "It's a fine line" several times to conclude the song.

"How Kind of You" finds McCartney singing all the vocals and playing all the instruments on the track, even a flugelhorn, with loops contributed by him and Godrich. The song gradually developed from just another pop number in A major to a richly textured composition, with drones and loops contributing to its dreamy tone. McCartney generated the lyrics from the quaint mannerisms of his posh British friends who, instead of saying something like, "thanks a lot," would say, "how kind of you." However, the song became quite personal, as McCartney addressed his thoughts to someone, possibly his late wife Linda Eastman, who cared for him deeply enough to rescue him from troubling situations.

The song's dreamy atmosphere is conveyed from the start in the verses through an E pedal point that lends a static quality to the harmonies sounding above. The last part of the verse is repeated and concludes in A major, after which the music moves to the parallel minor for an instrumental interlude that provides needed tonal/harmonic contrast. Indeed, this move to A minor is foreshadowed in the chord progressions of the verses where E6 chords alternate with Em. "How Kind of You" ends with an extended instrumental coda, with Fmaj7#11 chords alternating with ones on E before concluding on the tonic harmony A.

Because he loves to play acoustic guitar, McCartney took the guitar part of his famous song "Blackbird" from the *White Album* (1968), which is based on Bach's Bourée in E minor for lute, to generate that of "Jenny Wren." As a result, both songs feature similar two-part, finger-picking styles. More significantly, each song tells the story of a woman, who despite a distinct perspective (the woman in "Blackbird" is African American but in "Jenny Wren" she is British), has to deal with injustice. Although the title of the song bears the same namesake as the character found in Charles Dickens's *Our Mutual Friend*, "Jenny Wren" is a fictional person who, through McCartney's lyrics, sees the world realistically due to some emotional pain she experienced. The verses describe the character of Jenny, a happy-go-lucky girl whose heart was apparently broken by witnessing the injustice of poverty ("She saw poverty breaking up home"). Nevertheless, Jenny overcomes her hurt and sees the world as it is. She will regain her happiness ("sing again") once the world abandons its foolish ways. The chorus comments on Jenny's outlook on life, asking why people cast love aside, losing sight of life in the process.

While the song sounds in B♭ major, McCartney plays it in A major via a capo on the first fret. Diatonic chords support the vocal line of the verses that tell the story of Jenny, though with one creative twist at the end, a cadence on the mixture chord A minor, here serving as tonic harmony. This flirtation with the parallel minor is taken to the next level in the song's chorus, which is cast in the key of A minor, highlighting the persona's thoughts about Jenny's views on life. Finally, Pedro Eustache plays the duduk, an Armenian double-reed instrument, throughout the song, giving it an exotic, though melancholy flavor.

"At the Mercy" began life as an improvisation on the piano where McCartney found a chord progression and melody he liked that he eventually developed into a song about life's unexpected turns and humankind's ability to deal with them.[13] While the song is in D major, its opening chorus disorients any would-be listener due to its unorthodox sequence of chords (C7–Daug–D–D(♭5)–Bm/D–Em–Edim–Daug–D–D(♭5)–G7/D–D) and attendant chromatic melody. Things are also unorthodox harmonically in the verses, though in the instrumental interlude that separates chorus from bridge, things do settle down a bit. Overall, this song about humankind's stoic acceptance of life's vicissitudes is one of McCartney's most progressive songs from the standpoint of harmony.

McCartney has maintained that when you are composing songs, you can pretend to be someone else in order to motivate your writing. Just as he thought he was Ray Charles when writing "The Long and Winding Road" in 1969, McCartney imagined himself to be George Harrison when writing "Friends to Go." As he puts it, when he wrote the song, the feeling of

Harrison came over him, making him think that "George could've written this." The song's lyrics are ambiguous, which is frequently McCartney's intention when he writes songs. He did mention, however, while being interviewed for the documentary on the making of *Chaos and Creation in the Backyard*, that the lyrics may be related to him imagining that he was near some housing estate in the UK, where people lived in a block of flats. In that scenario, he was waiting on the other side for people to go so that he could move in. "Friends to Go" is in the key of E major and features a vocal line accompanied by a Harrison-like acoustic guitar part. Both chorus and bridge include mixture chords, both a McCartney and Beatles harmonic trademark.

"English Tea" sounds like it could have been one of McCartney's Beatle songs from the late 1960s. It is a humorous number that celebrates the English language as spoken by the British, and their love of tea, gardens, and croquet. Set in G major, the song begins with an intro played by a string quartet. Then McCartney enters with his "Beatley" vocal, accompanying himself on the piano. Through the song's verses and bridges, McCartney depicts English life through a series of often-pastoral images, even working in the word, "peradventure."

"Too Much Rain" was inspired by Charlie Chaplin's song, "Smile," and as McCartney has noted, is deeply indebted to Chaplin's work. The song has a positive, uplifting message, geared to anyone with unbearable burdens in their lives, encouraging one, in the final analysis, to persevere. After a piano-dominated intro, the verses encourage everyone to keep their proverbial chins up despite life's problems. Choruses 1–2 declare that it is not right for anyone to be burdened with a plethora of problems, whereas chorus 3, following up on the positive tone of verse 3, states optimistically that everything will be all right because there will be no more rain (i.e., problems). "Too Much Rain" is a typical "feel-good" song by McCartney. Cast in G major, it includes a verse–chorus–bridge framework in which melody and harmony flow effortlessly.

"A Certain Softness" is a Latin ballad that represents McCartney's love for old-fashioned, well-constructed love songs. It reflects the music he listened to while growing up in Liverpool, some of which dated before his father's time. As he puts it, his passion for well-crafted love songs, and all of these musical influences, sometimes flood into him and become a new song, as it did when he was on vacation in Greece writing "A Certain Softness." In the verses, the persona describes the attributes of the woman with whom he is fascinated. In the bridge, he concludes that he must worship the woman from afar, never telling her of his feelings, for to do so would break the spell she has cast upon him. The song's verses are in A minor, while its bridge is in A major. The melody shines in this song, as it reflects the seductive qualities of the lyrics with which it is associated.

"Riding to Vanity Fair" centers on the theme of rejection. It could have been inspired by the marital problems McCartney was having with Heather

Mills, which culminated in divorce. The track recounts the story of a difficult relationship and its accompanying roller-coaster emotions. In the verses, the persona describes how frustrated he is with the woman in his life. In the chorus, he declares that he has had enough and will try to forget her. The bridge finds the persona reflecting on the definition of friendship, which was not realized in his relationship, for the woman in his life, through the metaphor of "riding to Vanity Fair," rejected him.

Originally, "Riding to Vanity Fair" was an up-tempo song, but McCartney decided to slow it down, changing the mood completely. That change in tempo, coupled with the song's A aeolian framework, resulted in a dark and moody track. In the verses, the melody consists of a finely tuned balance between leaps and stepwise motion. The harmonic setting, however, is static, consisting of alternating Am6/9 and Am9 chords. Harmonic variety in the song comes via the chorus and bridge, where the key of C major is suggested.

"Follow Me" was one of the first songs McCartney did with Godrich for *Chaos and Creation in the Backyard*, recording it at RAK studios, London. It is an uplifting, quasi-religious song in the style of "Let It Be" that McCartney felt wrote itself. He premiered the song at the Glastonbury Festival in the UK with his new band (Rusty Anderson and Brian Ray on guitars, Paul "Wix" Wickens on keyboards, and Abe Laboriel, Jr., on drums) on 26 June 2004. The song may have been compiled from two separate numbers. The verse, a hymn of thanksgiving for that special someone in anyone's life who provides needed emotional support, is in C major, with McCartney singing a lyrical melody, accompanying himself at first on the acoustic guitar, and then supported later by other instruments. In the bridge, the lyrics begin in a darker vein, only to conclude optimistically with the discovery of a friend. Not only does the musical motion pick up here, but there is a suggestion of the key of G major. With the addition of vigorous string chords played by the Millennia Ensemble, McCartney has constructed a bridge that flows naturally from the verse, despite its origin as a separate song. Finally, the verse comes back to conclude the song.

Like "Follow Me," "This Never Happened Before," the album's twelfth track, was another early song McCartney did for the album with Godrich at RAK studios. When composing the song, McCartney devised a chord sequence for the verses that he believed went somewhere, allowing him to write the melody. "This Never Happened Before" is a love song, used, interestingly, to accompany the closing credits of the romantic film *The Lake House* (2006), starring Sandra Bullock and Keanu Reeves. McCartney summed up the song as two people in love who laugh and cry.

"This Never Happened Before" is one of the best songs on *Chaos and Creation in the Backyard*. Although notated in A minor in the album's accompanying piano-vocal songbook, the song is actually in E major despite suggesting A minor at times.[14] It opens with alternating Am7 and E chords in an instrumental intro that sets up the melancholy atmosphere of the song to come. To capture the persona's feelings of love in the verses, McCartney structures the melody around the interval of a fifth (A–E), which is expanded later to a sixth (G#–E). He accompanies the melody with an Am–G#m7–C#m–F#m7–Am–E–C#m–Am–E chordal succession. The bridge modulates to the key of G major, a relief from the darker mood of the verses, as the persona declares that lovers should not be separated and alone. However, he then focuses on the idea of loneliness, a darker thought captured by the music moving to the key of A minor via its retransitional dominant E, which, in turn, will be reinterpreted as the tonic harmony in the verses.

"Promise to You Girl," the album's eleventh track, is an upbeat pop song about commitment. It begins with an intro in the key of A minor sung by McCartney as persona in which he reflects on the past ("looking through the backyard of my life"). He decides that change is necessary in the future, as indicated by his wanting to sweep away the backyard's leaves. The intro segues into what I would call a pre-verse (a section of music that precedes a verse), cast in the parallel key of A major. The tempo picks up in the song's verse/refrain section as the persona recounts how he will be a faithful companion to the woman in his life. In each verse, words dealing with how the lovers will confront the world are accentuated by a mixture chord on F (♭VI). The reflective intro returns to end the song.

According to McCartney, Randy Newman may have influenced the sound of the tender love ballad, "Anyway." The piano's opening chord sequence in G major evokes, moreover, images of the Deep South in the US, such as Charleston, South Carolina or Savannah, Georgia. That sequence, incidentally, consists of G, Em7, C, and G chords, voiced in the lower tenor range of the piano (most notes lying below middle C). McCartney's observations about evoking the Deep South hold true for the song's verses, as they evince a gospel aura in which the persona pleads with his lover to stay in touch. The bridge gets more harmonically chromatic through an Eaug chord as the persona reflects on why he has failed at love. The chorus then modulates to D major as the persona gets over his doubts and encourages his lover to contact him.

Chaos and Creation in the Backyard closes with a surprise bonus track, "I've Got Only Two Hands." "Anyway" ends at 3:50. At 4:10, "I've Got Only Two Hands" begins and lasts for 3:12. It is a multisectional jam containing some avant-garde sounds which definitely grab the listener's attention.

ECCE COR MEUM (2006)

In 1997, Anthony Smith, former president (1998–2005) of Magdalen College, Oxford University, commissioned Paul McCartney to compose an oratorio in order to inaugurate a new concert hall there.[15] Smith wanted a composition that "could be sung by young people the world over—

something equivalent to Handel's *Messiah*." What resulted was McCartney's fourth major classical work, *Ecce Cor Meum* ("Behold My Heart"). McCartney took eight years to complete the work, though an early version was performed in Oxford's Sheldonian Theatre in November 2001.

To familiarize himself with English choral music in order to help him compose an oratorio, McCartney, with wife Linda Eastman, attended the daily services at Magdalen College where they heard pieces spanning over 500 years of English choral music. With the assistance of John Harle, who had worked with him on *Standing Stone*, McCartney was making some progress on his new classical work before the death of Eastman forced him to stop. He went into a long period of mourning in which all work came to a standstill. However, what at first seemed to be a setback inspired McCartney to forge ahead on a work that was to be a tribute to his late wife and helped to impart a sense of somber pathos to the work.

With *Ecce Cor Meum* planned as an oratorio in four movements for choir and orchestra, McCartney composed the music first, deciding later to look for a subject in order to write an attendant text. The title of the work was actually inspired by an inscription McCartney noticed above a crucifix in St. Ignatius Church, New York City, while taking part in a concert of John Tavener's music. Although the inscription from a Roman Catholic perspective has to do with the Sacred Heart of Jesus, McCartney freely adapted it for use in his composition. Like *Standing Stone*, McCartney composed the work using a computer hooked up to a synthesizer keyboard to translate what he played onto a musical score. After that point, he gave his computer-notated score to several people who helped him translate it into readable musical notation, as well as refine and orchestrate it.

Ecce Cor Meum is scored for two flutes, two oboes, two clarinets in B♭, two bassoons, two horns in F, two trumpets in B♭ (optionally doubling piccolo trumpets), tympani, percussion (side drum), harp, organ, and strings. The world premiere took place on 3 November 2006 at the Royal Albert Hall, London, with Kate Royal (soprano) and the Academy of Saint Martin in the Fields, London Voices, the Boys of Magdalen College Choir, Oxford, and King's College Choir, Cambridge conducted by Gavin Greenaway. The US premiere took place on 14 November 2006 at Carnegie Hall, New York City, with Kate Royal (soprano) and the Orchestra of Saint Luke's, the Concert Chorale of New York, and the American Boychoir conducted by Gavin Greenaway.

Ecce Cor Meum is in four movements, with a short lament-filled interlude forming the piece's emotional center. The text focuses on truth, love, honesty, and kindness, qualities important to McCartney. It is in English, although interspersed with a few Latin phrases.

In the first movement, *Spiritus*, sopranos, altos, tenors, and basses intone, in turn, plainchant-like phrases that ask for guidance with respect to the powerful emotion of love. Sopranos sing the movement's primary musical motif to a text that forms the oratorio's central theme: an appeal for divine guidance for help in finding love. Later in the movement, when the chorus asks for "new words for love," the boy sopranos reply in Latin, suggesting, according to Peter Quantrill, that the "act of discovery is one of recovering what has always been there." After its initial plainchant-like supplications, the music grows in dynamic and textural complexity, culminating with a fortissimo outburst from the choir recapitulating the movement's opening plea for help in finding love.

Gratia, the second movement, is a comforting response to the appeal for guidance that ended the first. The music begins with a poignant melody played by the strings. The text, "We may find a trace," is set to a soprano solo that develops the string melody. The soprano then soars above a lush choral and orchestral accompaniment with another McCartney-esque tune. The choir then takes center stage in the movement, developing the soprano's melodies. After several contrasting choral passages, the soprano resumes her music heard earlier in the movement. *Gratia* then comes to an ecstatic but quiet close.

The Interlude (*Lament*) is a moving pastoral elegy for oboe, strings, and wordless chorus that links the second and third movements. It lies at the heart of the work, for it is McCartney's emotional tribute to his late wife, Linda Eastman, whose figure is suffused throughout the piece.

Peter Quantrill describes the third movement, *Musica*, as a passage from "sorrow to light." The music begins plaintively with a harp solo, followed by various parts of the choir singing words that focus on the idea of being in the center of a beautiful song. Later, the basses anchor the upper voices with a new theme and its variation set to words focusing on being in the heart and light, respectively, of a sweet song. *Musica* builds in intensity as the soprano soloist, and then soprano soloist and chorus, take up, in turn, a new lyrical theme, with the piccolo trumpet playing fanfares reminiscent of "Penny Lane" and then a syncopated version of the new theme in ensuing passages. The basses anchor the choral texture again by singing their previously heard theme as an ostinato. *Musica* concludes with alternating C major and minor chords as it achieves a thunderous climax on the word, "sing," the embodiment of immersing oneself in beautiful song.

In the fourth movement, *Ecce Cor Meum*, the text takes a personal turn through its message that, despite being potentially separated in the future, the persona shows his beloved his heart through his music. Nonetheless, love is still the cornerstone that supplies a guiding light for everyone. Indeed, this universal belief in the power of love may be likened to Beethoven's belief in the power of joy. The chorus embarks on a long commentary on the oratorio's main themes concerning truth and love, all over a dynamic accompaniment in the orchestra. As noted by various commentators, there is an organ cadenza reminiscent of the style of writing found in pieces such as the Concerto for Organ, Strings, and Timpani in G minor by Francis Poulenc, a

French composer who blended rather effortlessly both the sacred and secular in his music. At the end, everyone celebrates love's victory by singing, "Ecce Cor Meum. . . . "

MEMORY ALMOST FULL (2007)

McCartney started working on *Memory Almost Full* in October 2003, before *Chaos and Creation in the Backyard* was finished. When *Chaos* was completed, he turned his attention to *Memory Almost Full*, completing it in February 2007. He enlisted the aid of David Kahne, who worked with him on *Driving Rain*, to produce the album. *Memory Almost Full* was McCartney's first release under the Starbucks' Hear Music label. More significantly, it enjoyed both critical and commercial success, something not seen since the days of *Flaming Pie* in 1997. The album debuted at No. 3 on the Billboard charts and sold well in the US, being certified gold by the Record Industry Association of America.

Memory Almost Full is another personal, retrospective statement from McCartney. It draws from his recollections of life in Liverpool. Its songs are often emotional statements about his life, as well as good old-fashioned rockers. Most of the album, moreover, was recorded before, during, and after his separation from Heather Mills. When *Memory Almost Full* was completed, McCartney felt that he should not delete any songs having to do with her.

"Dance Tonight," the first track on *Memory Almost Full*, is a rollicking, upbeat pop song, with McCartney singing and accompanying himself on the mandolin while stomping his feet.[16] He picked up the instrument at a shop in London and taught himself how to play it, feeling like a teenager learning a new instrument. "Dance Tonight" is a simple, heartfelt song in F major that begins with the rousing chorus—"Everybody's gonna dance tonight" (and its textual variations)—before proceeding to the bridge. The melody consists of repeated-note figures accompanied by F major's basic chords, F–Bb–C/F, while the bridge features Ebmaj7–F and Ebmaj7–C chordal successions. The song includes an instrumental interlude that supplies needed harmonic variety by sounding a chromatic line—F–F#–G, which, in turn, generates Bb, Bbaug, and Gm chords.

"Ever Present Past" is a reflective but fast rocker in C major focusing on time and the lack of it. In the song's verses, McCartney as persona laments that he may be too busy for his own good, ignoring the woman in his life. In the chorus, McCartney comments on the fleeting nature of time by recalling the things he did when he was a kid and how quickly they seemed to pass. The music's tempo and vocal line, particularly its descending and ascending scales and repetitive figures, convey the persona's preoccupation with time.

"See Your Sunshine" is a mid-tempo love song in C major in which the persona rejoices in the glow of love. Its verse–chorus–bridge structure is distinguished by different musical textures. In the verses, the persona describes the intensity of his love via a series of short isolated figures. In the choruses, things get more expansive as the persona reflects on the effect his woman has on him. After a musical refrain composed of vocal harmonies that rock back and forth in descending thirds, the more rhythmically active bridge enters, which may depict the intensity of the persona's emotions as the lyrics focus on descriptions of his woman. Throughout these sections, the music is enhanced by McCartney's "over-the-top" bass line. Finally, the song ends on the non-tonic harmony Dm7, which may suggest that the persona has not quite captured the affections of his loved one.

According to McCartney, "Only Mama Knows" is a novelette, but in the form of a rocker. It begins deceptively with synthesizer strings playing a mantra-like figure inspired by Phillip Glass over C#m7♭5, Cdim, and Em chords. After that point, McCartney rocks away in the key of E minor in the song's verses where he, as the song's persona, describes being abandoned by his mother. The song's choruses reflect on why his mother treated him so badly. Tonally, the chorus suggests B major before moving to a long interlude characterized by a sustained Em chord. The interlude's effect is to heighten the tension for further statements of the song's verse and chorus. To round off the song, the synthesizer string intro comes back as an outro.

"You Tell Me" opens with backward-masking-like tape sounds before McCartney begins this tender, melancholy ballad in B minor. The verses describe a nostalgic yearning for summers past by using the imagery of birds, honeybees, and butterflies to evoke those times. The song's sense of regret is reflected by the melody which proceeds on an inexorable path from F# down to B. Interestingly, the ballad builds in intensity, rather than ending softly, as more musical parts are added, including an electric guitar obbligato.

"Mr. Bellamy" is a mini-opera about a man who will not come down from the ledge of a skyscraper while people look on. The rescue workers arrive and encourage him not to jump, informing him that they will have him down soon. McCartney constructed "Mr Bellamy" so that the lyrics could poke in and out of the verse's signature piano riff. Given its conception as a mini-opera, "Mr. Bellamy" has multiple sections with changes of tempo. Beginning in C minor, the song ends with a vamp in E♭ major where the rescue workers tell Mr. Bellamy to come down.

With "Gratitude," McCartney wanted to express in song the numerous things in life for which he was grateful. The lyrics focus on thanking a person, presumably a woman, for the love and consideration she has given the song's protagonist. Cast in 3/4 time, "Gratitude" begins in A major, modulates to C major for the chorus, and then returns to A major for another round of verses via McCartney's signature mixture progression, Fmaj7–G7–A (♭VI–♭VII–I).

"Vintage Clothes" refers to McCartney's wardrobe from the 1960s. Although the song may be about how what went out is coming back in, its greater message centers on not clinging to the past but looking ahead to the future. But more importantly, "Vintage Clothes" is at the beginning of a five-song medley, something McCartney had not done since *Red Rose Speedway*. In any event, he thought it was time to revisit the medley idea again. Since "Vintage Clothes" is in the key of A major, it progresses smoothly to the A major of the next track, "That Was Me," a song that looks back to Liverpool. The lyrics provide details about McCartney's youth where he attended scout camps, participated in school plays, waited at bus stops, and played at the Cavern Club, among other activities. To match the lyrics, McCartney cast the song in an early rock 'n' roll style.

"Feet in the Clouds" continues the retrospective orientation of the medley, focusing on McCartney's days at the Liverpool Institute. Its key of E major allows for a segue from "That Was Me." The song reflects the dark atmosphere of the school motivated by its building constructed in 1825. But ultimately, the song was therapy for McCartney, as he was able to incorporate some vocal harmonies and perform them in a robotic manner to poke fun at an uninspiring time in his life.

McCartney believed that the "House of Wax," the next song of the medley, featured an expressive chord sequence in the key of C♯ minor that had the capacity to take you to a place that the vocal becomes. The lyrics of the "House of Wax" border on the surreal as the persona sings, for example, of lightning hitting the house of wax, with poets spilling out on the street. McCartney liked everything about the song, from writing the music and lyrics to performing and recording the track. "The End of the End" returns the music from the C♯ minor of the "House of Wax" to A major, the medley's home key. In the song, McCartney focuses on death and how to deal with it. On the day he dies, he wants to have jokes and funny stories told about him. *Memory Almost Full* closes with the hard-rocking "Nod Your Head" to end on a more optimistic note than the subject of death in "The End of the End."

Popular Music Icon

On 26 May 2008, Yale University awarded the Doctor of Music degree to Sir James Paul McCartney. In conferring the degree, the university remarked that no living musician compares with the legendary singer-songwriter. As of the writing of this book, McCartney's career spans 52 years, from when he first met John Lennon on 6 July 1957 at Saint Peter's Church in Woolton, to his recent successful summer tour of 2009. He played and sang in the Beatles, the greatest rock band ever, and became the group's driving force from the mid-1960s to their breakup in 1970. He formed and led Wings, one of the most successful rock bands of the 1970s.

During the following decade, he collaborated with a number of musicians, such as Stevie Wonder, Michael Jackson, Eric Stewart, and Elvis Costello, to update and revitalize his sound, which meant finally coming to terms with his work as a Beatle, something with which he had been struggling as a solo artist since his days with Wings:

> When we started Wings, we had to overcome the shadow of the Beatles. So we couldn't do any Beatle songs. And that was difficult, that was more difficult than now. Now, well, I don't care, I'll just look at my whole career and just choose anything I fancy doing.[1]

In the1990s, McCartney experienced a creative renaissance, beginning with *Flowers in the Dirt* in 1989, which paved the way for his acclaimed album, *Flaming Pie*, in 1997. Gone were any overt concerns about the market. He wanted to have fun making the music he enjoyed. In other words, instead of writing for the public, he wrote for the public in him. The 1990s saw the creation of two major classical works, the *Liverpool Oratorio* and *Standing Stone*, a bold step for any classical music composer, let alone a bass player and singer from Liverpool. The scope of his musical activities, which go beyond songwriting, playing in a band, or writing classical music, is mind-boggling.

In the first decade of the twenty-first century, McCartney has reached a plateau not imaginable back in the 1970s when he was maligned for his work in Wings. *Driving Rain, Chaos and Creation in the Backyard*, and *Memory Almost Full* all point to a highly creative and confident individual who will never cease to explore new musical territories. With his work on *The Beatles Anthology* in the 1990s, the release of the *Beatles Rock Band* in 2009, and the current popularity of the Beatles with people under 30, McCartney has not only won over new legions of fans but also has achieved a status as the greatest living popular music icon. In effect, there are now three generations of listeners who appreciate his music. In his solo music, he has transcended his work as a Beatle, and it is about time the public recognized that fact. Yet, he is not done with music; there is more to come before he leaves this world.

When being interviewed for the documentary on the making of *Chaos and Creation in the Backyard*, McCartney responded to a question often posed to him about why he is always writing music. People typically ask, "Why do you still do it [write songs]? You've written so many songs." He replies:

> Well, I love it. I think it comes from this love of listening to, what you think, is great music. It just gets a beautiful sort of feeling going in you. Everyone who loves music, feels that feeling. That's what's special about it. And it's kind of mystical. Why do these combinations of vibrations affect us so much? How come they really affect our emotions? I mean, I can't hear, God only knows, without welling up.[2]

In a word, writing music has been an emotional outlet for McCartney throughout his life, derived from his love of listening and the beautiful aesthetic experience that emerges from it. Through his music, he has conveyed a wide variety of emotions, some of which are deeply personal and at times painful. We can only be thankful for the love of music that has inspired his work as the world's premier singer-songwriter, for it has touched people throughout the world and is able to make them "well up" inside, too.

People also ask him, "Where does the song come from?" In the early 1980s, McCartney responded to that question by saying the following, which still holds true today:

> I've been asked that millions of times, and every composer you ever hear says— "Well, I sit down and it sort of comes through. I'm a vehicle." And it's true, you are. You sit down and have a bit of fun ... you love playing around on the old piano or the guitar. Suddenly, this little idea comes through ...[3]

Glossary of Technical Terms

The following glossary of technical terms is indebted to: James Bennighof, *The Words and Music of Paul Simon*, The Praeger Singer-Songwriter Collection, James E. Perone, ed. (Westport, CT: Praeger Publishers, 2007), xv–xviii, 167–80; Walter Everett, *The Beatles as Musicians: Revolver through the Anthology*, vol. 2 (New York: Oxford University Press, 1999), 309–19; and Ken Stephenson, *What to Listen for in Rock: A Stylistic Analysis* (New Haven and London: Yale University Press, 2002), 229–43.

Added-Note Chord: A chord that is analyzed as a triad with an added second, fourth, or sixth above the root.

Aeolian Mode: A diatonic scale with the pattern of whole and half steps corresponding to the notes A to A on the piano (whole–half–whole–whole–half–whole–whole).

Arpeggio: A chord played successively, ascending or descending.

Augmented-Sixth Chord: A chord based on the interval of an augmented sixth created by a lowered sixth scale degree ($\flat\hat{6}$) in the bass and raised fourth scale degree ($\sharp\hat{4}$) in an upper voice. The three types—Italian, German, and French—typically resolve to a dominant triad, as the interval of the augmented sixth resolves outward to the fifth scale degree ($\hat{5}$).

Authentic Cadence: A harmonic cadence consisting of V, V7, vii°, vii°7, or vii°7 progressing to I or i.

Basic Track: The initial recording of a song performed on drums, bass, rhythm guitar, and keyboard, upon which vocals, solos, and other parts could be overdubbed later.

Bridge: The contrasting middle section of a song that frequently begins in a non-tonic key and usually ends with retransitional dominant harmony, which propels the music back to the verse.

Cadence: The melodic, harmonic, or rhythmic pattern at the end of a phrase that articulates a complete musical thought.

Capo: A device guitarists use to raise the pitch of the strings by a desired number of half steps without requiring any changes in fingering. The guitarist clamps the capo behind a desired fret on the instrument's neck, thereby stopping all strings at that fret and creating a higher-pitched guitar.

Chord symbols: Roman numerals indicating the quality of the triad and its placement within a key. Uppercase Roman numerals denote major triads; lowercase Roman numerals, minor triads; uppercase Roman numerals followed by a plus sign, augmented triads; and lowercase Roman numerals followed by a small raised circle, diminished triads. An Arabic numeral following a Roman numeral may indicate a seventh, ninth, eleventh, or thirteenth chord. This book also employs a system common to sheet music, in which the root is indicated by a note name:

Symbol	Quality
C	major triad
C/G	major triad in second inversion
Cm	minor triad
C+	augmented triad
Cdim	diminished triad
Cmaj7	major seventh
C7	dominant seventh
Cm7	minor seventh
Cm7♭5	half-diminished seventh
Cdim7	diminished seventh
Csus	suspended chord

Chorus: The section of a song typically in the tonic key that often appears after the verse. Its text is constant, and may even contain the song's title.

Chromatic: Not part of the basic diatonic scale of a piece.

Chromatic-Third Relationship: Two major or minor triads whose roots are a third apart (e.g., C major and A major). Two keys have a chromatic-third relationship if their tonic chords are in that relationship.

Coda: A section of music that occurs after the major part of a composition has ended.

Common-tone diminished-seventh chord: A fully diminished seventh chord (symbolized ct°7) that shares one pitch with the chord that precedes or follows it.

Diatonic: Melody or harmony based on seven-note scales whose intervallic patterns are exemplified by the white keys on the piano.

Dominant: The fifth scale degree of a major or minor scale (such as E in A major or A minor), or a chord built on this note as root.

Doo-wop: A style of rhythm-and-blues singing popular in the 1940s and 1950s, often featuring a soloist backed up by a vocal ensemble.

Dorian mode: A diatonic scale with the pattern of whole and half steps corresponding to the notes D to D on the piano (whole–half–whole–whole–whole–half–whole).

Double-plagal cadence: The cadence involving two successive perfect fourth motions to the tonic (♭VII–IV–I).

Downbeat: The first beat of a measure.

Fret: One of several metal bars inset across the neck of a guitar or like instrument; a string depressed behind a fret vibrates only between the fret and the bridge, resulting in a higher pitch than it would if it were allowed to vibrate along its whole length.

Fugue: A composition or part of a composition in which the parts enter successively and in imitation.

Half Cadence: An inconclusive cadence on the dominant chord (V or V7).

Half Step: The smallest interval in Western music, exemplified by adjacent keys on the piano.

Harmonic Function: The tendency of one chord to progress to some other particular chord.

Hook: A pleasing and easily remembered musical figure in a popular song.

Incomplete progression: A harmonic progression that does not begin with the tonic.

Initiating Harmony: A harmony that occurs at the beginning of a section of a song.

Interval: The distance between two pitches.

Intro: The opening section of a song.

Legato: Played smoothly, without separation between notes.

Lick: A distinctive, brief musical figure played in popular music.

Linear Chord: A chord arising from the movement of musical lines.

LP: The 12-inch, long-playing 33-1/3-rpm vinyl format for an album, and the collection of songs associated with it.

Lydian II: A major triad built on scale degree 2 ($\hat{2}$) in a major key, but not functioning as V/V.

Key: The key of a song takes its name from the tonic scale degree of the major or minor tonality in which it is written.

Major Scale: A diatonic scale with the pattern of whole and half steps corresponding to the notes C to C on the piano (whole–whole–half–whole–whole–whole–half).

Melodic Motion: Rhythmic activity during a vocal phrase.

Mixolydian ♭VII: A major triad built on the lowered seventh scale degree ($\flat\hat{7}$) in a major key. The modal alternation of I with ♭VII is common in McCartney's solo music and is derived from folk and blues musical traditions.

Mixolydian mode: A diatonic scale with the pattern of whole and half steps corresponding to the notes G to G on the piano (whole–whole–half–whole–whole–half–whole).

Mixture Chord: A chord that typically appears in a major key whose spelling and quality derive from the parallel minor key.

Modal: Relating to the diatonic modes.

Modal Mixture: A combination of parallel major and minor modes.

Modulation: A change of key within a piece.

Natural-Minor Scale: A diatonic scale with the pattern of whole and half steps corresponding to the notes A to A on the piano (whole–half–whole–whole–half–whole–whole).

Neapolitan Chord: A major chord that is built on the lowered second scale degree ($\flat\hat{2}$).

Obbligato: A prominent musical line that accompanies the primary line.

Open-Fifth Chord: A chord whose notes are a fifth apart (e.g., C5).

Ostinato: A repetitive, usually accompanimental musical pattern.

Outro: The closing section of a song.

Overdub: Adding one recording to a preexisting one.

Parallel Keys: Two keys that share the same tonic. For example, C major and C minor are parallel keys.

Pedal Point: A note that is sustained or repeated while other parts or harmonies change against it.

Perfect Authentic Cadence: A conclusive harmonic cadence in which a root-position dominant or dominant-seventh chord (V or V7) progresses to a root-position tonic chord. The soprano voice moves from scale degrees two or seven to one ($\hat{2}-\hat{1}$ or $\hat{7}-\hat{1}$).

Period: A musical unit consisting of one phrase with a weak cadence followed by another ending with a more conclusive cadence.

Persona: A fictional, usually unnamed character who articulates the message or story behind a song's lyrics.

Phrase: A complete musical thought, with a beginning, middle, and end.

Pickup: One or more notes that lead into the next downbeat.

Plagal Cadence: The harmonic cadence consisting of IV or iv progressing to I or i. This motion can be considered as an expansion of the tonic triad.

Power Chord: An open fifth played on the guitar, loud and distorted.

Prolongation (of Harmony): The expansion of a harmony by means of contrapuntal motion or linear chords.

Refrain: An optional last line following a song's verse that does not vary during subsequent appearances and typically contains the title of the song.

Resolution: The way a harmony or pitch moves to the next harmony or pitch; usually associated with dissonance (instability) moving to consonance (stability).

Retransitional Dominant: The dominant harmony that typically concludes a song's bridge, facilitating a return to the tonic area of the verses.

Riff: A characteristic musical figure that recurs throughout a piece.

Scale: A group of notes arranged in particular order of whole and half steps.

Scale Degree: A name for each note of the scale.

Scat: A style of jazz singing characterized by improvisational, instrumental-sounding nonsense syllables.

Secondary Dominant: A major triad or dominant seventh chord that serves as a dominant-functioning harmony (V or V7) to a major or minor triad other than the tonic. Secondary dominants are represented by two Roman numerals separated by a forward slash: V7/V is read as "V7 of V," the dominant seventh of the dominant triad.

Sequence: A musical pattern that is restated successively on different pitches.

Single: A seven-inch 45-rpm recording that included one song per side, the A–side containing the stronger song.

Skiffle: A style of folk-like music popularized in the UK by Lonnie Donegan before the emergence of rock 'n' roll in the mid-1950s.

Stop time: An abrupt cessation of sound by rhythm instruments that underscores a continuing vocal or instrumental line.

Subdominant: The fourth scale step of a major or minor scale (such as F in the key of C major or C minor), or a chord that uses this note as its root.

Submediant: The sixth scale step of a major or minor scale (such as A in the key of C major or A♭ in the key of C minor), or a chord that uses this note as its root.

Syncopation: A shift of accent that occurs when a weak beat or parts of the beat are stressed.

Texture: Pattern of sound generated by the elements of a work.

Tonality: Organized relationships between musical tones with reference to a focal tone, the tonic.

Tonic: The first note of a major or minor scale that serves as the central note of a key, or a chord that uses this note as its root. In major and minor keys, and in most other scales, the tonic note identifies the key or scale.

Tonicization: The temporary conferral of "tonic" status to a scale degree other than the tonic.

Track: A term that either refers to an entire song on an album or to a portion of a recording tape.

Turnaround: A passage of music occurring at the end of one section of a song that leads harmonically and/or melodically to the next.

12-bar blues: The normal form of a blues chorus, with three lines of four bars each, progressing harmonically in the following manner: (1) bars 1–4, I–IV–I; (2) bars 5–8, IV–I; and (3) bars 9–12, V7–IV–I–V7.

Vamp: A repetitive introductory or accompanimental pattern that is played until a soloist enters.

Verse: A section of a song placed typically after the introduction that appears with two or three different sets of lyrics.

Verse–Chorus–Bridge: A form that consists of at least two repetitions of a verse-chorus pair followed by a bridge, which leads back to repetitions of earlier passages.

Vocalise: An exposed, improvisatory-sounding vocal line.

Whole Step: Two half steps.

Selected Discography/Videography

In this selected discography and videography of compact disc and digital video disc recordings by Paul McCartney, I have listed items in reverse chronological order. Individual CD recordings of his pop music are listed first, followed by his compilations and classical music, with DVD recordings listed at the end. Although they are certainly out there, I have not listed unofficial releases, bootlegs, and concert tapes, as well as recordings of McCartney's electronic music, music for films (exception being *Give My Regards to Broad Street*), or work recorded and produced under pseudonyms. Although original release dates are noted, I have not listed current release dates due to CDs and DVDs being released more than once. Finally, most of McCartney's albums are also available on iTunes and other music download Web sites.

Pop Music

Memory Almost Full. Paul McCartney. Originally released in 2007. Currently available as MPL/Starcon HMCD2-30618. With DVD and three bonus tracks on the CD.

Memory Almost Full. Paul McCartney. Originally released in 2007. Currently available as MPL/Starcon HMCD-30358.

Chaos and Creation in the Backyard: Special Edition. Paul McCartney. Originally released in 2005. Currently available as Capitol Records, Inc. CDP 0946 3 38759 2 0. With special edition DVD.

Driving Rain. Paul McCartney. Originally released in 2001. Currently available as Capitol Records, Inc. CDP 7243 5 35510 2 5.

Run Devil Run. Paul McCartney. Originally released in 1999. Currently available as Capitol Records, Inc. CDP 7243 5 22351 2 4.

Flaming Pie. Paul McCartney. Originally released in 1997. Currently available as Capitol Records, Inc. CDP 7243 8 56500 2 4.

Off the Ground. Paul McCartney. Originally released in 1993. Currently available as Capitol Records, Inc. CDP 7 80362 2.

Paul is Live. Paul McCartney. Originally released in 1993. Currently available as Capitol Records, Inc. CDP 7243 8 27704 2 8.

Paul McCartney Unplugged—The Official Bootleg. Paul McCartney. Originally released in 1991. Currently available as EMI/Parlophone CDP 7964132.

Tripping the Live Fantastic. Paul McCartney. Originally released in 1990. Currently available as Capitol Records, Inc. CDP 7 94778 2.

The Paul McCartney Collection: Flowers in the Dirt. Paul McCartney. Originally released in 1989. Currently available as EMI/Parlophone 0777 7 89138 2 5.

Paul McCartney: Back in the USSR: The Russian Album. Paul McCartney. Originally released in the U.S.S.R. on vinyl in 1988 by the Melodya label. Currently available as EMI/Parlophone CDP 7976152.

The Paul McCartney Collection: Give My Regards to Broad Street. Paul McCartney. Originally released in 1984. Currently available as EMI/Parlophone 0777 7 89268 2 5.

The Paul McCartney Collection: Pipes of Peace. Paul McCartney. Originally released in 1983. Currently available as EMI/Parlophone 0777 7 89267 2 6.

Tug of War. Paul McCartney. Originally released in 1982. Currently available as Capitol Records, Inc./Parlophone CDP 7 46057 2.

The Paul McCartney Collection: McCartney II. Paul McCartney. Originally released in 1980. Currently available as EMI Parlophone 0777 7 89137 2 6.

The Paul McCartney Collection: Back to the Egg. Wings. Originally released in 1979. Currently available as EMI/Parlophone 0777 7 89136 2 7.

The Paul McCartney Collection: London Town. Wings. Originally released in 1978. Currently available as EMI/Parlophone 0777 7 89265 2 8.

Wings at the Speed of Sound. Wings. Originally released in 1976. Currently available as EMI 0777 7 89140 2 0.

Wings Over America. Wings. Originally released in 1976. Currently available as EMI/Parlophone CDS 7 46715 8.

The Paul McCartney Collection: Venus and Mars. Wings. Originally released in 1975. Currently available as EMI/Parlophone 0777 7 89241 2 8.

Band on the Run: 25th Anniversary Edition. Paul McCartney & Wings. Originally released in 1973. Currently available as Capitol Records, Inc. CDP 7243 4 99176 2 0.

The Paul McCartney Collection: Red Rose Speedway. Paul McCartney & Wings. Originally released in 1972/3. Currently available as MPL/EMI Parlophone 0777 7 89238 2 4.

The Paul McCartney Collection: Wings Wild Life. Wings. Originally released in 1971. Currently available as EMI/Parlophone 0777 7 89237 2 5.

The Paul McCartney Collection: Ram. Paul and Linda McCartney. Originally released in 1971. Currently available as EMI/Parlophone 0777 7 89139 2 4.

Ram. Paul and Linda McCartney. Originally released in 1971. Currently available as Capitol Records, Inc. CDP 7 46612 2.

McCartney. Paul McCartney. Originally released in 1970. Currently available as Capitol Records, Inc./EMI Parlophone CDP 7 46611 2.

Pop Music Compilations

Wingspan: Paul McCartney: Hits and History. Paul McCartney. Originally released in 2001. Currently available as Capitol Records, Inc. CDP 7243 5 32946 2 5.

Paul McCartney: All the Best! Paul McCartney. Originally released in 1987. Currently available as Capitol Records, Inc. CDP 7 48287 2.

Classical Music

Ecce Cor Meum. Paul McCartney. Originally released in 2006. Currently available on CD as EMI/Angel Records 0946 3 70424 2 7.

Working Classical. Paul McCartney. Originally released in 1999. Currently available as EMI Classics 7243 5 56897 2 6.

Standing Stone. Paul McCartney. Originally released in 1997. Currently available as EMI Classics 7243 5 56484 2 6.

Liverpool Oratorio. Paul McCartney and Carl Davis. Originally released in 1991. Currently available as EMI Classics 0777 7 54372 2 5.

DVD

John, Paul, Tom & Ringo: The Tomorrow Show with Tom Snyder. Originally released in 2008. Includes an interview with Paul and Linda McCartney, and Wings members Denny Laine and Laurence Juber on 20 December 1979. Currently available on DVD as NBC Universal, Inc./Shout Factory SF 10129.

The McCartney Years. Paul McCartney. Originally released in 2007. Currently available on DVD as RHINO R2 285628.

Ecce Cor Meum. Paul McCartney. Originally released in 2007. Currently available on DVD as EMI Classics 50999 5 00733 9 9.

Paul McCartney: The Space Within Us: A Concert Film. Paul McCartney. Originally released in 2006. Currently available as MPL Communications Ltd./A & E Television AAE-76291.

Paul McCartney in Red Square: A Concert Film. Paul McCartney. Originally released in 2005. Currently available on DVD as MPL Communications Ltd./A & E Television AAE-71104.

Liverpool Oratorio. Paul McCartney/Carl Davis. Originally released in 2004. Currently available on DVD as EMI Classics SET 7243 5 99742 9 3.

Paul Is Live: In Concert on the New World Tour. Paul McCartney. Originally released in 2003. Currently available on DVD as Rounder Records 116 613 190–99.

Paul McCartney Back in the U.S. Concert Film. Paul McCartney. Originally released in 2002. Currently available on DVD as MPL Communications Ltd./Capitol Records, Inc. C9 7243 4 77989 9 3.

Wingspan: An Intimate Portrait. Paul McCartney. Originally released in 2001. Currently available on DVD as MPL Communications Ltd./Capitol Records, Inc. C9 7243 4 77909 9 7.

Paul McCartney: Live at the Cavern Club! Paul McCartney. Originally released in 2000. Currently available on DVD as MPL Communications Ltd./Image Entertainment as ID0384MPDVD.

Working Classical. Paul McCartney. Originally released in 2000. Currently available on VHS (not DVD) as PBS Home Video B8247.

Standing Stone. Paul McCartney. Originally released in 1999. Currently available on DVD as EMI Classics 7243 4 92243 9 1.

Paul McCartney's Get Back World Tour Movie. Paul McCartney. Originally released in 1990. Currently available on DVD as Lions Gate Home Entertainment 16943.

Paul McCartney's Give My Regards to Broad Street. Starring Paul McCartney, Bryan Brown, Ringo Starr, Barbara Bach, Linda McCartney, Tracey Ullman, Ralph Richardson. Originally released in 1984. Currently available on DVD as MPL Communications Ltd./Twentieth[-]Century Fox Film Corporation 24543 11370

Notes

INTRODUCTION

1. The following biographical sketch of Paul McCartney is indebted to The Beatles, *The Beatles Anthology* (San Francisco: Chronicle Books, 2000); Geoffrey Giuliano, *Blackbird: The Life and Times of Paul McCartney*, updated edition (Cambridge, MA, and New York: Da Capo Press, Inc., 1997); Garry McGee, *Band on the Run: A History of Paul McCartney and Wings* (New York: Taylor Trade Publishing, 2003); Barry Miles, *Paul McCartney: Many Years from Now* (New York: Henry Holt and Company, 1998); Christopher Sandford, *McCartney* (New York: Carroll & Graf Publishers, 2007); and Bob Spitz, *The Beatles: The Biography* (New York: Little, Brown and Company, 2005).

2. Spitz, *The Beatles: The Biography*, 76.

3. Miles, *Paul McCartney: Many Years from Now*, 4.

4. Spitz, *The Beatles: The Biography*, 82.

5. Miles, *Paul McCartney: Many Years from Now*, 9.

6. When McCartney and Harrison met, McCartney lived at 12 Ardwick Road, Speke, Liverpool 24, whereas Harrison lived at 25 Upton Green, Speke, Liverpool 24.

7. The Beatles, *The Beatles Anthology*, 21, 27.

8. Ibid., 20.

9. Ibid.

10. McCartney performed "I Lost My Little Girl" for the first time publicly on 25 January 1991 for MTV's Unplugged television series in which rock musicians performed their songs with acoustic instruments. On that particular night, McCartney, Robbie McIntosh, Hamish Stuart, Paul Wickens, Linda McCartney, and Blair Cunningham played a two-and-a-half-hour concert before an audience of about 200 people at the Limehouse Television Studios, Wembley, London. The concert was taped by

MTV and aired in an edited version on 3 April 1991. "I Lost My Little Girl" is included as the second track of the album, *Paul McCartney: Unplugged - The Official Bootleg*, which contains 17 songs from the MTV performance. See Bill Harry, *The Paul McCartney Encyclopedia* (London: Virgin Books Ltd, 2002), 438–39, 874–75. The television performance of the song is included on volume three of the DVD Collection, *The McCartney Years* (produced by Paul McCartney, directed by Dick Carruthers, 406 minutes, MPL Communications/Rhino, 2007).

11. *The Beatles Anthology*, 20.

12. Made popular by Lonnie Donegan (1931–2002), skiffle was a popular British musical genre of the 1950s, a contemporary counterpart to American rockabilly. Derived from American folk music of the first half of the twentieth century, skiffle consisted of an odd blend of blues, country, and jazz elements, played by means of homemade or improvised instruments. At the Woolton village fête, The Quarry Men were playing instruments such as a banjo, guitar, tea-chest bass, and drums.

13. See Harry, *The Paul McCartney Encyclopedia*, 499.

14. Ibid., 400.

15. Ibid., 401. The fourth club in Hamburg (not identified by Harrison) that the Beatles played at was the Star Club in April 1962.

16. Ibid., 535.

17. *The Real Buddy Holly Story* (produced by Paul McCartney, directed by Richard Spence, 86 minutes, White Star/MPL Communications, Inc. & BBC TV, 1987/2004, DVD).

18. The original songs on the *Please, Please Me* album were credited to McCartney/Lennon. At Lennon's insistence, the credits were changed to Lennon/McCartney for all subsequent albums.

19. The official British releases of Beatle albums (excluding compilations) are: (1) *Please, Please Me* (1963); (2) *With the Beatles* (1963); (3) *A Hard Day's Night* (1964); (4) *Beatles for Sale* (1964); (5) *Help!* (1965); (6) *Rubber Soul* (1965); (7) *Revolver* (1966); (8) *Sgt. Pepper's Lonely Hearts Club Band* (1967); (9) *Magical Mystery Tour* (1967); (10) *The Beatles* (1968); (11) *Yellow Submarine* (1969); (12) *Abbey Road* (1969); and (13) *Let It Be* (1970). In the US, Capitol Records released different versions of these albums during the 1960s, as well as new albums altogether. This hodgepodge packaging by Capitol irritated the Beatles, motivating them to create their famous "butcher shot" for their Capitol album, *Yesterday and Today*. In any event, Capitol's practice ceased with the release of *Sgt. Pepper's Lonely Hearts Club Band*.

20. See especially Walter Everett, *The Beatles as Musicians: Revolver through the Anthology* (New York: Oxford University Press, 1999), 8–11.

21. The following observations about McCartney's musical contributions to the Beatles are indebted to Everett, *The Beatles as Musicians: Revolver through the Anthology*, 12, 14.

22. I shall refer to Linda Eastman McCartney throughout the book as Linda Eastman, or simply Eastman, in order to avoid referring to her and her husband informally as Linda and Paul.

23. *The Beatles Anthology*, 315.

24. For a detailed look at this part of McCartney's life—the demise of the Beatles to McCartney's lawsuit against his fellow band mates (1969–71), see Miles, *Paul McCartney: Many Years from Now*, 568–82.

25. Sir Lew Grade of ATV and Northern Songs sued McCartney, challenging his assertion that Eastman was a cowriter on almost half of the album's songs. Since Eastman was not associated with Northern Songs, Grade was losing 50 percent of the royalties due his company. See McGee, *Band on the Run*, 12.

26. McCartney had asked Hugh McCracken and Dave Spinoza, session players on *Ram*, to join his new band, but they turned him down.

27. McGee, *Band on the Run*, 138.

28. Ibid., 145.

29. Although perhaps simmering below the surface during the earlier days of the Beatles, McCartney and Lennon openly criticized each other's music during the recording of *Abbey Road* in 1969. Their hostility toward each other's work continued through the 1970s.

30. Harry, *The Paul McCartney Encyclopedia*, 403.

31. Ibid., 457.

32. In late 1979, McCartney commissioned playwright Willy Russell to write a script for a film that would highlight him and his music. He eventually became dissatisfied, however, with Russell's work, and having turned down other proposed scripts for the film, decided to write a screenplay himself. In 1982, while being chauffeured in a car, and caught in traffic, in London, McCartney conceived of a plot for his film. In the story line, an unsavory banker and his cohorts would takeover McCartney's company unless McCartney found the missing master tapes of his new album before midnight. Thus, McCartney's script for *Give My Regards to Broad Street* was born. See John Blaney, *Lennon and McCartney: Together Alone: A Critical Discography of Their Solo Work* (London: A Jawbone Book, 2007), 168.

33. Harry, *The Paul McCartney Encyclopedia*, 526.

34. Ibid., 25.

35. *Wingspan: An Intimate Portrait* (produced by Paul McCartney, directed by Alistair Donald, 120 minutes, MPL Communications Ltd./Inc., 2001, DVD).

36. For the best examination of McCartney's music as a Beatle, see Walter Everett's two-volume set, *The Beatles as Musicians: Revolver through the Anthology*, and *The Quarry Men through Rubber Soul* (New York: Oxford University Press, 1999/2001). Most studies that cover McCartney's solo career, such as Geoffrey Giuliano's *Blackbird: The Life and Times of Paul McCartney* (1997), Garry McGee's *Band on the Run: A History of Paul McCartney and Wings* (2003), or Christopher Sandford's *McCartney* (2007), are biographical accounts that avoid discussions of compositional techniques, music/text relationships, and instrumentation in his music. Still, other books on McCartney, such as Barry Miles's *Paul McCartney: Many Years from Now* (1997) or Bill Harry's *The Paul McCartney Encyclopedia* (2002), either focus on McCartney's Beatle days or provide trivia about his life and career. Although providing valuable information about McCartney's solo music, such as the genesis of albums and individual songs, instrumentation, and musical lineups, along with some insightful commentary about his work as a songwriter, John Blaney's *Lennon and McCartney: Together Alone: A Critical Discography of Their Solo Work* (2007), or Howard Elson's *McCartney: Songwriter* (London: Comet Books, 1986), do not address the more musical aspects of McCartney's work.

37. Many of the CDs that I base my commentary on are drawn from *The Paul McCartney Collection*. See the selected discography/videography for information.

38. See the selected bibliography for information about these sheet-music publications and classical music scores.

CHAPTER 1

1. In *Lennon and McCartney: Together Alone* (p. 30), John Blaney states that McCartney began recording songs for his new album in September 1969. This contradicts McCartney's statement in his press release issued in a limited run on the album's inner sleeve that he began recording songs for *McCartney* just before Christmas 1969. See Harry, *The Paul McCartney Encyclopedia*, 558.

2. This commentary is reprinted in Harry, *The Paul McCartney Encyclopedia*, 560–62. All references to McCartney's commentary, along with information about each song's instrumentation, are taken from this source.

3. I am indebted to Thomas Cody for this observation.

4. Blaney, *Lennon and McCartney: Together Alone*, 32.

5. In the sheet music-publication issued by MPL Communications, "Every Night" is in F major. See Paul McCartney, *Wingspan: Paul McCartney: Hits and History*, (Milwaukee, WI: MPL Communications in association with the Hal Leonard Corporation, 2001), 110–12.

6. Blaney, *Lennon and McCartney: Together Alone*, 32.

7. In the sheet music-publication issued by MPL Communications, "Junk" is in B♭ major. See Paul McCartney, *Wingspan: Paul McCartney: Hits and History*, 118–20.

8. Blaney, *Lennon and McCartney: Together Alone*, 33.

9. See Harry, *The Paul McCartney Encyclopedia*, 549.

10. In the sheet music-publication issued by MPL Communications, "Man We Was Lonely" is in B♭ major. See Paul McCartney, *Wingspan: Paul McCartney: Hits and History*, 121–23.

11. Blaney, *Lennon and McCartney: Together Alone*, 33.

12. The Beatles, *Anthology 3*, liner notes, Apple Corps Ltd./EMI Records Ltd. CDP 7243 8 34451 2 7, 1996, compact disc recording.

13. Harry, *The Paul McCartney Encyclopedia*, 555.

14. According to Ian Peel (*The Unknown Paul McCartney: McCartney and the Avant-Garde*, with a forward by David Toop [London: Reynolds & Hearn Ltd, 2002], 71), the documentary was entitled "The Tribe That Hides from Man" and shown on ITV.

15. McGee, *Band on the Run*, 4.

16. Ibid., 9. According to *The McCartney Recording Sessions: 1971* (http://webpages.charter.net/ram71/mrs.htm), accessed 16 June 2009, Spinoza played guitar on "3 Legs" and "Eat at Home," while McCracken played guitar on the rest of *Ram*.

17. Blaney, *Lennon and McCartney: Together Alone*, 46.

18. See McGee, *Band on the Run*, 10; and John Blake, *All You Needed Was Love: The Beatles After the Beatles* (New York: Perigree Books, G. P. Putnam's Sons, 1981), 141.

19. Blaney, *Lennon and McCartney: Together Alone*, 45–46.

20. George Formby, Jr. (1904–61), née George Hoy Booth, was an English singer and comedian from the British music-hall tradition. Audiences loved his wry sense of humor and folksy demeanor.

21. Blaney, *Lennon and McCartney: Together Alone*, 46.

22. Ibid.

23. Ibid.

24. Mark Lewisohn, ed., *Wingspan: Paul McCartney's Band on the Run* (Boston: Bulfinch Press, 2002), 25.

25. *The McCartney Years* (2007), vol. 1.

26. Everett refers to the raised supertonic in relation to the music of the Beatles as a modally derived Lydian II♯. See Everett, *The Beatles as Musicians: Revolver through the Anthology*, 310.

27. See Blaney, *Lennon and McCartney: Together Alone*, 47.

28. Harry, *The Paul McCartney Encyclopedia*, 628.

29. Ibid., 533.

30. See Blaney, *Lennon and McCartney: Together Alone*, 47.

31. See Everett, *The Beatles as Musicians: Revolver through the Anthology*, 316–17.

32. Ibid., 316.

33. Harry, The Paul McCartney Encyclopedia, 42.

34. Blaney, *Lennon and McCartney: Together Alone*, 47.

35. "B(inst.)" refers to an instrumental B section; "A(inst.[orchestra]/vocal)" refers to an instrumental A section played by the orchestra, followed by a vocal A section; and "B(outro [inst.])" refers to an instrumental B section used as an outro. I shall use such designations throughout the book.

36. Blaney, *Lennon and McCartney: Together Alone*, 40.

37. Peel, *The Unknown Paul McCartney*, 73.

CHAPTER 2

1. Lewisohn, ed., *Wingspan*, 29.

2. Ibid., 33, 155. Bob Dylan recorded *New Morning* (1970), the album to which McCartney refers, in one week.

3. Harry, *The Paul McCartney Encyclopedia*, 899.

4. Ibid., 64–65.

5. In the sheet music-publication issued by MPL Communications, "Bip Bop" is in D major. See Paul McCartney, *Wingspan: Paul McCartney: Hits and History*, 163–65.

6. Harry, *The Paul McCartney Encyclopedia*, 900.

7. Blaney, *Lennon and McCartney: Together Alone*, 58.

8. Ibid.

9. Lewisohn, ed., *Wingspan*, 40.

10. See Harry, *The Paul McCartney Encyclopedia*, 368.

11. Blaney, *Lennon and McCartney: Together Alone*, 75.

12. Lewisohn, ed., *Wingspan*, 51.

13. Ibid., 53–54.

14. Geoffrey Giuliano, *Blackbird: The Life and Times of Paul McCartney*, 363–64.

15. Harry, *The Paul McCartney Encyclopedia*, 513.

16. Blaney, *Lennon and McCartney: Together Alone*, 75. Rupert the Bear was a beloved children's cartoon character created by Mary Tourtel for the *Daily Express* in 1920. As a child, McCartney adored the strip, and reacquainted himself with the character when he began reading Rupert the Bear stories to his stepdaughter, Heather. Consequently, McCartney bought the film rights to Rupert the Bear in April 1970 in order to develop a short animated film about the character, which he did with *Rupert and the Frog Song*, issued on videocassette in November 1985. See Harry, *The Paul McCartney Encyclopedia*, 767–70.

17. Blaney, *Lennon and McCartney: Together Alone*, 76.

18. Ibid., 77.

19. Harry, *The Paul McCartney Encyclopedia*, 725–26.

20. See Blaney, *Lennon and McCartney: Together Alone*, 73–74, and Harry, *The Paul McCartney Encyclopedia*, 416–17.

21. In an interview with Paul Gambaccini of *Rolling Stone* magazine in 1974, McCartney muddies the waters as to whether "Hi, Hi, Hi" was controversial due to its drug or sexual references: "[The song] could easily be taken as a natural high, could be taken as [a] booze high and everything. It doesn't have to be drugs, you know, so I'd kind of get away with it. Well the first thing they saw was drugs, so I didn't get away with that, and then I just had some line 'Lie on the bed and get ready for my polygon.'" See Paul Gambaccini, "The *Rolling Stone* Interview with Paul McCartney," originally published in *Rolling Stone* 153 (31 January 1974): 32–34, 38–40, 42, 44, 46; [http://www.rollingstone.com/news/coverstory/9359339], accessed 1 July 2009.

22. Harry, *The Paul McCartney Encyclopedia*, 86.

23. Blaney, *Lennon and McCartney: Together Alone*, 77.

24. Christopher Sandford, *McCartney*, 215, 220.

25. McGee, *Band on the Run*, 60.

26. Mark Lewisohn, "The Recording of *Band on the Run*," in Paul McCartney, *Band on the Run: 25th Anniversary Edition*, Paul McCartney & Wings, liner notes, originally released in 1973, currently available as Capitol Records, Inc. CDP 7243 4 99176 2 0.

27. See Jon Landau, "McCartney Takes a Stand" (review of *Band on the Run*); originally published in *Rolling Stone* 153 (31 January 1974): 50; [http://www.rollingstone.com/artists/paulmccartney/albums/album/ 112198/review/6211633/band_on_the_run], accessed 26 June 2009.

28. Lewisohn, "The Recording of *Band on the Run*."

29. Lewisohn, ed., *Wingspan*, 57.

30. Lewisohn, "The Recording of *Band on the Run*."

31. Blaney, *Lennon and McCartney: Together Alone*, 86.

32. Ibid.

33. "Jet" was the second time that McCartney titled one of his songs after a dog, the first one being "Martha My Dear" from the *White Album* of 1968, named after his sheepdog, Martha.

34. Harry, *The Paul McCartney Encyclopedia*, 71.

35. As seen by their performance of "Bluebird" on *Rockshow*, McCartney, Laine, and McCulloch play the song in F major. See Paul McCartney, *The McCartney Years*, vol. 3. The sheet-music publications of "Bluebird" in the *Band on the Run* songbook ([Milwaukee, WI: MPL Communications, Inc. in association with the Hal Leonard

Corporation, 1977], 16–17), and *Wingspan: Paul McCartney: Hits and History* (105–6), notate the song in the key of E♭ major. In the *Paul McCartney Chord Songbook Collection* ([London: Wise Publications, 2003], 50–52), "Bluebird" is likewise set in E♭ major. In the *Paul McCartney Guitar Chord Songbook: Sixty Songs* ([Milwaukee, WI: MPL Communications, Inc. in association with the Hal Leonard Corporation, 2007], 21–23), "Bluebird" is cast in C major.

36. In "Mrs. Vanderbilt," McCartney borrowed the phrase "Down in the jungle, living in a tent" from the act of British music-hall comedian Charlie Chester. See Lewisohn, "The Recording of *Band on the Run*."

37. See Blaney, *Lennon and McCartney: Together Alone*, 87.

38. Harry, *The Paul McCartney Encyclopedia*, 508.

39. The sheet-music publications of "Let Me Roll It" in the *Band on the Run* songbook (28–29), and *Wingspan: Paul McCartney: Hits and History* (90–91), notate the song incorrectly as being in the key of A major. Furthermore, they list the F♯m chord of each verse, as well as the intro and outro, incorrectly as an F♯ chord. The *Paul McCartney Guitar Chord Songbook* (70–71) lists the chords and key of the song correctly.

40. Lewisohn, "The Recording of *Band on the Run*."

41. Ibid.

42. When released as part of the Paul McCartney Collection in 1993, *Band on the Run* included "Helen Wheels" and its B–side, "Country Dreamer," as bonus tracks.

43. See Blaney, *Lennon and McCartney: Together Alone*, 78.

44. The following account of the genesis of "Picasso's Last Words (Drink to Me)" is taken from "The *Rolling Stone* Interview with Paul McCartney," *Rolling Stone* 153 (31 January 1974): 33; [http://www.rollingstone.com/news/coverstory/9359339], accessed 1 July 2009.

CHAPTER 3

1. McGee, *Band on the Run*, 61–63.

2. See McGee, *Band on the Run*, 73–76, and Blake, *All You Needed Was Love*, 194.

3. McCartney had intended to release an album entitled *Hot Hits and Cold Cuts* in December 1974 before he and Wings recorded and released *Venus and Mars*. The album was to include A– and B–sides of Wings singles along with unreleased tracks. For some reason, McCartney did not release the projected album. Although he revisited the project during the 1980s, McCartney ultimately decided not to pursue the project when a bootleg version of *Cold Cuts* was released in 1986. See Harry, *The Paul McCartney Encyclopedia*, 263–64.

4. For a sampling of these reviews, see McGee, *Band on the Run*, 81–83.

5. See Blaney, *Lennon and McCartney: Together Alone*, 109.

6. See Harry, *The Paul McCartney Encyclopedia*, 535.

7. See Paul Gambaccini, ed., *Paul McCartney: In His Own Words* (New York/London: Flash Books, 1976), 94.

8. Blaney, *Lennon and McCartney: Together Alone*, 110.

9. Lewisohn, ed., *Wingspan*, 91.

10. Blaney, *Lennon and McCartney: Together Alone*, 110.

11. Ibid.

12. *Wingspan: An Intimate Portrait.*

13. Harry, *The Paul McCartney Encyclopedia*, 275.

14. *Paul McCartney: All the Best!*, originally released in 1987, currently available as Capitol Records, Inc. CDP 7 48287 2; *Wingspan: Paul McCartney: Hits and History*, originally released in 2001, currently available as Capitol Records, Inc. CDP 7243 5 32946 2 5.

15. See Lewisohn, ed., *Wingspan*, 74, and McGee, *Band on the Run*, 65.

16. McGee, *Band on the Run*, 93.

17. Ibid., 210–11.

18. Blaney, *Lennon and McCartney: Together Alone*, 113.

19. Harry, *The Paul McCartney Encyclopedia*, 787.

20. Blaney, *Lennon and McCartney: Together Alone*, 113.

21. Howard Elson, *McCartney: Songwriter* (London: Comet Books, 1986), 152.

22. McGee, *Band on the Run*, 93.

23. Harry, *The Paul McCartney Encyclopedia*, 888–89.

24. Blaney, *Lennon and McCartney: Together Alone*, 98.

25. Ibid., 99.

26. The following information about *London Town* is indebted to McGee, *Band on the Run*, 109–15, 119–20.

27. See Lewisohn, ed., *Wingspan*, 135.

28. See Blaney, *Lennon and McCartney: Together Alone*, 124.

29. Harry, *The Paul McCartney Encyclopedia*, 87.

30. Ibid., 442. Harry does not identify the girlfriend.

31. Blaney, *Lennon and McCartney: Together Alone*, 122.

32. Elson, *McCartney: Songwriter*, 203.

33. John Blaney claims that McCartney denies writing "Girlfriend" for Jackson. McCartney composed the song while vacationing in Switzerland and recorded a demo in November 1974, around the time that McCartney and Jackson met. However, Blaney acknowledges that McCartney, at a later point in time, may have wanted Jackson to record "Girlfriend" when he mentioned the song to Jackson, referring to it as sounding like the Jackson Five. See *Lennon and McCartney: Together Alone*, 124–25.

34. See Blaney, *Lennon and McCartney: Together Alone*, 125.

35. Harry, *The Paul McCartney Encyclopedia*, 915.

36. Blaney, *Lennon and McCartney: Together Alone*, 125.

37. Elson, *McCartney: Songwriter*, 203.

38. Blaney, *Lennon and McCartney: Together Alone*, 125.

39. Elson, *McCartney: Songwriter*, 203.

40. Blaney, *Lennon and McCartney: Together Alone*, 125.

41. Lewisohn, ed., *Wingspan*, 129.

42. The following discussion about "Mull of Kintyre" is indebted to Lewisohn, ed., *Wingspan*, 128–33.

43. McGee, *Band on the Run*, 122.

44. Peel, *The Unknown Paul McCartney*, 96.

45. Ibid.

46. Ibid., 99.

47. Blaney, *Lennon and McCartney: Together Alone*, 127.

48. Harry, *The Paul McCartney Encyclopedia*, 893.

49. Peel, *The Unknown Paul McCartney*, 97.
50. Elson, *McCartney: Songwriter*, 122.
51. Blaney, *Lennon and McCartney: Together Alone*, 127.
52. Peel, *The Unknown Paul McCartney*, 100.
53. Harry, *The Paul McCartney Encyclopedia*, 16.
54. Blaney, *Lennon and McCartney: Together Alone*, 130.
55. Peel, *The Unknown Paul McCartney*, 98.
56. Harry, *The Paul McCartney Encyclopedia*, 41.
57. See Paul McCarmey, *The McCartney Years*. vol. 1.
58. Blaney, *Lennon and McCartney: Together Alone*, 126–27.
59. McGee, *Band on the Run*, xiii.

CHAPTER 4

1. See Elson, *McCartney: Songwriter*, 126, and Paul Gambaccini, "Paul McCartney's One-Man Band," *Rolling Stone* 320 (26 June 1980): 20.
2. Peel, *The Unknown Paul McCartney*, 103.
3. Blaney, *Lennon and McCartney: Together Alone*, 136.
4. Elson, *McCartney: Songwriter*, 126–27, 205.
5. Blaney, *Lennon and McCartney: Together Alone*, 138.
6. Ibid.
7. In the sheet music-publication issued by MPL Communications, "Nobody Knows" is in B♭ major. See Paul McCartney, *McCartney II* (Milwaukee, WI: MPL Communications, Inc. in association with the Hal Leonard Corporation, 1980), 28–33.
8. Blaney, *Lennon and McCartney: Together Alone*, 138.
9. Peel, *The Unknown Paul McCartney*, 104.
10. Blaney, *Lennon and McCartney: Together Alone*, 138.
11. See Harry, *The Paul McCartney Encyclopedia*, 74, and Blaney, *Lennon and McCartney: Together Alone*, 139.
12. Blaney, *Lennon and McCartney: Together Alone*, 139.
13. Harry, *The Paul McCartney Encyclopedia*, 383.
14. In the sheet music-publication issued by MPL Communications, "Goodnight Tonight" is in F major. See *Wingspan: Paul McCartney: Hits and History*, 59–62.
15. See Blaney, *Lennon and McCartney: Together Alone*, 152.
16. Ibid., 154.
17. In the *Paul McCartney Chord Songbook Collection* (276–77), the chord symbols above the lyrics in "The Pound Is Sinking" are listed as one half step lower than the actual pitch of the song (Em instead of Fm).
18. Blaney, *Lennon and McCartney: Together Alone*, 155.
19. The following information about the recording of "Get It" is derived from Blaney, *Lennon and McCartney: Together Alone*, 155.
20. Paul McCartney, Commentary to "Ebony and Ivory," *The McCartney Years*, vol. 1.
21. Blaney, *Lennon and McCartney: Together Alone*, 151.
22. "Ebony and Ivory" is the final track on *Tug of War* and the last one discussed in relation to this album. When *Tug of War* was released in 1993 as part of *The Paul McCartney Collection*, it contained no bonus tracks.

23. Peel, *The Unknown Paul McCartney*, 105.

24. Harry, *The Paul McCartney Encyclopedia*, 720.

25. Ibid., 721.

26. Blaney, *Lennon and McCartney: Together Alone*, 159.

27. Ibid.

28. Paul McCartney, Commentary to "Say, Say, Say," *The McCartney Years*, vol. 1.

29. Blaney, *Lennon and McCartney: Together Alone*, 160.

30. Ibid., 159.

31. Harry, *The Paul McCartney Encyclopedia*, 473.

32. Elson, *McCartney: Songwriter*, 207.

33. Blaney, *Lennon and McCartney: Together Alone*, 160.

34. Ibid.

35. Ibid.

36. Elson, *McCartney: Songwriter*, 208.

37. Blaney, *Lennon and McCartney: Together Alone*, 168.

38. The following information about "Spies Like Us" is indebted to Harry, *The Paul McCartney Encyclopedia*, 804–5, and Paul McCartney, Commentary to "Spies Like Us," *The McCartney Years*, vol. 2.

39. For McCartney, collaborating with Eric Stewart reminded him of working with John Lennon. See Blaney, *Lennon and McCartney: Together Alone*, 176.

40. Harry, *The Paul McCartney Encyclopedia*, 821.

41. Blaney, *Lennon and McCartney: Together Alone*, 176.

42. Ibid.

43. Ibid.

44. Harry, *The Paul McCartney Encyclopedia*, 660–61.

45. Blaney, *Lennon and McCartney: Together Alone*, 175.

46. Ibid., 174.

47. Ibid., 177.

48. Ibid., 178.

49. Kurt Loder, "The *Rolling Stone* Interview: Paul McCartney," *Rolling Stone* 482 (11 September 1986): 48.

50. Ibid.

51. As heard on *Press to Play*, "It's Not True" is a remixed version by Julian Mendelssohn, with a saxophone solo inserted in place of the guitar solo played by Carlos Alomar on the version released as the B–side to the single, "Press."

52. James Henke, "Can Paul McCartney Get Back?" *Rolling Stone* (15 June 1989): 148.

53. Everett, *The Beatles as Musicians: Revolver through the Anthology*, 283.

54. Harry, *The Paul McCartney Encyclopedia*, 640.

55. Blaney, *Lennon and McCartney: Together Alone*, 188.

56. Harry, *The Paul McCartney Encyclopedia*, 762.

57. Blaney, *Lennon and McCartney: Together Alone*, 189.

58. Henke, "Can Paul McCartney Get Back?" 48.

59. Ibid.

60. "Interview with George Martin," in Tony Barrow and Robin Bextor, *Paul McCartney: Now and Then*, ed. Julian Newby (London: Carlton Books Ltd, 2004), 83.

61. Blaney, *Lennon and McCartney: Together Alone*, 190.

62. Harry, *The Paul McCartney Encyclopedia*, 892.

63. Paul McCartney, "Put It There," *The McCartney Years*, vol. 2.

64. Blaney, *Lennon and McCartney: Together Alone*, 190.

65. See Paul McCartney, Commentary to "This One," *The McCartney Years*, vol. 2.

66. Blaney, *Lennon and McCartney: Together Alone*, 190.

67. Ibid., 192.

68. Ibid.

CHAPTER 5

1. The following narrative describing the genesis and musical form of the *Liverpool Oratorio* is indebted to "Ghosts of the Past," disc 2 of *Paul McCartney's Liverpool Oratorio*, Paul McCartney/Carl Davis, produced by Paul McCartney, 90 minutes, MPL Communications/EMI Classics, 2004; *Liverpool Oratorio*, liner notes, Paul McCartney and Carl Davis, originally released in 1991, currently available as EMI Classics 0777 7 54372 2 5; and the *Liverpool Oratorio*, vocal score, text by Paul McCartney (London, UK: Faber Music Ltd. in association with MPL Communications Ltd, 1991), iii–vi.

2. For an in-depth look at the McCartney-Davis collaboration, I encourage the reader to view the documentary "Ghosts of the Past," disc 2 of *Paul McCartney's Liverpool Oratorio* DVD.

3. The following account of the genesis of *Off the Ground* is indebted to Blaney, *Lennon and McCartney: Together Alone*, 212–13.

4. Blaney, *Lennon and McCartney: Together Alone*, 213.

5. Harry, *The Paul McCartney Encyclopedia*, 592.

6. Blaney, *Lennon and McCartney: Together Alone*, 213.

7. See Harry, *The Paul McCartney Encyclopedia*, 64, for a genesis of the song.

8. Blaney, *Lennon and McCartney: Together Alone*, 214.

9. Harry, *The Paul McCartney Encyclopedia*, 86.

10. Henke, "Can Paul McCartney Get Back?," 42.

11. The following account of the genesis of *The Beatles Anthology* is indebted to Everett, *The Beatles as Musicians: Revolver through the Anthology*, 286–87.

12. Henke, "Can Paul McCartney Get Back?," 42.

13. See Everett, *The Beatles as Musicians: Revolver through the Anthology*, 287.

14. See Blaney, *Lennon and McCartney: Together Alone*, 224.

15. Harry, *The Paul McCartney Encyclopedia*, 800.

16. Ibid., 921.

17. Ibid

18. Blaney, *Lennon and McCartney: Together Alone*, 226.

19. Harry, *The Paul McCartney Encyclopedia*, 799–800.

20. Blaney, *Lennon and McCartney: Together Alone*, 223.

21. Ibid., 226.

22. The piano-vocal score incorrectly lists this chord as Bm. See Paul McCartney, *Flaming Pie* (Milwaukee, WI: MPL Communications, Inc. in association with the Hal Leonard Corporation, 1997), 51.

23. Harry, *The Paul McCartney Encyclopedia*, 409.

24. Ibid., 876.

25. See Harry, *The Paul McCartney Encyclopedia*, 801–2.

26. Paul McCartney, *The McCartney Years*, vol. 2.

27. Harry, *The Paul McCartney Encyclopedia*, 744.

28. The following discussion of "Beautiful Night" is indebted to Harry, *The Paul McCartney Encyclopedia*, 57–60.

29. The following narrative describing the genesis and musical form of *Standing Stone* is indebted to "The Documentary of the Creation of the Work," side 2 of *Standing Stone*, Paul McCartney, produced by Paul McCartney, 133 minutes, MPL Communications/EMI Classics, 1999; and *Standing Stone*, liner notes, Paul McCartney, originally released in 1997, currently available as EMI Classics 7243 5 56484 2 6.

CHAPTER 6

1. See Harry, *The Paul McCartney Encyclopedia*, 299–300.

2. Peel, *The Unknown Paul McCartney*, 45.

3. Blaney, *Lennon and McCartney: Together Alone*, 255–56.

4. Ibid., 256.

5. Ibid., 256–57.

6. Ibid., 257.

7. Harry, *The Paul McCartney Encyclopedia*, 41.

8. Blaney, *Lennon and McCartney: Together Alone*, 257.

9. Ibid.

10. Ibid., 253.

11. Peel, *The Unknown Paul McCartney*, 215.

12. The following background information about the album, as well as its songs, is derived from Paul McCartney, DVD Documentary, "Between Chaos and Creation," *Chaos and Creation in the Backyard: Special Edition*, originally released in 2005, currently available as Capitol Records, Inc., CDP 0946 3 38759 2 0.

13. Blaney, *Lennon and McCartney: Together Alone*, 272.

14. See "This Never Happened Before," *Chaos and Creation in the Backyard* (Milwaukee, WI: MPL Communications, Inc. in association with the Hal Leonard Corporation, 2005), 65–68.

15. The following narrative describing the genesis and musical form of *Ecce Cor Meum* is indebted to "Creating *Ecce Cor Meum*," *Ecce Cor Meum*, Paul McCartney, produced by Paul McCartney, 107 minutes, MPL Communications/EMI Classics, 2007; *Ecce Cor Meum*, liner notes, Paul McCartney, originally released in 2006, currently available as EMI/Angel Records 0946 3 70424 2 7; and *Ecce Cor Meum*, vocal score, text by Paul McCartney (London, UK: Faber Music Ltd. in association with MPL Communications Ltd, 2006), iii.

16. Information about each song is indebted to McCartney's track-by-track commentary found on disc 2 of *Memory Almost Full*, Paul McCartney, originally released in 2007, currently available as MPL/Starcon HMCD-30358.

CHAPTER 7

1. Caroline Grimshaw, comp. and ed., *Each One Believing: Paul McCartney: On Stage, Off Stage, and Backstage* (San Francisco: Chronicle Books, 2004), 4.

2. Paul McCartney, "Between Chaos and Creation."

3. Elson, McCartney: Songwriter, 145.

Selected Bibliography

BOOKS, ARTICLES, AND ESSAY COLLECTIONS

Bacon, Tony, and Gareth Morgan. *Paul McCartney: Bassmaster*. San Francisco: Backbeat Books, 2006.

Barrow, Tony, and Robin Bextor. *Paul McCartney: Now and Then*. Edited by Julian Newby. London: Carlton Books Ltd, 2004.

Beatles, The. *The Beatles Anthology*. San Francisco: Chronicle Books, 2000.

Bennighof, James. *The Words and Music of Paul Simon*. The Praeger Singer-Songwriter Collection, James E. Perone, ed. Westport, CT: Praeger Publishers, 2007.

Blake, John. *All You Needed Was Love: The Beatles After the Beatles*. New York: Perigree Books, G. P. Putnam's Sons, 1981.

Blaney, John. *Lennon and McCartney: Together Alone: A Critical Discography of Their Solo Work*. London: A Jawbone Book, 2007.

Bonici, Ray. "Paul McCartney Wings It Alone." Originally published in *Music Express* 36 (April/May 1982). [http://beatles.ncf.ca/mpl.html], accessed 14 July 2009.

Brown, Geoff. "McCartney: Life after Death!" *Melody Maker* (30 November 1974): 8–9, 63.

Cocks, Jay. "McCartney Comes Back." *Time* 107, no. 23 (31 May 1976): 40–44.

Coleman, Ray. *Lennon*. New York: McGraw-Hill Book Co., 1985.

———. *McCartney: Yesterday and Today*. London: Boxtree, 1995.

DeCurtis, Anthony. "Paul McCartney." *Rolling Stone* (5 November–10 December 1987): 39–40, 44.

Dowlding, William J. *Beatlesongs*. New York: Simon & Schuster, 1989.

Elson, Howard. *McCartney: Songwriter*. London: Comet Books, 1986.

Emerick, Geoff, with Howard Massey. *Here, There and Everywhere: My Life Recording the Music of the Beatles*. New York: Gotham, 2006.

Everett, Walter. *The Beatles as Musicians: The Quarry Men through Rubber Soul*, Vol. 1. New York: Oxford University Press, 2001.

———. *The Beatles as Musicians: Revolver through the Anthology*, Vol. 2. New York: Oxford University Press, 1999.

———. "Voice Leading and Harmony as Expressive Devices in the Early Music of the Beatles: *She Loves You*." *College Music Symposium* 32 (1992): 19–37.

Everett, Walter, ed. *Expression in Pop-Rock Music: A Collection of Critical and Analytical Essays*. Studies in Contemporary Music and Culture, ed. Joseph Auner, vol. 2. New York and London: Garland Publishing, Inc., 2000.

Flippo, Chet. *Yesterday: The Unauthorized Biography of Paul McCartney*. New York: Doubleday, 1988.

Frith, Simon. *Music for Pleasure: Essays in the Sociology of Pop*. New York: Routledge, 1988.

Gambaccini, Paul. "Paul McCartney's One-Man Band." *Rolling Stone* (26 June 1980): 11, 20.

———. "British Rockers Unite in Concerts for Kampuchea." *Rolling Stone* (21 February 1980): 17–18.

———. "A Conversation with Paul McCartney." *Rolling Stone* (12 July 1979): 39–46.

———. "The *Rolling Stone* Interview with Paul McCartney." Originally published in *Rolling Stone* (31 January 1974): 32–34, 38–40, 42, 44, 46. [http://www.rollingstone.com/news/coverstory/9359339], accessed 1 July 2009.

Gambaccini, Paul, ed. *Paul McCartney: In His Own Words*. New York/London: Flash Books, 1976.

Giuliano, Geoffrey. *Blackbird: The Life and Times of Paul McCartney*, updated edition. Cambridge, MA, and New York: Da Capo Press, Inc., 1997.

Gracen, Jorie B. *Paul McCartney: I Saw Him Standing There*. New York: Billboard Books, 2000.

Grimshaw, Caroline, comp. and ed. *Each One Believing: Paul McCartney: On Stage, Off Stage, and Backstage*. San Francisco: Chronicle Books, 2004.

Harry, Bill. *The Paul McCartney Encyclopedia*. London: Virgin Books Ltd., 2002.

Henke, James. "Can Paul McCartney Get Back?" *Rolling Stone* (15 June 1989): 40–44, 48, 148.

Hertsgaard, Mark. *A Day in the Life: The Music and Artistry of the Beatles*. New York: Dell Publishing, 1995.

Krims, Adam. "What Does It Mean to Analyze Popular Music?" *Music Analysis* 22, nos. 1–2 (2003): 181–209.

Landau, Jon. "McCartney Takes a Stand" (review of *Band on the Run*). Originally published in *Rolling Stone* (31 January 1974): 48, 50. [http://www.rollingstone.com/artists/paulmccartney/albums/album/112198/review/6211633/band_on_the_run], accessed 26 June 2009.

Lennon, Cynthia. *John*. New York: Crown Publishers, 2005.

Lewisohn, Mark. *The Beatles Recording Sessions: The Official Abbey Road Studio Session Notes, 1962–1970.* New York: Harmony Books, 1988.

———. "The Recording of *Band on the Run.*" In Paul McCartney, *Band on the Run: 25th Anniversary Edition.* Paul McCartney & Wings. Liner Notes. Originally released in 1973. Currently available as Capitol Records, Inc. CDP 7243 4 99176 2 0, 1998.

Lewisohn, Mark, ed. *Wingspan: Paul McCartney's Band on the Run.* Boston: Bulfinch Press, 2002.

Loder, Kurt. "The *Rolling Stone* Interview: Paul McCartney." *Rolling Stone* (11 September 1986): 46–48, 100–103.

McGee, Garry. *Band on the Run: A History of Paul McCartney and Wings.* New York: Taylor Trade Publishing, 2003.

Mellers, Wilfrid. *Twilight of the Gods: The Music of the Beatles.* New York: Schirmer Books, 1973.

Miles, Barry. *Paul McCartney: Many Years from Now.* New York: Henry Holt and Company, 1997.

Moore, Allan F. *The Beatles: Sgt. Pepper's Lonely Hearts Club Band.* Cambridge, UK: Cambridge University Press, 1997.

———. "The So-Called 'Flattened Seventh' in Rock." *Popular Music* 14, no. 2 (May 1995): 185–201.

Moore, Allan F., ed. *Analyzing Popular Music.* Cambridge, UK: Cambridge University Press, 2003.

Ono, Yoko. "Linda McCartney Remembered." *Rolling Stone* (11 June 1998): 31.

Orth, Maureen. "Paul Soars." *Newsweek,* 17 May 1976, 100.

Peel, Ian. *The Unknown Paul McCartney: McCartney and the Avant-Garde.* With a Forward by David Toop. London: Reynolds & Hearn Ltd, 2002.

Reck, David R. "Beatles Orientalis: Influences from Asia in a Popular Song Tradition." *Asian Music* 16, no. 1 (1985): 83–149.

Rifkin, Joshua. "On the Music of The Beatles." In *The Lennon Companion: Twenty-Five Years of Comment,* edited by Elizabeth Thomson and David Gutman, 113–26. New York: Schirmer Books, 1987.

Russell, Jeff. *The Beatles Complete Discography.* New York: Universe Publishing, 2006.

Salewicz, Chris. *McCartney.* New York: St. Martin's Press, 1986.

Sandford, Christopher. *McCartney.* Revised and updated edition. New York: Carroll & Graf Publishers, 2006.

Spitz, Bob. *The Beatles: The Biography.* New York: Little, Brown and Company, 2005.

Stephenson, Ken. *What to Listen for in Rock: A Stylistic Analysis.* New Haven and London: Yale University Press, 2002.

Urish, Ben, and Ken Bielen. *The Words and Music of John Lennon.* The Praeger Singer-Songwriter Collection, James E. Perone, ed. Westport, CT: Praeger Publishers, 2007.

Wagner, Naphtali. " 'Domestication' " of Blue Notes in the Beatles' Songs." *Music Theory Spectrum* 25, no. 2 (Fall 2003): 353–66.

Wenner, Jann S. *Lennon Remembers: The Rolling Stone Interviews from 1970.* New ed. London and New York: Verso, 2000.

Musical Scores
Popular Music

Fujita, Tetsuya et al. *The Beatles: Complete Scores*. London: Hal Leonard Publishing Corporation and Wise Publications, 1993.

McCartney, Paul. *Back to the Egg: Wings*. Milwaukee, WI: MPL Communications, Inc. in association with the Hal Leonard Corporation, 1979.

———. *Band on the Run*. Milwaukee, WI: MPL Communications, Inc. in association with the Hal Leonard Corporation, 1977.

———. *Chaos and Creation in the Backyard*. Milwaukee, WI: MPL Communications, Inc. in association with the Hal Leonard Corporation, 2005.

———. *Driving Rain*. Milwaukee, WI: MPL Communications, Inc. in association with the Hal Leonard Corporation, 2001.

———. *Flaming Pie*. Milwaukee, WI: MPL Communications, Inc. in association with the Hal Leonard Corporation, 1997.

———. *Flowers in the Dirt*. Milwaukee, WI: MPL Communications, Inc. in association with the Hal Leonard Corporation, 1989.

———. *McCartney II*. Milwaukee, WI: MPL Communications, Inc. in association with the Hal Leonard Corporation, 1980.

———. *Memory Almost Full*. [Milwaukee, WI]: MPL Communications, Ltd/Inc. in association with the Hal Leonard Corporation, 2007.

———. *The Music of Paul McCartney 1963–1973*. Milwaukee, WI: MPL Communications Ltd. in association with the Hal Leonard Corporation, 2003.

———. *The Music of Paul McCartney 1973–2001*. Milwaukee, WI: MPL Communications, Inc. in association with the Hal Leonard Corporation, 2003.

———. *Off the Ground*. Milwaukee, WI: MPL Communications, Inc. in association with the Hal Leonard Corporation, 1993.

———. *Paul McCartney Chord Songbook Collection*. London: Wise Publications, 2003.

———. *Paul McCartney Guitar Chord Songbook: Sixty Songs*. Milwaukee, WI: MPL Communications, Inc. in association with the Hal Leonard Corporation, 2007.

———. *Red Rose Speedway*. Milwaukee, WI: MPL Communications, Inc. in association with the Hal Leonard Corporation, 1977.

———. *Run Devil Run*. London: Wise Publications in association with the Hal Leonard Corporation, 1999.

———. *Spies Like Us*. Milwaukee, WI: MPL Communications, Inc. in association with the Hal Leonard Corporation, 1985.

———. *Tripping the Live Fantastic*. Milwaukee, WI: MPL Communications, Inc. in association with the Hal Leonard Corporation, 1991.

———. *Wingspan: Paul McCartney: Hits and History*. Milwaukee, WI: MPL Communications, Inc. in association with the Hal Leonard Corporation, 2001.

———. *Wings at the Speed of Sound*. Milwaukee, WI: MPL Communications, Inc. in association with the Hal Leonard Corporation, 1976.

Classical Music

McCartney, Paul. *Ecce Cor Meum*. Vocal Score. London, UK: Faber Music Ltd. in association with MPL Communications Ltd., 2006.

————. *A Leaf.* Milwaukee, WI: MPL Communications, Inc. in association with the Hal Leonard Corporation, 1994/95.

McCartney, Paul, and Carl Davis. *Liverpool Oratorio.* Vocal Score. Text by Paul McCartney. London, UK: Faber Music Ltd. in association with MPL Communications Ltd, 1991.

WEB SITES

BBC News. "The Seven Ages of Paul McCartney." [http://news.bbc.co.uk/2/hi/entertainment/5087006.stm], accessed 14 July 2009.

"Hal Leonard Corporation." [http://www.halleonard.com/], accessed 25 June 2009.

"The McCartney Recording Sessions." [http://webpages.charter.net/ram71/mrs.htm], accessed 16 June 2009.

"MPL Communications Ltd." [http://www.mplcommunications.com/], accessed 25 June 2009.

"Paul McCartney.com." [http://www.paulmccartney.com/index.php], accessed 25 June 2009.

Index

The letter *n* following a page number indicates the note number.

About the Author

Vincent P. Benitez is Assistant Professor of Music at the Pennsylvania State University where he teaches undergraduate and graduate courses in music theory and analysis. He is the author of *Olivier Messiaen: A Research and Information Guide* (2008) and has published further articles on Messiaen in *Music Analysis, Messiaen the Theologian* (Ashgate), *Dutch Journal of Music Theory*, the *Journal of Musicological Research*, the fourth volume of the *Poznan Studies on Opera, Music Theory Online*, and the *College Music Symposium*. Benitez has additional research interests in the analysis of seventeenth- and eighteenth-century music, the history of music theory, and popular music, publishing articles and reviews on these topics in *The American Organist, BACH, Diapason, GAMUT*, and the *Indiana Theory Review*.